Preface

THIS BOOK BRINGS TOGETHER PIECES OF A WORLD THAT fell apart in the eighteenth century. It was a world, or underworld, that lived from the production and diffusion of illegal literature in prerevolutionary France. In its day it was invisible to all but the initiate, and since then it has been buried under so much history that it might seem to be beyond excavation. Why even try to put it back together?

I would answer in the first place that the reconstruction of worlds is one of the historian's most important tasks. He undertakes it, not from some strange urge to dig up archives and sift through old paper, but because he wants to talk with the dead. By putting questions to documents and listening for replies, he can sound dead souls and take the measure of the societies they inhabited. If we lost all contact with the worlds we have lost, we would be condemned to live in a two-dimensional, time-bound present, and our own world would turn flat.

That may sound rather grand as a way to introduce a book about Grub Street hacks, pirate publishers, and under-the-cloak peddlers of forbidden books. But the subject is more important than it may seem; for a great deal of literature has been forbidden throughout the course of history, and still is today, as anyone knows who has watched the samizdat and the "flying university" contend with the prison camp in Eastern Europe. The underground was especially important in the eighteenth century, when censorship, the police, and a monopolistic guild of booksellers attempted to contain the printed word within limits set by the official orthodoxies. When it conveyed heterodox ideas, the word spread through the underground. But how? Historians know very little about the way legal literature was written, printed, distributed, and read under the Old Regime. They know still less about prohibited books. Yet most of what passes today for eighteenth-century French literature circulated on the shady side of the law in eighteenth-century France. This book provides a tour of those circuits.

I was able to uncover them because seventeen years ago I walked into a historian's dream: an enormous cache of untouched archives, the papers of the Société typographique de Neuchâtel in the municipal library of Neuchâtel, Switzerland. The Société typographique was one of the largest of the many publishing houses that grew up around France's borders in order to supply the demand for pirated and prohibited books within the kingdom. Its papers contain the richest vein of information about an eighteenth-century publisher anywhere in existence. After working through them, I decided to consult complementary sources in France—archives of the police, the Bastille, and the booksellers' guild—and to write a series of studies of the book as a force in eighteenth-century Europe. The first installment, *The Business of Enlightenment: A Publishing History of the Encyclopédie, 1775–1800,* appeared in 1979. This is the second.

Having explored as much of the literary underground as possible, I realized that it could be pictured more effectively by a set of sketches than by a grand tableau. Sketching in history provides a way of catching men in motion, of holding subjects up to unfamiliar light and examining their

The Literary Underground
of the Old Regime

THE
LITERARY
UNDERGROUND
OF THE
OLD REGIME

Robert Darnton

HARVARD UNIVERSITY PRESS

Cambridge, Massachusetts, and
London, England

1982

Library of Congress Cataloging in Publication Data

Darnton, Robert.
The literary underground of the Old Regime.

Includes bibliographical references and index.
1. Underground literature—France.   2. France—
History—Revolution, 1789-1799—Causes and character.
I. Title.
DC133.3.D37   944.04'2   82-2918
ISBN 0-674-53656-8   AACR2

complexities from different angles. It also can convey the sense of coming up against surprising varieties of humanity in the course of research. While working through the archives, dossier-by-dossier, letter-by-letter (there are 50,000 letters in the Neuchâtel collection), I was constantly struck by the impression of a life looming up from obscurity, taking on a distinct, personal shape, and playing itself out while writing, printing, or peddling books. It is an extraordinary sensation to open a dossier of fifty or a hundred letters that have lain unread since the eighteenth century. Will they come from a Parisian garret, where a young author is scribbling away, his vision suspended between Parnassus and the threats rising from the landlady on the ground floor? Will they recount the travails of a paper-maker on a remote mountainside as he curses the weather for spoiling his size (finish) and damns the ragpickers for missing deliveries? Perhaps their semilegible scrawl will have to be read aloud so that the ear can pick up messages that baffle the eye, and the outline of a smuggling operation will come into focus. They may take you into a printing shop where workers heave at presses, or under counters where seditious books are stocked, or around circuits where salesmen spread Enlightenment from horseback, or down great rivers to entrepôts like Amsterdam and Marseille and far-flung literary marketplaces: Lisbon, Naples, Frankfurt, Leipzig, Warsaw, Budapest, Moscow.

The letters could come from anywhere and reveal anything, for they often take you by surprise. Just when you think your author is about to snare a dowry, he is run out of town by *lettre de cachet*. Just when a crate of books is due in port, it is seized by privateers. Your businessman turns into a confidence man; your philosopher becomes a police spy. Humanity keeps changing shape under your eyes as you watch the publishers' speculations unravel and the wagon-loads of books rumble across the continent. The world that printing set in motion had a *comédie humaine* of its own, so rich and complex that it cannot be compressed within the covers of a single volume. So I have tried to sketch its most interesting sectors, leaving systematic study for a later work.

While investigating the baroque characters who inhabited the literary underground, I ran into some classic historical problems. How deeply did the Enlightenment penetrate into French society? How much did radical ideas contribute to the destruction of the Old Regime? And what were the connections between Enlightenment and Revolution in France? When reexamined from the perspective of publishers' archives, those questions seem less abstract and more down-to-earth than in their textbook formulations. If they cannot be answered in an absolute sense, they can be reduced to manageable proportions and worked through in narrative form as a series of case studies. This book presents the cases.

In doing so, it attempts to argue for a broadening of intellectual history and to suggest that a mixed genre, the social history of ideas, could contribute to a fresh assessment of the age of the Enlightenment. By reading and rereading the great books of the eighteenth century, historians and literary scholars have built up a picture of the Enlightenment as a distinct phase in western civilization. Without disputing the value of their labor, I would like to urge the importance of going beyond the books in order to confront a new set of questions: How did writers pursue careers in the Republic of Letters? Did their economic and social condition have much effect on their writing? How did publishers and booksellers operate? Did their ways of doing business influence the literary fare that reached their customers? What was that literature? Who were its readers? And how did they read?

Those questions could be played on almost any period of history, but they have special importance for the understanding of the Old Regime. During the eighteenth century, a general reading public emerged in France; public opinion gathered force; and ideological discontent welled up with other currents to produce the first great revolution of modern times. Books contributed a great deal to this ferment, but their contribution cannot be appreciated merely by studying their texts. We need to know more about the world behind the books, beginning with Grub Street, where so many of the texts took shape, and continuing through printing shops and smuggling routes into the back-room businesses and under-the-cloak operations of an enormous literary underground. This book provides only a preliminary reconnoitering of that territory, but it should be enough to open up a world that we had lost and to help us see into some lives that had vanished in the past.

Contents

1. The High Enlightenment and the Low-Life of Literature   *1*

2. A Spy in Grub Street   *41*

3. A Pamphleteer on the Run   *71*

4. A Clandestine Bookseller in the Provinces   *122*

5. A Printing Shop across the Border   *148*

6. Reading, Writing, and Publishing   *167*

Notes   *211*
Acknowledgments   *251*
Index   *253*

The Literary Underground
of the Old Regime

The High Enlightenment and the Low-Life of Literature

Where does so much mad agitation come from? From a crowd of minor clerks and lawyers, from unknown writers, starving scribblers, who go about rabblerousing in clubs and cafés. These are the hotbeds that have forged the weapons with which the masses are armed today. —P. J. B. GERBIER, JUNE 1789

The nation's rewards must be meted out to those who are worthy of them; and after having repulsed despotism's vile courtiers, we must look for merit dwelling in basements and in seventh-story garrets ... True genius is almost always sans-culotte.
—HENRI GRÉGOIRE, AUGUST 1793

 THE SUMMIT VIEW OF EIGHTEENTH-CENtury intellectual history has been described so often and so well that it might be useful to strike out in a new direction, to try to get to the bottom of the Enlightenment, and even to penetrate into its underworld, where the Enlightenment may be examined as the Revolution has been studied recently—from below.

Digging downward in intellectual history calls for new methods and new materials, for grubbing in archives instead of contemplating philosophical treatises. As an example of the dirt that such digging can turn up, consider the following letter from a bookseller in Poitiers to his supplier in Switzerland: "Here is a short list of philosophical books that

I want. Please send the invoice in advance: *Venus in the Cloister or the Nun in a Nightgown, Christianity unveiled, Memoirs of Mme la marquise de Pompadour, Inquiry on the Origin of Oriental Despotism, The System of Nature, Theresa the Philosopher, Margot the Campfollower.*"[1] Here, couched in the idiom of the eighteenth-century book trade, is a notion of the philosophical that was shared by men who made it their business to know what Frenchmen wanted to read. If one measures it against the view of the philosophic movement that has been passed on piously from textbook to textbook, one cannot avoid feeling uncomfortable: most of those titles are completely unfamiliar, and they suggest that a lot of trash somehow got mixed up in the eighteenth-century idea of philosophy. Perhaps the Enlightenment was a more down-to-earth affair than the rarefied climate of opinion described by textbook writers, and we should question the overly highbrow, overly metaphysical view of intellectual life in the eighteenth century. One way to bring the Enlightenment down to earth is to see it from the viewpoint of eighteenth-century authors. After all, they were men of flesh and blood, who wanted to fill their bellies, house their families, and make their way in the world. Of course, the study of authors does not solve all the problems connected with the study of ideas, but it does suggest the nature of their social context, and it can draw enough from conventional literary history for one to hazard a few hypotheses.[2]

A favorite hypothesis in histories of literature is the rise in the writer's status throughout the eighteenth century. By the time of the High Enlightenment, during the last twenty-five years of the Old Regime, the prestige of French authors had risen to such an extent that a visiting Englishman described them exactly as Voltaire had described English men of letters during the early Enlightenment: "Authors have a kind of nobility."[3] Voltaire's own career testifies to the transformation of values among the upper orders of French society. The same milieux who had applauded the drubbing administered to him by Rohan's toughs in 1726 cheered him like a god during his triumphal tour of Paris in 1778. Voltaire himself used his apotheosis to advance the cause of his "class"—the men of letters united by common values, interests, and enemies into a new career group or "estate." The last twenty years of his correspondence read like a continuous campaign to proselytize for his "church," as he called it, and to protect the "brothers" and the "faithful" composing it. How many youths in the late eighteenth century must have dreamt of joining the initiates, of lecturing monarchs, rescuing outraged innocence, and ruling the republic of letters from the Académie Française or a château like Ferney. To become a Voltaire or d'Alembert, that was the sort of glory to tempt young men on the make. But how did one make it as a philosophe?

Consider the career of Jean-Baptiste-Antoine Suard, a typical philosophe of the High Enlightenment. Others—Marmontel, Morellet, La Harpe, Thomas, Arnaud, Delille, Chamfort, Roucher, Garat, Target, Maury, Dorat, Cubières, Rulhière, Cailhava—might do just as well. The advantage of Suard's case is that it was written up by his wife. A philosophe's rise to the top is indeed revealing when seen from his wife's viewpoint, and especially when, as in the case of Mme. Suard, the wife had an eye for domestic detail and the importance of balancing the family accounts.[4]

Suard left the provinces at the age of twenty and arrived in Paris just in time to participate in the excitement over the *Encyclopédie* in the 1750s. He had three assets: good looks, good manners, and a Parisian uncle, as well as letters of introduction to friends of friends. His contacts kept him going for a few months while he learned enough English to support himself as a translator. Then he met and captivated the Abbé Raynal, who functioned as a sort of recruiting agent for the sociocultural elite known as *le monde*.[5] Raynal got Suard jobs tutoring the well-born, encouraged him to write little essays on the heroes of the day—Voltaire, Montesquieu, Buffon—and guided him through the salons. Suard competed for the essay prizes offered by provincial academies. He published literary snippets in the *Mercure;* and having passed at Mme. Geoffrin's, he began to make frequent appearances in *le monde*—a phrase that recurs with the regularity of a leitmotif in all descriptions of Suard.[6] With doors opening for him in the salons of d'Holbach, Mme. d'Houdetot, Mlle. de Lespinasse, Mme. Necker, and Mme. Saurin, Suard walked into a job at the *Gazette de France:* lodging, heating, lighting, and 2,500 livres a year for putting polish on the materials provided every week by the ministry of foreign affairs.

At this point Suard took his first unorthodox step: he got married. Philosophes did not generally marry. The great figures of the early Enlightenment—Fontenelle, Duclos, Voltaire, d'Alembert—remained bachelors; or, if they fell into matrimony, as in the case of Diderot and Rousseau, it was with someone of their own station—shop girls and servants.[7] But the elevated status of the philosophe in Suard's time made marriage conceivable. Suard picked a girl of good bourgeois stock like himself; overcame the objections of her brother, the publisher Panckoucke, and of Mme. Geoffrin, who held old-fashioned ideas about the incompatibility of professional writing and family life; and set up house in the apartment that went with his job on the *Gazette de France.* Mme. Suard trimmed her wardrobe to fit their tight budget. Friends like the Prince de Beauvau and the Marquis de

Chastellux sent them game from the hunts every week. And princely patrons like Mme. de Marchais sent carriages to carry the couple off to dinners, where the bride marveled at "the rank and the merit of the guests."[8] This was something new: Madame Philosophe had not accompanied her husband on his forays into *le monde* before. Mme. Suard followed her husband everywhere and even began to form a salon of her own, at first a modest supper for literary friends. The friends and patrons responded so enthusiastically that something of a cult grew up around the *petit ménage,* as it was known from a poem celebrating it by Saurin. Formerly a fringe character picked up for amusement by the salons and readily turned out into the street for drubbings, begging, and *embastillement,* the philosophe was becoming respectable, domesticated, and assimilated into that most conservative of institutions, the family.

Having made it into *le monde,* Suard began to make money. By taking over the entire administration of the *Gazette de France,* he and his collaborator, the Abbé Arnaud, boosted their income from 2,500 to 10,000 livres apiece. They succeeded by appealing over the head of a bureaucrat in the ministry of foreign affairs, who was "astonished that men of letters shouldn't consider themselves rich enough with 2,500 livres of revenue,"[9] to the foreign minister, the Duc de Choiseul, whose sister, the Duchesse de Grammont, was an intimate of the Princesse de Beauvau, who was a friend of the Suards and of Mme. de Tessé, who was the protector of Arnaud. Such obliging noblesse was vulnerable to the vagaries of court politics, however, and when d'Aiguillon replaced Choiseul, the Suards were turned out of their *Gazette* apartment. Once again *le monde* rallied to the defense of its *petit ménage.* Suard received a compensatory pension of 2,500 livres from d'Aiguillon, who was persuaded by Mme. de Maurepas, who was moved by the Duc de Nivernais, who was touched by the sight of Mme. Suard weeping in the Académie Française and by the prodding of d'Alembert and La Harpe. Then a gift of 800 livres in *rentes perpétuelles* arrived from the Neckers. The Suards rented a house in the rue Louis-le-Grand. Suard managed to get the lucrative post of literary correspondent to the Margrave of Bayreuth. His friends arranged a pension for him of 1,200 livres on the income from the *Almanach Royal*. He sold his collection of English books to the Duc de Coigny for 12,-000 livres and bought a country house. He became a royal censor. Election to the Académie Française came next, bringing an income of up to 900 livres in *jetons* (doubled in 1786) and far more in indirect benefits, such as a position as censor of all plays and spectacles, worth 2,400 livres and later 3,700 livres a year. When the *Journal de Paris* was suspended for printing an irreverent verse about a foreign princess, the keeper of the seals called in Suard, who agreed to purge all future copy and to share the profits: another 1,200 livres. "He took a cabriolet, which transported him after he fulfilled the duties of his posts, to the lovely house he had given to me,"[10] Mme. Suard reminisced. They had reached the top, enjoying an income of 10,000, perhaps over 20,000, livres a year and all the delights of the Old Regime in its last days. The Suards had arrived.

The most striking aspect of the Suard success story is its dependence on "protection"—not the old court variety of patronage, but a new kind, which involved knowing the right people, pulling the right strings, and "cultivating," as it was known in the eighteenth century. Older, established writers, wealthy bourgeois, and nobles all participated in this process of co-opting young men with the right style, the perfect pitch of bon ton, into the salons, academies, privileged journals, and honorific posts. The missing element was the market: Suard lived on sinecures and pensions, not on sales of books. In fact, he wrote little and had little to say—nothing, it need hardly be added, that would offend the regime. He toed the party line of the philosophes and collected his reward.

But how many rewards of that kind were there, and how typical was Suard's *cas typique?* Part of the answer to those questions lies in a box in the Archives Nationales containing a list of 147 "Men of Letters Who Request Pensions" and ten dossiers crammed with material on writers and their sources of support.[11] The list reads like a "Who's Who" of the literary world drawn up by officials in the Contrôle général to guide Calonne, who had decided in 1785 to increase and systematize the award of literary pensions, *gratifications,* and *traitements.* Calonne was also guided by a committee composed of Lenoir, the former lieutenant general of police, Vidaud de Latour, the director of the book trade, and two courtier-academicians, the Maréchal de Beauvau and the Duc de Nivernais. Hardly a revolutionary group. The pension list, with the recommendations of Calonne's officials and his own notes scrawled in the margins, gives a corresponding impression. It shows a strong bias in favor of established writers, especially academicians. Here Morellet appears with his 6,000 livres a year from the Caisse de Commerce; Marmontel with 3,000 livres as *historiographe de France* and 2,000 livres as perpetual secretary of the Académie Française. La Harpe complains of receiving a mere 600 livres from the *Mercure,* the Maréchal de Beauvau pushes to get him pensioned for 1,500, and the pension is granted, despite a subordinate official's observation that La Harpe also collects 3,000 livres for lecturing in the Lycée. And so the list goes, one figure of the High Enlightenment succeeding another: Chamfort (granted 2,000 livres in addition to 1,200 on the *maison du roi*), Saint-Lambert (requested 1,053 livres, decision delayed), Bernardin de Saint-Pierre (1,000 livres), Cailhava (1,000 livres), Keralio, Garat, Piis, Cubières, Des Essarts, Aubert, and Lemierre.

Blin de Sainmore, a solid citizen in the republic of letters' lesser ranks, exemplified the qualities required for getting a pension. He was a royal censor, *historiographe de l'Ordre du Saint-Esprit,* and protégé of the Princesse de Rochefort. "I will further add, Monseigneur, that I am the head of a family, that I was born without fortune, and that I have nothing for the support and education of my family except the post of historiographer of the king's orders, whose income is barely sufficient for me alone to live in a decent style."[12] Thus the pensions went for charity as well as good works. Saurin's widow applied because his death had left her destitute, since he had lived entirely from "the beneficence of the government."[13] And Mme. Saurin specified:

Pension of the Académie Française	2,000
Pension on the General Farms	3,000
As the son of a converted [Protestant] minister	800
As a censor	400
On an office of *trésorier du pavé de Paris*	2,400
Total	8,600

This beneficence generally went to serious, deserving writers but not to anyone unconnected with *le monde.* Academicians were first on the government's list—to such an extent that one ministerial aide jotted in a margin, "There is some danger that the title of academician might become a synonym for pensioner of the King."[14] Ducis demanded 1,000 livres a year for life on the grounds that "most of our confrères, either of the Académie Française or the Académie des Inscriptions, have obtained pensions that have the character of a permanent grace."[15] This favoritism offended Caraccioli, who wrote testily,

> I am pretentious enough to believe that you will have heard of my works, all of which have religion and sound morality as their object. I have been writing in this genre for thirty-five years; and despite the frivolity of the century, [my works] have spread everywhere and have been translated into various languages. Nevertheless, under ministers who preceded you and who made me the most beautiful promises, I never obtained anything, although living in a modest state that might well be called indigence. And I have seen *gratifications* as well as pensions pour down.[16]

As Caraccioli's comments suggest, "sound" opinions were considered a necessary qualification for a pension. In some cases the government subsidized writers who had produced propaganda for it. It looked favorably on the Abbé Soulavie, because "he has submitted some manuscripts on financial matters to M. le Contrôleur Général."[17] Conversely, the government avoided making payments to anyone whose loyalties were in doubt. It turned down J.-C.-N. Dumont de Sainte-Croix, a minor author on jurisprudence, because, according to the marginal note next to his name, "All the new systems of this genre would merit some encouragement, if they were made only to be known by the government and not by the public, which is incited to rebel against the established laws instead of becoming enlightened as to the means of making them better." Then, in another hand: "Nothing."[18] Rivarol also received nothing, but only because he already had a secret pension of 4,000 livres: "He is very clever, and an encouragement, which could be paid to him each year, if he remains faithful to sound principles, would be a way of preventing him from

following his inclination toward those which are dangerous."[19]

So several considerations determined the state's patronage. As in the case of modern institutions like the French
Centre National de la Recherche Scientifique, the monarchy
supported serious savants, perhaps even with the intention
of recruiting a fresh intellectual elite.[20] It also dispensed
charity. And it used its funds to encourage writing that
would make the regime look good. In each instance, however, it restricted its subsidies to men with some standing in
the world of letters. A few fringe characters like Delisle de
Sales, Mercier, and Carra presumed to apply for the pensions; but they received nothing. Lenoir later revealed that
he and his colleagues had turned down Carra, Gorsas, and
Fabre d'Eglantine because "the academicians described them
as the excrement of literature."[21] While the literary rabble
held out its hands to the government, the government gave
its handouts to writers situated safely within *le monde*.

It dispensed them on a large scale. A note by a subordinate official put the total payments at 256,300 livres per
year, to which 83,153 livres were added in 1786. But that
sum represented only the direct dole from the royal trea-
suries. Far more money flowed into the purses of "sound"
writers from the appointments at the government's dis-
posal. Journals, for example, provided an important source
of income for the privileged few in the literal sense of the
word. Royal privileges reserved certain subjects for the
quasi-official periodicals like the *Mercure, Gazette de France,*
and *Journal des savants,* which exploited their monopolies
without worrying about competitors (the government permitted some discreet foreign journals to circulate, provided
they passed the censorship and paid compensation to a privi-

leged journal) and turned over part of the take to writers named by the government. In 1762 the *Mercure* paid out 30,400 livres to twenty subluminaries of the High Enlightenment.[22] Then there were many sinecures. Not only did the king require an official historiographer, he also subsidized *historiographes de la marine, des bâtiments royaux, des menus-plaisirs,* and *de l'Ordre du Saint-Esprit.* The branches of the royal family were loaded with readers, secretaries, and librarians—more or less honorific posts that one had to work *for* but not *at,* that one acquired by waiting in antechambers, improvising eulogies, cultivating acquaintances in salons, and knowing the right people. Of course it always helped to be a member of the Académie Française.[23]

The dozens of volumes about the history and *petite histoire* of the academy in the eighteenth century,[24] whether written in love or in hatred, reveal a dominant theme: the Enlightenment's successful campaign to win over the French elite. After the *chasse aux Pompignans* of 1760, the election of Marmontel in 1763, and d'Alembert's elevation to the perpetual secretaryship in 1772, the academy fell to the philosophes. It became a sort of clubhouse for them, an ideal forum for launching attacks against *l'infâme,* proclaiming the advent of reason, and co-opting new philosophes as fast as the old-guard academicians would die off. This last function, virtually a monopoly of the philosophic salons, assured that only party men would make it to the top. And so Voltaire's church was besieged by converts. The spectacle of a new generation taking up the torch warmed the old man's heart. When he congratulated Suard on his election, Voltaire exulted, "Voilà, God be thanked, a new career assured ... At last I see the real fruits of philosophy, and I begin to believe that I shall die content."[25] Thus Suard and his circle, the high priests of the High Enlightenment, took over the summit of the literary world, while the mid-century philosophes declined and died. The new men included both writers like Thomas, Marmontel, Gaillard, La Harpe, Delille, Arnaud, Lemierre, Chamfort, and Rulhière, and philosophically minded *grands,* powerful courtiers and clergymen, like the Marquis de Chastellux; the Maréchal de Duras; Boisgelin, Archbishop of Aix; and Loménie de Brienne, Archbishop of Sens.

The fusion of *gens de lettres* and *grands* had been a favorite theme of philosophic writing since the mid-century. Duclos had proclaimed it triumphantly in his *Considérations sur les moeurs de ce siècle* (1750). Writing had become a new "profession," which conferred a distinguished "estate" upon men of great talent but modest birth, he explained. Such writers became integrated into a society of courtiers and wealthy patrons, and everyone benefited from the process: the *gens du monde* gained amusement and instruction, and the *gens de lettres* acquired polish and standing. It went without saying that promotion into high society produced some commitment to the social hierarchy. Duclos had a keen eye for all the subtleties of status and rank; and although he took pride in the man of letter's ability to rise by sheer talent, he showed equal respect for what made a man of *le monde:* "One is an *homme du monde* by birth and by position."[26]

Voltaire, the archapologist for *le mondain,* shared the same attitudes. His article entitled "Gens de lettres" in the *Encyclopédie* emphasized that in the eighteenth century "the spirit of the age made them [men of letters] for the most part as suitable for *le monde* as for the study. They were kept out of society until the time of Balzac and Voiture. Since then they have become a necessary part of it." And his article "Goût" in the *Dictionnaire philosophique* revealed the elitist bias in his conception of culture: "Taste is like philosophy. It belongs to a very small number of privileged souls ... It is unknown in bourgeois families, where one is contantly occupied with the care of one's fortune." Voltaire—who incessantly cultivated courtiers, tried to become one himself, and at least managed to buy his way into the nobility—thought that the Enlightenment should begin with the *grands:* once it had captured society's commanding heights, it could concern itself with the masses—but it should take care to prevent them from learning to read.

D'Alembert believed in essentially the same strategy, but he did not share his "master's" taste for the court.[27] His *Essai sur les gens de lettres et les grands* (1752), published two years before his election to the Académie Française, amounted to a declaration of independence for writers and writing as a proud new profession (not in the present sociological sense of the term, but as it was used by Duclos). Yet despite some strong language advocating a "democratic" republic of letters in contrast to the humiliating practices of patronage, d'Alembert stressed that society was and ought to be hierarchical and that the *grands* belonged on top.[28] By the time he wrote his *Histoire des membres de l'Académie française* (1787), when he ruled the academy as Duclos's successor in the perpetual secretaryship, d'Alembert reformulated Duclos's theme in a conservative vein. He castigated the "horde of literary rebels" (*frondeurs littéraires*) for venting their frustrated ambitions in attacks on the academy. He defended the academy's mixture of *grands seigneurs* and writers. And he emphasized the role of courtiers, as experts in the realm of taste and language, in a very elitist Enlightenment—a process of gradual, downward diffusion of knowledge, in which the principle of social equality could play no part.

> Is a great effort of philosophy necessary to understand that in society, and especially in a large state, it is indispensable to have rank defined by clear distinctions, that if virtue and talent alone have a claim to our true homage, the superiority of birth and position commands our deference and our respect . . . ? And how could men of letters envy or misconstrue the so legitimate prerogatives of other estates?[29]

As spokesmen for the writer's new estate (but not for the brand of philosophe represented by Diderot and d'Holbach), Duclos, Voltaire, and d'Alembert urged their "brethren" to profit from the mobility available to them in order to join the elite. Rather than challenge the social order, they offered a prop to it.

But what was the meaning of this process? Was the establishment becoming enlightened or the Enlightenment established? Probably both, although it might be best to avoid the overworked term "establishment"[30] and to fall back on the eighteenth-century expression already cited, *le monde.* After fighting for their principles in the mid-century and consolidating their victories during the last years of Louis XV's reign, the great philosophes faced the problem that has plagued every victorious ideology: they needed to find acolytes worthy of the cause among the next generation. Admittedly, "generation" is a vague concept.[31] Perhaps there are no real generations but only demographic "classes." Still, the great philosophes form a fairly neat demographic unit: Montesquieu 1689–1755, Voltaire 1694–1778; and then Buffon 1707–1788, Mably 1709–1785,

Rousseau 1712-1778, Diderot 1713-1784, Condillac 1715-1780, and d'Alembert 1717-1783. Contemporaries were naturally struck by the deaths, not the births, of great men. Voltaire, Rousseau, Diderot, Condillac, d'Alembert, and Mably all died between 1778 and 1785; and their deaths left important places to be filled by younger men, who were born, for the most part, in the 1720s and 1730s.

As age overcame them, the great philosophes made the rounds of the salons, searching for successors. They tried to find another d'Alembert—and came up with Marmontel, the champion of *Gluckisme.* They tried to persuade themselves that Thomas could thunder like Diderot and La Harpe bite like Voltaire. But it was no use. With the death of the old Bolsheviks, the Enlightenment passed into the hands of nonentities like Suard: it lost its fire and became a mere tranquil diffusion of light, a comfortable ascent toward progress. The transition from the heroic to the High Enlightenment domesticated the movement, integrating it with *le monde* and bathing it in the *douceur de vivre* of the Old Regime's dying years. As Mme. Suard remarked after reporting the receipt of their last pension, "I have no more events to recount, other than the continuation of a soft and varied life, until that horrible and disastrous epoch [the Revolution]."[32]Her husband, turned censor, refused to approve Beaumarchais's not so very revolutionary play, *Le Mariage de Figaro.* And Beaumarchais put most of his energy into speculation, and ultimately into building the biggest townhouse in Paris—"a house that is talked about"—the arriviste's dream.[33]

The establishment of the Enlightenment did not blunt its radical edge, however, because just as a generation gap separated the high philosophes from their predecessors, a generation split cut them off from the low-life of literature, from their contemporaries who failed to make it to the top and fell back into Grub Street.

Perhaps the literary world has always divided into a hierarchy whose extremes might be labeled a *monde* of mandarins on the one hand and Grub Street on the other. Such milieux existed in the seventeenth century and exist today. But the social and economic conditions of the High Enlightenment opened up an unusual gulf between the two groups during the last twenty-five years of the Old Regime, and this split, if examined in depth, ought to reveal something about one of the standard questions posed by the prerevolutionary era: what was the relation between the Enlightenment and the Revolution?

At first glance, it seems that the writer's lot should have improved substantially by the reign of Louis XVI. The relevant data, flimsy as they are, all point in the same direction: a considerable expansion in demand for the printed word.[34] Literacy probably doubled in the course of the century, and the general upward swing of the economy, combined with improvements in the educational system, very likely produced a larger, wealthier, and more leisured reading public. Certainly book production soared, whether measured by demands for privileges and *permissions tacites* or indirectly by the number of censors, booksellers, and printers. But there is little evidence that writers benefited from any publishing boom. On the contrary, everything indicates that while the mandarins fattened themselves on pensions, most authors sank into a sort of literary proletariat.

Admittedly, information about the growth of Grub Street comes from anecdotal sources, not statistics. Mallet du Pan claimed that three hundred writers, including a heavy dose of hacks, applied for Calonne's pensions, and he

concluded, "Paris is full of young men who take a little fa-
cility to be talent, of clerks, accountants, lawyers, soldiers,
who make themselves into authors, die of hunger, even beg,
and turn out pamphlets."[35] Crébillon fils, who reportedly
gave out *permissions de police* for 40,000–50,000 verses of pamphlet poetry every year, was besieged by a "multitude of
versifiers and would-be authors" who flooded into Paris
from the provinces.[36] Mercier found these "famished scribblers," "these poor hacks" (*écrivailleurs affamés, ces pauvres
barbouilleurs*) everywhere,[37] and Voltaire constantly hammered at the theme of the "ragged rabble" (*peuple crotté*)
crowding the bottom of the literary world. He placed "the
miserable species that writes for a living"—the "dregs of
humanity," "the riff-raff of literature" (*lie du genre humain,
canaille de la littérature*)—at a social level below prostitutes.[38] Writing in the same spirit, Rivarol and Champcenetz published a mock census of the undiscovered Voltaires
and d'Alemberts crammed into the garrets and gutters of
Paris. They produced articles on well over five hundred of
these poor hacks, who scribbled for a while in obscurity,
and then vanished like their dreams of glory, except for a
few: Carra, Gorsas, Mercier, Restif de la Bretonne, Manuel,
Desmoulins, Collot d'Herbois, and Fabre d'Eglantine. The
names of those future revolutionaries look strange in Rivarol's roll-call of "the five or six hundred poets" lost in the
legions of "la basse littérature," but Rivarol put them
rightly in their place.[39]

That place was Grub Street, and its population, combus-
tible at any time, was exploding during the last twenty-five
years of the Old Regime. Of course the interpretation may
be only a demographic fantasy based on subjective literary
sources, but the sources seem suggestive enough to warrant
giving the fantasy rein. They continually stress the theme of

the provincial lad who reads some Voltaire, burns with the ambition to become a philosophe, and leaves home only to smolder helplessly and expire down and out in Paris.[40] Even Duclos worried about this corollary to his formula for success.[41] And Voltaire, obsessed by the overpopulation of young writers in Paris ("Egypt of old had fewer locusts"), claimed that he attacked Grub Street in order to warn youth away from it.[42] "The number of those who are lost as a result of this passion [for the "career of letters"] is prodigious. They render themselves incapable of any useful work . . . They live off rhymes and hopes and die in destitution."[43] Voltaire's attacks wounded Mercier, who rose to the defense of the "poor devils" in opposition to the pampered, pensioned darlings of the academies and salons. Mercier protested that the "poor" of the "low literature" (*basse littérature*) in the Faubourg Saint-Germain had more talent and integrity than the "rich" in the "high literature" (*haute littérature*) of the Faubourg Saint-Honoré. But even he concluded pessimistically, "Ah! keep away from this career you who do not want to know poverty and humiliation."[44] Linguet, another anti-voltairean, devoted a whole book to the same theme. A constant target of would-be authors in search of a protector, he had reason to lament that "secondary schools have become a seedbed of child authors, who hurriedly scribble tragedies, novels, histories, and works of all sorts" and then "spend the rest of their lives in destitution and despair."[45]

The provincials flocked to Paris in search of glory, money, and the improved estate that seemed promised to any writer with sufficient talent. They did not necessarily share the motivations of the early philosophes, who were often nobles and clergymen enjoying enough leisure to write when the spirit moved them and who wrote before the time when "literature became a *métier,*" as Meister distastefully observed.[46] J. J. Garnier, a writer with a highly developed sense of professionalism, noted that by 1764 many men of letters were moved by "the hope of gaining reputation, influence, wealth etc. The avenues of advancement having been closed to them because of their humble birth and modest fortunes, they observed that the career of letters, open to everyone, offered another outlet for their ambition."[47] Mercier agreed that the immigrant from the provinces could hope to shake off his humble origins and climb to the top in Paris.[48] But the top of Paris, the *tout Paris,* had little room for ambitious young men on the make, perhaps because, as sociologists claim, rising status groups tend to become exclusive; perhaps because of a literary version of the Malthusian crush; perhaps because France suffered from a common ailment of developing countries: a surplus population of overeducated and underemployed littérateurs and lawyers. In any case, it seems that the attractiveness of the new career celebrated by Duclos and the new church proclaimed by Voltaire resulted in a record crop of potential philosophes, far more than could be absorbed under the archaic system of protections. Of course the lack of statistics and the confusion of social categories in prerevolutionary France (how does one define a "man of letters"?—someone with a literary reputation, someone who has published a book, or someone who lives by his pen?) make these hypotheses unverifiable. But there is no need for a complete census of eighteenth-century writers in order to make sense of the tension between the men of Grub Street and the men of *le monde* on the eve of the Revolution. The facts of literary life at that time speak for themselves.

The most salient fact is that the marketplace could not support many more writers than in the days when Prévost and Le Sage proved that it was possible—barely possible—to live from the pen instead of pensions. Although publishers offered somewhat better terms than earlier in the century, authors were caught between the masters of the publishing-bookselling guilds, who paid little for manuscripts, and pirate publishers, who paid nothing at all.[49] None of the great mid-century philosophes relied much on sales except for Diderot, who never fully extricated himself from Grub Street. Mercier claimed that in his day only thirty hard-core "professionals" supported themselves by writing.[50] The open, "democratic" market that could feed large numbers of enterprising authors did not appear in France until well into the nineteenth century. Before the day of the steam press and the mass reading public, writers lived by the kind of scavenging along the road to riches that worked so well for Suard—or they dropped by the wayside, in the gutter.

Once he had fallen into Grub Street, the provincial youth who had dreamt of storming Parnassus never extricated himself. As Mercier put it, "He falls and weeps at the foot of an invincible barrier . . . Forced to renounce the glory for which he so long has sighed, he stops and shudders before the door that closes the career to him."[51] The nephews and grandnephews of Rameau really faced a double barrier, both social and economic; for after Grub Street had left its mark on them, they could not penetrate into polite society where the plums were passed around. So they cursed the closed world of culture. They survived by doing the dirty work of society—spying for the police and peddling pornography; and they filled their writings with imprecations against the *monde* that humiliated and corrupted them. The prerevolutionary works of men like Marat, Brissot, and Carra do not express some vague, "anti-Establishment" feeling; they seethe with hatred of the literary "aristocrats" who had taken over the egalitarian "republic of letters" and made it into a "despotism."[52] It was in the depths of the intellectual underworld that these men became revolutionaries and that the Jacobinical determination to wipe out the aristocracy of the mind was born.

To explain why Grub Street had no exit and why its prisoners felt such hatred for the *grands* at the top it is necessary to say a word about the cultural modes of production during the late eighteenth century; and that word is the term one meets everywhere in the Old Regime: privilege.[53] Books themselves bore privileges granted by the grace of the king. Privileged guilds, whose organization showed the hand of Colbert himself, monopolized the production and distribution of the printed word. Privileged journals exploited royally granted monopolies. The privileged Comédie Française, Académie Royale de Musique, and Académie Royale de Peinture et de Sculpture legally monopolized the stage, opera, and the plastic arts. The Académie Française restricted literary immortality to forty privileged individuals, while privileged bodies like the Académie des Sciences and the Société Royale de Médecine dominated the world of science. And above all these corps rose the supremely privileged cultural elite who kept *le monde* all to themselves.

It may have been appropriate for a corporate society to organize its culture corporately, but such archaic organization constrained the expansive forces that might have opened up the cultural industries and supported more of the overpopulated underworld of letters. As it was, the bookdealers' guilds acted far more effectively than the police in suppressing unprivileged books, and underprivileged youths like Brissot were forced into destitution, not so much because their early works were radical as because the monopolies prevented them from reaching the market.[54] Writers

therefore fed their families either from the pensions and sinecures reserved for the members of *le monde* or from the
scraps tossed into Grub Street.

The corporate organization of culture was not simply an
economic matter, for it contradicted the basic premises
under which the young writers had flocked to Paris in the
1770s and 1780s. They had come with the conviction that
the republic of letters really existed as it had been described
in the works of the great philosophes—as the literary counterpart to the "atomic" individualism of Physiocratic theory, a society of independent but fraternal individuals, in
which the best men won but all derived dignity, as well as a
living, from service to the common cause. Experience
taught them that the real world of letters functioned like
everything else in the Old Regime: individuals got ahead as
best they could in a labyrinth of baroque institutions. To
have an article published in the *Mercure,* to get a play accepted by the Comédie Française, to steer a book through
the Direction de la Librairie, to win membership in an academy, entry into a salon, or a sinecure in the bureaucracy required resorting to the old devices of privilege and protection, not merely the demonstration of talent.

Talent certainly carried some to the top. Maury was the
son of a poor cobbler in a village of the Venaissain, Marmontel of a poor tailor in the Limousin, Morellet of a
small-time paper merchant of Lyons, Rivarol (who called
himself a count) of an innkeeper in Languedoc; La Harpe
and Thomas were orphans. All rose through skill and schol-
arships, and they were not the only examples of rapid upward mobility. But as de Tocqueville observed, it was the erratic opening up of mobility, not the absence of it, that
produced social tensions. Nowhere was this general phenomenon more important than in the world of letters, be-

cause the attractiveness of writing as a new kind of career produced more writers than could be integrated into *le monde* or supported outside of it. To the outsiders, the whole process looked rotten, and they were not inclined to blame their failures on their own inability: on the contrary, they tended to see themselves as successors to Voltaire. They had knocked on the door of Voltaire's church, and the door remained closed. Not only did their status fail to rise as fast as their expectations; it plummeted, dragging them down to a world of opposites and contradictions, a *monde* turned upside down, where estate could not be defined at all, and dignity dissolved in destitution. Seen from the perspective of Grub Street, the republic of letters was a lie.

If the institutional realities of the established literary world contradicted its principles, at least from the viewpoint of those who failed to reach the top, what were the realities of life for those at the bottom? Grub Street had no principles, and it had no institutions of a formal kind. It was a world of free-floating individuals—not Lockean gentlemen abiding by the rules of some implicit game, but Hobbesian brutes struggling to survive. It was as far removed from *le monde* as was the café from the salon.[55]

Despite the democratic play of wit, the salon remained a rather formal institution. It did not allow any putting of elbows on the table or any admission to those without introductions. During the last decades of the Old Regime, the salon became increasingly a preserve for the high philosophes, who generally abandoned the cafés to the lower species of littérateur. The café functioned as the antithesis of the salon. It was open to everyone, just one step from the street, although there were degrees in its closeness to street life. While the great names gathered in the Procope or La Régence, lesser figures congregated in the notorious Caveau of the Palais-Royal, and the humblest hacks frequented the cafés of the boulevards, blending into an underworld of "swindlers, recruiting agents, spies, and pickpockets; here one finds only pimps, buggers, and *bardaches*."[56]

Grub Street may have lacked the corporate structure of the established culture, but it was not sheer anarchy. It had institutions of a sort. For example, the *musées* and *lycées* that sprang up in such numbers during the 1780s responded to the needs of obscure writers for a place to exhibit their wares, to declaim their works, and to make contacts. These clubhouses formalized the functions of the cafés. The *musées* of Court de Gébelin and P. C. de La Blancherie seem even to have served as counteracademies and antisalons for the multitude of philosophes who could not get a hearing elsewhere. La Blancherie published a journal, *Les Nouvelles de la République des lettres et des arts,* which vented some of the frustrations of the *musée* members both by sniping at academicians and by reviewing works that were beneath the notice of the *Journal de Paris* and the *Mercure.*[57] But the most effective sniper and the most influential outsider of prerevolutionary France was Simon-Henri Linguet. While respecting the crown and the church, Linguet blasted at France's most prestigious institutions, especially the Parisian bar and the Académie Française. His polemical genius made his pamphlets, judicial *mémoires,* and journals best-sellers; and his tirades against aristocratic and despotic corporateness reverberated up and down Grub Street, setting the tone for some of the antielitist propaganda of the Revolution.[58]

Grub Street therefore had a few organs and organizations to express itself. Perhaps it even had an inchoate stratification system of its own, for the underground contained several levels. Having cultivated an established philosophe or got some verses published in the *Almanach des muses,* some writers lived just below *le monde.* Mirabeau maintained a mandarin style of life even when in prison and in debt. He kept a stable of pamphleteers (who referred to him simply as *le comte*) to produce the works published under his name.[59] Lesser figures put together the encyclopedias, dictionaries, digests, and anthologies that circulated in such profusion in the last half of the eighteenth century. Even cruder hack work could be relatively respectable—writing for ministers, pamphleteering for the *baissiers* fighting the *haussiers* on the Bourse, and producing *nouvelles à la main;* or it could be demeaning—manufacturing smut, peddling prohibited works, and spying for the police. Many writers lived on the fringes of the law, calling themselves lawyers or law clerks and taking on the odd jobs available in the *basoche* of the Palais de Justice. Some, at the bottom of the literary underworld, sank into criminality. Charles Théveneau de Morande, one of Grub Street's most violent and virulent pamphleteers, lived in a demimonde of prostitutes, pimps, blackmailers, pickpockets, swindlers, and murderers. He tried his hand at more than one of these professions and gathered material for his pamphlets by skimming the scum around him. As a result, his works smeared everything, good and bad alike, with a spirit of such total depravity and alienation that Voltaire cried out in horror, "There has just appeared one of those satanic works [Morande's *Gazetier cuirassé*] where everyone from the monarch to the last citizen is insulted with furor; where the most atrocious and most absurd calumny spreads a horrible poison on everything one respects and loves."[60]

Grub Street stifled respect and love. Its grim struggle for survival brought out baser sentiments, as is suggested by the following excerpts from reports submitted to the Parisian police by its legions of spies and secret agents, many of them underworld writers themselves with their own dossiers in the archives of the police.

GORSAS: proper for all kinds of vile jobs. Run out of Versailles and put in Bicêtre [a jail for especially disreputable criminals] by personal order of the king for having corrupted children whom he had taken in as lodgers, he has withdrawn to a fifth floor on the rue Tictone. Gorsas produces *libelles*. He has an arrangement with an apprentice printer of the Imprimerie Polytype, who has been fired from other printing shops. He [Gorsas] is suspected of having printed obscene works there. He peddles prohibited books.

AUDOUIN: calls himself a lawyer, writes *nouvelles à la main,* peddler of forbidden books; he is connected with Prudhomme, Manuel, and other disreputable authors and book peddlers. He does all kinds of work; he will be a spy when one wants.

DUPORT DU TERTRE: solicits a position in the offices of the police; is a lawyer who is not often employed in the Palais, although he is not without merit. He failed to get a position in the Domaines. He lives in a modest, fourth-story apartment; he hardly gives off an air of wealth [*il ne respire pas l'opulence*]. He is generally well spoken of; he has a good reputation in his neighborhood.

DELACROIX: lawyer, writer, expelled from the bar. He produces [judicial] *mémoires* for shady cases; and when he has no *mémoires* to write, he writes scurrilous works.

MERCIER: lawyer, a fierce, bizarre man; he neither pleads in court nor consults. He hasn't been admitted to the bar, but he takes the title of lawyer. He has written the *Tableau de Paris,* in four volumes, and other works. Fearing the Bastille, he left the country, then returned and wants to become attached to the police.

MARAT: bold charlatan. M. Vicq d'Azir asks, in the name of the Société Royale de Médecine, that he be run out of Paris. He is from Neuchâtel in Switzerland. Many sick persons have died in his hands, but he has a doctor's degree, which was bought for him.

CHENIER: insolent and violent poet. He lives with Beauménil of the Opéra, who, in the decline of her charms, fell in love with him. He mistreats her and beats her—so much that her neighbors report that he would have killed her had they not come to her rescue. She accuses him of having taken her jewels; she describes him as a man capable of any crime and doesn't hide her regrets at having let herself be bewitched by him.

FRERON: who has neither the wit nor the pen of his father, is generally despised. It is not he who writes the *Année littéraire,* although he has its privilege. He hires young unemployed lawyers. He's an insolent coward, who has received his share of beatings—and doesn't boast about it—most recently from the hand of the actor Desessarts, whom he had called a "ventriloquist" in one of his issues. He is connected with Mouvel, who was expelled from the Comédie for pederasty.

PANIS: young lawyer of the Palais, protected by M. le Président d'Ormesson because of Panis's parents, who are his [d'Ormesson's] *fermiers;* is employed by Fréron on the *Année littéraire.* Panis has as a mistress a woman branded by the hand of the executioner.[61]

Life in Grub Street was hard, and it took a psychological toll, because "the excrement of literature" had to face not merely failure but degradation, and they had to face it alone. Failure breeds loneliness, and the conditions of Grub Street were peculiarly suited to isolate its inhabitants. Ironically, the basic unit of life in *la basse littérature* was the garret (stratification went more by story than by neighborhood in eighteenth-century Paris). In their fourth- and fifth-floor *mansardes,* before Balzac had romanticized their lot, the undiscovered philosophes learned that they were what Voltaire had called them: the *canaille de la littérature.* But how could they come to terms with such knowledge?

Fabre d'Eglantine is a case in point. A drifter and a déclassé who saw himself as the successor of Molière, he went down in the police dossiers as a "poor poet, who drags about in shame and destitution; he is despised everywhere; among men of letters he is considered an execrable subject" (*poète médiocre qui traîne sa honte et sa misère; il est partout honni; il passe parmi les gens de lettres pour un exécrable sujet*).[62] Sometime before the Revolution, Fabre wrote a play that reads like an escapist fantasy of an author trapped in Grub Street. The hero, an unappreciated twenty-eight-year-old genius from the provinces, writes his heart out in a Parisian garret, mocked and exploited by the evil elite that dominates French literature: mercenary publishers, crass journal editors, and the perfidious *beaux-esprits* who monopolize the salons. He is about to succumb to disease and poverty when, by a stroke of good fortune, a virtuous bourgeois tycoon discovers him, appreciates his talent and superior morality, and carries him off to the provinces, where he writes masterpieces happily ever after. The play breathes hatred of the cultural elite and a fierce egalitarianism, which confirms La Harpe's description of the prerevolutionary Fabre as an embittered failure, "envenomed with hatred, like all the persons of his sort, against everyone who called himself an *homme du monde,* against everything that had a rank in society—a rank that he did not have and should not have had."[63]

Others probably sought refuge in similar fantasies. Marat dreamed of being whisked away to preside over an academy of sciences in Madrid.[64] Both he and Carra found solace in imagining that they had outstripped Newton, despite society's failure to appreciate them. But no amount of fantasy could erase the contradictions between life at the top and the bottom of the world of letters and between what those at the bottom were and what they wanted to be. The established writers enjoyed an estate; they derived honor and wealth from the established cultural institutions. But the literary proletariat had no social location. Its ragged pamphleteers could not call themselves men of letters; they were just *canaille,* condemned to gutters and garrets, working in isolation, poverty, and degradation, and therefore easy prey to the psychology of failure—a vicious combination of hatred of the system and hatred of the self.

The Grub Street mentality made itself heard with exceptional vehemence during the last years of the Old Regime. It spoke through the *libelle,* the hack writers' staff of life, their meat, their favorite genre and a genre that deserves to be rescued from the neglect of historians, because it communicates the Grub Street view of the world: a spectacle of knaves and fools buying and selling one another and forever falling victim to *les grands.* The *grand monde* was the real target of the *libelles.* They slandered the court, the church, the aristocracy, the academies, the salons, everything elevated and respectable, including the monarchy itself, with a scurrility that is difficult to imagine today, although it has had a long career in underground literature. For pamphleteers had lived by libel since the time of Aretino. They had exploited all the great crises in French history, in the propaganda produced by the Catholic League during the religious wars, for example, and in the *Mazarinades* of the Fronde. But the ultimate crisis of the Old Regime gave them an unusual opportunity, and they rose to the occasion with what seems to have been their greatest barrage of antisocial smut.[65]

Although a survey of *libelles* published between 1770 and 1789 cannot be undertaken here,[66] it should be possible to capture some of their flavor by explicating one of their texts. Perhaps the most outspoken *libelle*—a pamphlet so sensational and so widely read that it became virtually a prototype of the genre—was the work that especially horrified Voltaire: *Le Gazetier cuirassé* by Charles Théveneau de Morande. Morande mixed specific calumny and general declamation in brief, punchy paragraphs, which anticipated the style of gossip columnists in the modern yellow press. He promised to reveal "behind-the-scenes secrets" (*secrets des coulisses*)[67] in the tradition of the *chronique scandaleuse.* But he provided more than scandal:

> The devout wife of a certain Maréchal de France (who suffers from an imaginary lung disease), finding a husband of that species too delicate, considers it her religious duty to spare him and so condemns herself to the crude caresses of her butler, who would still be a lackey if he hadn't proven himself so robust.[68]

This sexual sensationalism conveyed a social message: the aristocracy had degenerated to the point of being unable to reproduce itself;[69] the great nobles were either impotent or deviant;[70] their wives were forced to seek satisfaction from their servants, representatives of the more virile lower classes; and everywhere among *les grands* incest and venereal disease had extinguished the last sparks of humanity.[71] Vivid detail communicated the message more effectively than abstractions; for although the reader might at first merely be shocked by a particular incident,

> The Count of Noail——, having taken some scandalous liberties with one of his lackeys, this country bumpkin knocked over Monseigneur with a slap that kept his lordship in bed for eight days . . . The lackey . . . is a Picard of the first order who had not yet been instructed how to serve a Spanish grandee, Knight of the Royal Orders, Lieutenant General, Governor of Vers——, Prince of P——, Lord of Arpa——, Grand Cross of Malta,

Knight of the Golden Fleece, and secular member of the Society of Jesus, etc., etc., etc., etc.[72]

he would know what to conclude after he had recovered from the shock. Morande led the reader toward general conclusions by piling up anecdotes and slanting them in the same direction—against *le monde.* He showed that the summit of society had decayed beyond the point of recovery, both morally and physically:

The public is warned that an epidemic disease is raging among the girls of the Opera, that it has begun to reach the ladies of the court, and that it has even been communicated to their lackeys. This disease elongates the face, destroys the complexion, reduces the weight, and causes horrible ravages where it becomes situated. There are ladies without teeth, others without eyebrows, and some completely paralyzed.[73]

Morande's chronicle of cuckoldry, buggery, incest, and impotence in high places therefore reads as an indictment of the social order. And Morande did not merely leave the reader with a general impression of corruption. He associated the aristocracy's decadence with its inability to fulfill its functions in the army, the church, and the state.

Of approximately two hundred colonels in the infantry, cavalry, and dragoons in France, one hundred and eighty know how to dance and to sing little songs; about the same number wear lace and red heels; at least half can read and sign their names; and in addition not four of them know the first elements of their craft.[74]

As the king's confessor was disgraced for having been discovered flirting with some pages, there is now open competition for that position, which will go to the prelate who will be easiest on the king's conscience. The Archbishop of R—— has been proposed but rejected, because of the scandalous relations he has maintained for such a long time with one of his grand vicars. The cardinals of Gèv—— and of Luy—— were designated to serve by alternate semesters; but since the first doesn't know how to read and the second hasn't recovered from being slapped [a reference to a scandal involving homosexuality], one can't be sure of His Majesty's decision.[75]

Morande constantly stressed the connection between sexual and political corruption by news flashes like the following: "Having a pretty wife of whom he was very jealous, the unfortunate Baron of Vaxen was sent to prison by a *lettre de cachet* in order to learn the customs of *le monde,* while the duke [La Vrillière, one of Louis XV's favorite ministers] sleeps with his wife."[76] The monarchy had degenerated into despotism, this message stood out on every page: the ministers have hired an extra team of secretaries just to sign *lettres de cachet;* the Bastille and Vincennes are so overcrowded that tents have been set up inside their walls to house the guards; a new elite police corps, modeled on Louis XIV's dragonades, has been created to terrorize the provinces; the government is experimenting with a new machine that can hang ten men at a time; and the public executioner has resigned, not because he is worried about automation, but because the new Maupeou ministry offends his sense of justice. In case any reader could possibly miss the point, Morande stated it explicitly: "According to Chancellor Maupeou, a monarchical state is a state where the prince has the right of life and death over all his subjects, where he is proprietor of all the wealth in the kingdom, where honor and equity are founded on arbitrary principles, which must always conform with the interests of the sovereign."[77]

What was the king's place in this political system? "The chancellor and the Duke d'Aiguillon have come to dominate the king so much that they leave him only the liberty of sleeping with his mistress, petting his dogs, and signing marriage contracts."[78] Deriding the idea of a divine origin to royal sovereignty,[79] Morande reduced the king to the level of the ignorant, crapulous court. He made Louis XV look ridiculous, a trivial figure even in his despotism: "A notice has been published in the hopes of finding the scepter of one of the greatest kings of Europe. After a very long search, it was found in the *toilette* of a pretty woman called a countess, who uses it for playing with her cat."[80] The real rulers of France and the villains of the book were the Countess DuBarry and the ministerial triumvirate of Maupeou, Terray, and d'Aiguillon. Seizing on Mme. DuBarry as a symbol of the regime, Morande dwelt on every detail about her that he could fabricate or extract from café gossip: her supposedly illegitimate birth to a servant girl who had been seduced by a monk, her career as a common whore, her use of the king's power to help her former colleagues by forbidding the police to set foot in brothels, her lesbianic relations with her maid, and so on. Similarly, Morande showed that the ministers used their authority to fatten their purses, procure mistresses, or simply enjoy villainy for its own sake.

Grotesque, inaccurate, and simplistic as it was, this version of political news should not be dismissed as merely mythical, because myth making and unmaking proved to be powerful forces in the last years of a regime, which, though absolutist in theory, had become increasingly vulnerable in practice to the vagaries of public opinion. To be sure, the eighteenth-century French "public" did not exist in any coherent form; and insofar as it did exist, it was excluded from direct participation in politics. But its exclusion produced a political naiveté that made it all the more vulnerable to Morande's style of gazeteering. For instead of discussing issues, the *gazetier cuirassé* defamed individuals. He buried Maupeou's reforms—probably the regime's last chance to survive by destroying some of the vested interests that were devouring it—in a torrent of mudslinging. That the Maupeou program would have benefited the common people did not matter to Morande, because he and his fellow hacks had no interest in reform. They hated the system in itself; and they expressed their hatred by desanctifying its symbols, destroying the myths that gave it legitimacy in the eyes of the public, and perpetrating the countermyth of degenerate despotism.

Far from being limited to Morande's works, these themes became increasingly important in *libelle* literature as the Old Regime approached its finale. *Le Gazetier cuirassé* merely set the tone for an outpouring of antigovernment pamphlets that extended from the "Maupeouana" of the early 1770s to the "Calonniana" of the late 1780s. The most prolific producer of the latter was Jean-Louis Carra, an outcast from the closed circles of established science, who stated frankly that his efforts to damn the ministry had been provoked by the refusal of one of Calonne's pensions.[81] Morande's motives had not been nobler. He meant to make money, both by exploiting the market for sensationalism and by blackmailing the persons he libeled.

Did slander on such a scale, its crass motivation notwithstanding, amount to a call for revolution? Not really, because the *libelles* lacked a program. They not only failed to give the reader any idea of what sort of society should replace the Old Regime; they hardly contained any abstract ideas at all. In denouncing despotism, Morande cried out for liberty; and in fulminating against aristocratic decadence, he seemed to advocate bourgeois standards of decency, if only by contrast.[82] But he did not defend any clear set of principles. He referred to himself as *le philosophe cynique*[83] and slandered everything, even the philosophes.[84] The same spirit animated most other *libelles;* it was a spirit of nihilism rather than of ideological commitment.

Yet the *libelles* showed a curious tendency to moralize, even in their pornography. The climax of one of Morande's obscene pamphlets about courtiers and courtesans came in an indignant description of Mme. DuBarry:

> passing directly from the brothel to the throne, toppling the most powerful and redoubtable minister, overthrowing the constitution of the monarchy, insulting the royal family, the presumptive heir to the throne, and his august consort by her incredible luxury, by her insolent talk, [and insulting] the entire nation, which is dying of hunger, by her vainglorious extravagance and by the well-known depredations of all the *roués* surrounding her, as she sees groveling at her feet not only the *grands* of the kingdom and the ministers, but the princes of the royal blood, foreign ambassadors, and the church itself, which canonizes her scandals and her debauchery.[85]

This tone of moral outrage was typical of the *libelles* and seems to have been more than a rhetorical pose. It expressed a feeling of total contempt for a totally corrupt elite. So if the *libelles* lacked a coherent ideology, they communicated a revolutionary point of view: they showed that social rot was consuming French society, eating its way downward from the top. And their pornographic details got the point across to a public that could not assimilate the *Social Contract* and that soon would be reading *Le Père Duchesne.*

This gutter Rousseauism—a natural idiom for the *Rousseau du ruisseau*[86]—may have been related to Rousseau's rejection of the culture and morality of France's upper classes. For the men of Grub Street saw Jean-Jacques as one of their own. In following his career, they could not only imagine the realization of their hopes but also find consolation for their failures. *Débourgeoisé* like such typical *libellistes* as Brissot and Manuel, Rousseau had risen from their ranks into *le monde,* seen it for what it was, exposed elitist culture itself as the very agent of social corruption, and returned with his semiliterate, working-class wife to a humble existence in the neighborhood of Grub Street, where he died pure and purged. The hacks respected him and despised Voltaire— Voltaire the *mondain,* who had stigmatized Rousseau as a "poor devil" and who died in the same year, in the bosom of *le monde.*[87]

Is it surprising then that the writers whom Voltaire scorned as *la canaille de la littérature* should have moralized in the manner of Rousseau in their politico-pornography? To them the Old Regime was obscene. In making them its spies and smut-peddlers, it had violated their moral core and desecrated their youthful visions of serving humanity honorably in Voltaire's church. So they became rank atheists and poured out their souls in blasphemies about the society that had driven them down into an underworld of criminals and deviants. The scatology of their pamphlets—their frequent references, for example, to venereal disease passed on from the Cardinal de Rohan to the queen and all the great figures of the court during the Diamond Necklace Affair— communicates a sense of total opposition to an elite so corrupt as to deserve annihilation. No wonder that the government kept secret files on the *libellistes* and consigned the *libelles* to the bottom of its graduated scale of illegality, or that the very catalogues of them circulated secretly, in handwritten notes, like the list of "philosophical books" quoted above. The *libellistes* spoke for a subintelligentsia that was not merely unintegrated but beyond the pale and that wanted not to reform society in some polite, liberal, Voltairean way, but to overturn it.

There is a danger of using the word "revolutionary" too

liberally and of exaggerating the ideological distance between the top and the bottom of the literary world in the Old Regime. The first philosophes were revolutionary in their fashion: they articulated and propagated a value system, or an ideology, that undermined the traditional values Frenchmen inherited from their Catholic and royalist past. The men of Grub Street believed in the message of the philosophes; they wanted nothing more than to become philosophes themselves. It was their attempt to realize this ambition that made them see *philosophie* in a different light and to hold it up to the realities not only of society in general but also of the cultural world. The great philosophes had had a sharp eye for realities also, and their successors of the next generation may have been as realistic as the most hard-bitten hacks: nothing suggests that the view from the top is more distorted than the view from the bottom. But the difference in viewpoints was crucial—a difference of perspective not principle, of mentality not philosophy, a difference to be found less in the content of ideas than in their emotional coloring. The emotional thrust of Grub Street literature was revolutionary, although it had no coherent political program nor even any distinctive ideas of its own. Both the philosophes and the *libellistes* were seditious in their own way: in becoming established, the Enlightenment undercut the elite's faith in the legitimacy of the social order; and in attacking the elite, the *libelles* spread disaffection deeper and more widely. Each of the opposing camps deserves its place among the intellectual origins of the Revolution.

Once the Revolution came, the opposition between the high- and low-life of literature had to be resolved. Grub Street rose, overthrew *le monde,* and requisitioned the positions of power and prestige. It was a cultural revolution, which created a new elite and gave them new jobs. While Suard, Marmontel, and Morellet found themselves stripped of their income, Brissot, Carra, Gorsas, Manuel, Mercier, Desmoulins, Prudhomme, Loustalot, Louvet, Hébert, Maret, Marat, and many more of the old literary proletariat led new lives as journalists and bureaucrats.[88] The Revolution turned the cultural world upside down. It destroyed the academies, scattered the salons, retracted the pensions, abolished the privileges, and obliterated the agencies and vested interests that had strangled the book trade before 1789. Newspapers and theaters sprang up at such a rate that one could even speak of an industrial revolution within the cultural revolution.[89] And in destroying the old institutions, the new elite meted out a crude, revolutionary justice: Manuel took over the police department that had once hired him secretly for the suppression of *libelles*, and he published its archives in *libelle* from (carefully purging all references to his and Brissot's careers as police spies); Marat, a victim of academic persecution before the Revolution, led the movement that eventually destroyed the academies; and Fabre and Collot, frustrated actor-playwrights in the Old Regime, struck down the monopoly of the *comédiens du roi* and very nearly struck off their heads. In a sequel to his prerevolutionary census, Rivarol interpreted the Revolution as the work of the status-hungry surplus population of men who had failed to make it in the old order.[90]

Of course the cultural revolution did not fit perfectly into the pattern of Rivarol's counterrevolutionary propaganda any more than it corresponded to Taine's counterrevolutionary history. Many of the old elite, even academicians like Condorcet, Bailly, Chamfort, and La Harpe, did not oppose the destruction of the institutions in which they had prospered. The literary hacks scattered in a dozen directions, supporting different factions in different phases of the conflict. Some of them, particularly during the Girondist period and the Directory, showed that they wanted nothing more than to participate in a revival of *le monde*. And at least during the years 1789–1791, the Revolution realized many of the ideas propagated by the High Enlightenment. But the Revolution at its most revolutionary expressed the antielitist passions of Grub Street. It would be wrong to interpret tred of mandarins. The Jacobin pamphleteers believed in their propaganda. They wanted to slough off their corrupt old selves and to become new men, newly integrated in a republic of virtue. As cultural revolutionaries, they wanted to destroy "the aristocracy of the mind" in order to create an egalitarian republic of letters in an egalitarian republic. In calling for the abolition of academies, Lanjuinais put their case perfectly: "The academies and all other literary corps must be free and not privileged; to authorize their formation under any kind of protection would be to make them into veritable guilds. Privileged academies are always seedbeds of a literary aristocracy."[91] From there it was but one step to Grégoire's injunction: "We must look for merit dwelling impoverished in basements and in seventh-story garrets ... True genius is almost always *sans-culotte*."[92] Perhaps the propagandists of the garrets functioned as the ideological carriers who injected the crude, Jacobinical version of Rousseauism into the Parisian *sans-culotterie*.[93] Hébert certainly played that role—Hébert, who had rotted in obscurity before the Revolution and, at one point, had tried to persuade the Variétés to perform one of his plays only to get a job checking seat tickets in the *loges*.[94]

It would seem to be necessary, therefore, in looking for the connection between the Enlightenment and the Revolution, to examine the structure of the cultural world under the Old Regime, to descend from the heights of metaphysics and to enter Grub Street. At this low level of analysis, the High Enlightenment looks relatively tame. Voltaire's *Lettres philosophiques* may have exploded like a "bomb"[95] in 1734, but by the time of Voltaire's apotheosis in 1778, France had absorbed the shock. There was nothing shocking at all in the works of his successors, for *they* had been absorbed, fully integrated into *le monde.* Of course one must allow for exceptions like Condorcet, but the Suard generation of philosophes had remarkably little to say. They argued over Gluck and Piccini, dabbled in pre-Romanticism, chanted the old litanies about legal reform and *l'infâme,* and collected their tithes. And while they grew fat in Voltaire's church, the revolutionary spirit passed to the lean and hungry men of Grub Street, to the cultural pariahs who, through poverty and humiliation, produced the Jacobinical version of Rousseauism. The crude pamphleteering of Grub Street was revolutionary in feeling as well as in message. It expressed the passion of men who hated the Old Regime in their guts, who ached with hatred of it. It was from such visceral hatred, not from the refined abstractions of the contented cultural elite, that the extreme Jacobin revolution found its authentic voice.

A Spy
in Grub Street

 JACQUES-PIERRE BRISSOT'S LIFE READS LIKE a parable of his times. He made sure it would because he wrote the script himself. In his memoirs, he appears as the embodiment of the revolutionary spirit, uncorruptible and uncompromising, a philosophe turned man of action, having imbibed Enlightenment as a child, rejected the authority of church and state as a youth, and plotted revolution as an adult. Brissot's biographers and most authorities on the French Revolution have accepted the memoirs as an accurate picture of the complete prerevolutionary man. As Daniel Mornet put it, "From his youth on, he is the complete image of all the aspirations of a generation."[1] When seen through business letters and police reports, however, a man can look very different from the way he presents himself in his memoirs. A new examination of Brissot's career, based on new sources, should add some shadows and flesh tones to the traditional portraits of him. It is undertaken, not in order to expose the nakedness of the man behind the memoirs, but rather to understand the making of a revolutionary and the era he is believed to typify.

Brissot's prerevolutionary career seems most vulnerable to inspection at its most critical point, the two months he spent in the Bastille during the summer of 1784. As he contemplated it from his prison cell, the Old Regime may well have looked like a conspiracy to snuff out free spirits such as himself. The thirteenth son of a tavernkeeper in Chartres, he had set out seven years earlier to win a place as a respectable citizen in the republic of letters, whose capital lay in Paris. He had published thousands of pages on the appropriate subjects—the fallacies of St. Paul, the absurdities of the French legal system, the glories and weaknesses of the British constitution—and had taken the appropriately encyclopedic view of things, as could be seen by the very titles of his *Correspondance universelle sur ce qui intéresse le bonheur de l'homme et de la société* and *De la vérité ou méditations sur les moyens de parvenir à la vérité dans toutes les connaissances humaines.* He had made the conventional philosophic pilgrimages to the Switzerland of Rousseau and the England of Voltaire and Montesquieu. He had appealed for support to Voltaire and D'Alembert. He had competed in the essay contests sponsored by various academies and had won two prizes. He had even earned two *lettres de cachet.* But although he had done everything a young writer should do, Paris had refused to recognize him as a philosophe.

Undaunted, he had moved to London, investing all his energy, all his ambition, and all the 4,000 or 5,000 livres that he had inherited after his father's death in 1779 into a plan to establish a "Lycée" or world center for philosophers, which would include a journal, a correspondence system, and a clubhouse. The world's philosophers, however, had failed to rally around Brissot's modest home at 26 Newman Street. Very few of them corresponded with him or subscribed to his journal—so few that Brissot's partner, Desforges d'Hurecourt, who had arrived in the spring of 1784 to find the Lycée a one-man, nonprofit organization lacking even the promised clubhouse, concluded that he had been swindled and demanded the return of the 13,000 livres he claimed he had sunk into the enterprise. At this time the landlord and the tax collector also began clamoring for money, and Brissot's printer had him thrown into prison for debt. Brissot scraped up enough money to buy his way out but was forced to drop everything in order to find a replacement for Desforges among the speculators of Paris. While seeking to recover from the loss of his capital, Brissot lost the main market for his journal, because Vergennes, the foreign minister, revoked the permission for it to circulate in France. Then, on July 12, at one o'clock in the morning, the crowning blow fell: he was locked up in the Bastille on suspicion of having produced some pamphlets satirizing French officials.[2]

Brissot had expended his youth in failures and frustrated ambitions. It had brought him to this, the Bastille, and his future, as he contemplated it in his thirtieth year, must have seemed worse than his past. His first child, Félix, had been born on April 29, 1784, shortly before Brissot's departure for France, and both the infant and the mother were ailing. The Lycée was ruined; the journal could not be revived, and Desforges had begun a long, costly, and ultimately unresolved legal battle to recover his 13,000 livres and to convict Brissot for swindling. Brissot had lost all of his own investment in the Lycée and still owed large sums to his printer, paper supplier, and others. No assets remained to offset those debts, for Desforges had even sold the furniture in the Newman Street house. Imprisoned and stripped of virtually all his possessions, where was Brissot to find the 13,335 livres that he needed, as he later maintained,[3] in order to avoid leaving his London affairs in bankruptcy? Where was he to find a job, a home for his family, a way out of the Bastille? He had failed to become a philosophe: what *was* to become of him?

Temporary solutions were available for some of these problems. Brissot's mother-in-law took his wife and baby into her home at Boulogne-sur-Mer for a few months, and Mme. de Genlis, his wife's former employer at the Palais Royal, helped negotiate his release from the Bastille on September 10. But another problem made his situation almost hopeless. Since August 31, 1779, he had been corresponding with the Société typographique de Neuchâtel. The correspondence, now in the Bibliothèque de la ville de Neuchâtel, provides a detailed record of his evolution as a pamphleteer and a measure of his desperate circumstances in the second half of 1784. Brissot's first letters fairly vibrate with the enthusiasm of a young man setting out to make himself into a philosophe, but by 1784 his enthusiasm disappeared under a load of financial problems. He foolishly undertook to pay for his own publications (although who else would finance the philosophizing of an unknown son of a provincial tavernkeeper?) and filled the Society's books with commissions. They make a sad list of failures: about a dozen pamphlets and treatises, including his *Bibliothèque philosophique du législateur, Théorie des lois criminelles, De la vérité, Testament politique de l'Angleterre,* and the first volume of his *Correspondance universelle.* Brissot gambled that the sale of the works would pay for the cost of their publication and would establish his place as a young Voltaire or d'Alembert. He succeeded only in acquiring a reputation as a minor, rather outspoken pamphleteer and 12,301-9-0 livres[4] in debts to the Society, in addition to the thousands that he owed in London.

The Society began dunning Brissot for payment of his printing bills as soon as it learned of his release from the Bastille. He parried its demands by offering to let it take over his stock of unsold books—a classic ploy of impecunious authors, as the Society had learned at a heavy cost on other occasions. Still, Brissot had nothing else to offer, and there was some hope of selling his *Bibliothèque philosophique du législateur,* a ten-volume compilation of philosophical works on the law, which seemed likely to have more appeal than his own treatises with the general reading public. Before pursuing that last hope, however, Brissot needed to remove one more obstacle to his recovery. The Paris police had confiscated a shipment of the fifth volume of the *Bibliothèque philosophique.* Without the fifth volume, the ten-volume set would be worthless. So wherever he turned, the powers of the Old Regime seemed to bar his way. The desperate state of his affairs can be appreciated from the following letter, which he sent to the printers in Neuchâtel six weeks after he got out of the Bastille.

Boulogne-sur-Mer, 22 October 1784

Messieurs,

I seize my first free moment, which I have had at last at Boulogne, to straighten out our accounts. I have examined them with the utmost care. They do not answer completely the points that I raised in my detailed letter of 3 February 1784 . . . But I set aside this and all other articles. I want to finish. I want to bid a solemn farewell to speculations in publishing and to renounce a career which I entered too imprudently. I had too little knowledge of the world, and especially of the world in which I did business. I was deceived, taken for a ride everywhere. Fortunately, it is not too late, and I want to withdraw. Your account is one of the last and the only large one of its kind that I have to terminate. I shall do what I can to settle it soon. You had an accurate idea of my position, when you believed me too weak to sustain this enterprise [the London Lycée]. I thought the beginning would bring in enough to support the end. But everyone wanted satisfaction at the same time, and I was crushed. Now we are approaching the liquidation. I can liberate myself and even expect a certain profit, if you will lend an ear to the arrangements that I propose in the accompanying memorandum. Before reading it, give the deepest consideration to two points: first, my honesty, which commits me to the end of my life to repay my debts, whatever they may be; second, my present situation. You know my misfortune. But the worst suffering of all, because it extends into the future, is unknown to you. My imprisonment in the Bastille has ruined me. I must abandon my establishment [the Lycée]. This loss costs me more than 20,000 livres, involves me in a major lawsuit, and in fact would completely annihilate me were it not for the support that a friend has extended to me in my collapse. I owe to this extraordinary generosity more than 10,000 livres, which were necessary to save me and to sustain my journal, which is all I have been able to salvage from my sad disaster. You can well imagine that in such a precarious situation I dare not contract any more obligations, first because I do not want to make any that I cannot repay, and secondly because it is time at last for me to stop abusing the generosity of my friends and exhausting their purses merely in order to increase my own misery. All that is not consoling for you, I know. It would suit you better to receive cash rather than an account of my misfortune. But what can I do when I don't have any? Offer you my possessions, seeing that you are in a position to make use of them and even to make some profit from them. It is in this spirit that I have formulated the propositions herewith enclosed.[5] You may modify them, increase or diminish them. Be persuaded that I am open to anything that will suit your interests and that will promote a settlement. If you have other propositions to make, send them to me. Your delicacy is too well known to me for me to have any doubts as to the friendliness of your procedures. To a hardened creditor I would say: all the rigor in the world will not help you one iota. It will even make you lose. But to you I say: by leniency and conciliation you will be paid, and you can even save some resources for an unhappy friend whom you have esteemed. I am convinced that this motive alone will determine you to give me a satisfactory reply. I pray you do not delay it, because I am taking steps to get my *Bibliothèque* allowed in France and am pretty well certain of receiving that favor. For that reason, please send immediately by the stagecoach of Besançon two stitched copies of volumes six through nine to M. Lenoir, Lieutenant-Général de Police à Paris, and volume ten, too, if it is printed. If it is not, you should send it as soon as it is. I should think that you have printed the tenth volume so that the complete set can be put on sale this winter. You should put the name of Belin, bookseller in the rue St. Jacques, on the title page along with that of Desauges.[6] Send me notice of the shipment made to M. Lenoir.

I have the honor to be with all possible consideration, Messieurs, your most humble and obedient servant.

Brissot de Warville[7]

This reply satisfied the Société typographique in some respects. It indicated that Brissot could pry his books out of the hands of the police and that a wealthy friend was helping him stave off bankruptcy. To be sure, he set an exorbitant price on the books that he offered in lieu of payment of his bills, but the Society could bargain him down, and it eventually did so, in the course of some arduous negotiations. The main thing was to get some assurance about Brissot's solvency and prospects from his benefactor, who turned out to be the man he would promote as minister of finance in 1792, the Genevan speculator Etienne Clavière. After bailing out Brissot in 1784, Clavière was to keep him afloat for the next five years.[8] The Neuchâtel printers knew both men very well. So they wrote to Clavière for assurances that Brissot would honor his debt, and on November 15, 1784, they received the following reply:

My knowledge of Monsieur de Warville's affairs and the opinion I have of his resources in the future persuade me that his offer to you is the utmost he can do in his condition . . . He has decided at present to remain in France. It is a sort of restriction that has been imposed upon him, and he expects to occupy himself with such useful and instructive writing as his knowledge and talent should make him able to produce. It is not impossible that some day he should obtain a lucrative position from the government. It

seems that his honesty and capacity for work has been appreciated
... Be assured, Messieurs, that M. de Warville is in a precarious
state and that the friends who have saved him can only count for
reimbursement on the little that will be left over from the works
he has printed and whatever his pen can produce. His ill-consid-
ered presumption of success drew him into enterprises more
ruinous than he ever imagined. He is full of determination, but
his friends who know his situation cannot help but worry about
the way he will find to extricate himself.[9]

These letters might seem to confirm the conventional
picture of Brissot. They show that the climactic effort of his
struggle to win a place in the world of letters had collapsed
under blows from the arbitrary powers of the Ancien
Régime. The seizure of his *Bibliothèque* shipment, the suspension of his journal's privilege, and his *embastillement,* on
top of his financial problems, had ruined him. Only Clavière's help saved him from bankruptcy, and that help only
postponed the reckoning of 20,000 to 30,000 livres of
debts—a sum that would have taken him at least fifty years
to earn at the salary he had received as a law clerk before he
gave way to his ambition to become a philosophe. Brissot's
desperate circumstances must have driven him to bitter
thoughts about the political system that used the full
weight of the state to crush the ambitions of a provincial
bourgeois. Those two months in the Bastille must have
made him into a revolutionary—but not the revolutionary
celebrated in the history books, for the letters printed above
raise some doubts about his relation to the powers of the
French state. How was it that a man just released from the
Bastille could expect, as a "favor," that the head of the police would release an illegal book from the state's machinery
of thought control? How was it that the government had

come to esteem its former prisoner so much that it considered hiring him? Jean Paul Marat would have had an answer to those questions:

> There he was once again, out on the pavement, without a penny, and to top off his misery burdened with a wife and child. It is now notorious that having come to the end of his rope, he decided to offer his services to the lieutenant of police Lenoir, who made a royal observer of him for wages of 50 écus a month. He exercised this noble profession at the time of the fall of the Bastille but had to leave it when his patron fled . . . Bailly, who took over the municipal administration and had already prostituted himself to the government, stopped [Brissot] short by threatening to show to the public his name inscribed on the list of police spies; then he promised to favor and protect him, if he would fall in line on [Bailly's] side.[10]

Marat's accusation has never been taken seriously because of its brutally polemical nature. Marat used it to strike back against the Girondins who, in June 1792, were attempting to flush him out of his hiding places and arrest him as an agitator. In his agitation, Marat made some factual errors, such as a statement that Brissot worked for the Duc d'Orléans (as well as Lenoir) *after* his American trip of 1788. But Marat also revealed some facts—about Brissot's relations with book dealers in Paris and London, for example—that only a close friend of Brissot's would have known. Marat could claim with some justice in 1792 that "no one has been better placed than I to see to the bottom of his soul,"[11] because he had then known Brissot for thirteen years. In 1783 Brissot was "my very dear friend" to him: "You know, dear friend, the place that you have in my heart."[12] Marat's testimony therefore seems worthy of some

consideration, and the problem of whether Brissot spied for
the police warrants further investigation, for it provides a
key test of the accuracy of the typical revolutionary man
pictured in Brissot's memoirs and biographies.

Brissot's three biographers, writing under the inescapable
influence of his memoirs, barely bring up the question of
his spying. One doesn't mention it at all,[13] another refers to
it briefly as an example of the attacks made against him,[14]
and the third dismisses it as too slanderous for serious consideration.[15] Taine accredited the charge in order to illustrate the nastiness of the revolutionary leaders,[16] and Mathiez mentioned it to exemplify Girondin nastiness, although
he carefully attributed it to Brissot's enemies.[17] No such
scruples restrained Pierre Gaxotte from repeating the
charge, without bothering about evidence, in the antirevo-
lutionary spirit of Taine.[18] Among the defenders of the Revolution, Michelet, Lescure, and Louis Blanc attempted to
defend Brissot, at least by implication,[19] but the chief coun-
sel for the defense was Alphonse Aulard, whose habit of
drawing morals from the lives of the revolutionaries ("All
his life the statesman adored his mother as he adored
France; the great patriots of the Convention were all dutiful
sons,"[20] he told the children of the Third Republic in his
biography of Danton) inspired an indignant rebuttal of
Taine. In his copy of *Les origines de la France contemporaine,*
Aulard underscored Taine's portrait of Brissot: "This
wretch, born in a bakery, raised in an attorney's office, former police agent at 150 francs a month, former associate of
blackmailers and peddlers of calumny, adventurer of the
pen, scribbler, and all-around hack."[21] And he cited this
passage in an attack on Brissot's attackers: "They should
hesitate before such an honest confession [Brissot's memoirs, which Aulard accepted as the picture of the true Bris-

sot] to say that this generous propagator of philosophic ideas was only a vile police agent at 150 francs a month, as someone claimed in print very recently without condescending to produce a shadow of proof."[22] Taine did not disdain documentation for want of evidence: like most writers concerned with the Girondin-Montagnard conflict, he carefully selected his material from the torrent of denunciations and personal abuse that filled the debates of the revolutionary assemblies and the columns of the revolutionary journals. It seems best, then, to turn from the historians to the revolutionaries themselves in order to examine Brissot's reputation as a police spy.

The spying charge led the list of accusations against Brissot in the indictment of the Girondins presented by André Amar to the Committee of General Security on October 8, 1793. Speaking for the victorious Montagnards, Amar attached the epithet "police agent under the kings" to Brissot's name and pointed him toward the guillotine. It was a brief remark, tossed off by way of introduction to an analysis of Brissot's role in the Revolution, and it did not appear in the report against Brissot and the other Girondins that Saint-Just delivered for the Committee of Public Safety to the Convention on July 8;[23] but Brissot took it seriously enough to refute it at some length in his "Projet de défense devant le Tribunal Révolutionnaire." Once more imprisoned, but this time with his life at stake, he attempted to justify his career to both the Revolutionary Tribunal and posterity. As in his memoirs, which were written under the same circumstances, he presented himself as a disinterested idealist, the very antithesis of a police spy:

> And I always showed myself to be an implacable enemy of the inquisitorial reign of the police! And my only dealings with the minister and with the police was to have been struck down by

three *lettres de cachet* for my writings in favor of liberty, to have
been put by them in the Bastille for two months, to have seen
almost all my works forbidden and seized by them! And from
1779 until the destruction of the police in 1789, I published
works against the government every year; and the police, having
kept me constantly surrounded by their spies, never stopped
hounding me! How then could I have been the agent of a minister who was persecuting me and whom I was unmasking?[24]

Brissot may have felt a need to insist on his innocence
because his enemies had been repeating Marat's denuncia-
tion of June 4, 1792, with increasing frequency as the struggle between the Girondins and the Montagnards became
more and more fierce. On November 14, 1792, François
Chabot brought a violent attack on Brissot in the Jacobin
Club to a climax by accusing Brissot of being a "former police spy,"[25] and Anacharsis Cloots echoed this accusation in
a speech to the Jacobins on November 26.[26] An anonymous
pamphlet published between June and October 1793 prepared the country for Brissot's execution by denouncing
"the infamous role he played under the secondary tyrants of
the police." It cast him in this role as soon as he first arrived
in Paris and then added enough fictitious detail to make
him into an unrecognizable villain.[27] Robespierre made
Brissot's corruptibility official dogma in a speech denouncing the "cowardly police spy" to the Convention of June 24,
1793.[28]

But it was Camille Desmoulins who did more than anyone else to spread Brissot's reputation as a spy. Desmoulins
reportedly exclaimed after the Revolutionary Tribunal sen-
tenced the Girondins to death on October 31, 1793, "Oh
my God, my God; I am the one who is killing them. Oh my
God, it is my *Brissot démasqué* that is killing them."[29] This
pamphlet, the cleverest, most effective attack ever made

against Brissot, contained a letter that Desmoulins attributed to the Baron de Grimm: "You tell me that Brissot de Warville is a good republican. Yes, but he was a spy for M. Lenoir, at 150 livres a month. I defy him to deny it, and I can say furthermore that he was dismissed from the police because Lafayette, who was plotting intrigues at that time, had bribed him and taken him into his service."[30] As Desmoulins must have known, the letter was really a diatribe against Volney by Rivarol, entitled *Réponse de M. le Baron de Grimm ... à la lettre de M. Chasseboeuf de Volney,* dated January 1, 1792. The remark about Brissot had nothing to do with the main theme of the letter. Rivarol apparently added it as a sort of postscript in order to vent some personal resentment or to support his argument that the Revolution recruited its leaders from ambitious mediocrities, who, unlike himself, had not been able to make it to the top during the Ancien Régime.[31]

Rivarol was but one of Brissot's enemies from the early stages of the Revolution who provided ammunition for the Montagnard attacks of 1792 and 1793. Brissot put his finger on some of the Montagnards' other sources when he defended himself against the accusation of spying in his "Projet de défense": "This infamous slander, first imagined by some aristocrats and spread by Gouy d'Arsy and by Théodore Lameth, was repudiated by me in all the newspapers. I formally challenged him to produce any proof, and these vile calumniators did not dare to reply to me. Such are the men whom the republicans are copying today in order to slander one of the most zealous defenders of republicanism!"[32]

The Marquis de Gouy d'Arsy, an aristocrat and slave owner who had passed as a radical in 1789, turned against Brissot in early 1791, because Brissot, then a spokesman for the radical cause and a leader of the Société des Amis des Noirs, was directing a campaign to get the Constituent Assembly to abolish the slave trade. Pitting as it did the commercial interests of the coastal towns against the revolutionary principles of liberty and equality and the humanitarian sentiments of the time, the slave trade issue provoked some envenomed pamphleteering. In a characteristic pamphlet against Brissot, Gouy d'Arsy charged that, far from serving humanity, the "friend of the blacks" had been in the service of the Parisian police; and Brissot replied with an equally outspoken pamphlet, containing a defiant statement of his innocence, which he reprinted in his newspaper, *Le Patriote français,* of February 3, 1791: "You have me corresponding with the former lieutenant of police Lenoir; you make me out to have been a confidential agent of his. He put me in the Bastille. That is the only mark of confidence he ever gave me. I did not know him before, and I never saw him afterwards. Prove the contrary, I defy you."[33]

Brissot confronted another accuser with the same defiance in *Le Patriote français* of March 20, 1792: "He insinuated that I was in the pay of the old police. I challenged him to (1) sign his name, (2) repeat his charge, (3) supply some proof. He then signs, says nothing of the slander, and cites no proof. Thus he is convicted by his very silence as a slanderer." The enemy this time was François de Pange, an aristocrat who wanted to keep the Revolution from moving beyond the limits of a conservative constitutional monarchy. In the spring of 1792, he and several other Feuillant sympathizers filled the *Journal de Paris* with attacks on Brissot, who by then had become one of the most powerful members of the Legislative Assembly. Pange posed as a spokesman of the informed public's opinion of Brissot:

"Some inquisitive persons . . . wrote that he was seen in the pay of the old police"; and he made clear his attempt to accredit this rumor by observing that it might explain Brissot's praise of the French monarchy, the police, and even Lenoir himself—"a minister who is a friend of humanity," Brissot had called him—in a pamphlet published in 1781.[34] To Brissot's demand for proof of his alleged spying, Pange merely replied that Brissot's pamphlet proved him worthy of it; and Pange's friend André Chénier elaborated on this argument in a letter to the *Journal de Paris* of March 19, 1792. Pange and Chénier had no real interest in proofs or even in the accusation; they wanted to discredit the radical stand of the "Brissotins" by presenting Brissot as an opportunist hypocrite: "He is a peddler of ideas, who has always sounded the preference of the public in order to flog only those that would bring in a profit."[35]

The charge of spying was equally irrelevant to the quarrel that arose between Brissot and Théodore Lameth in March 1791. Lameth backed a group of conversative citizens from Lons-le-Saunier, who claimed affiliation with the Parisian Jacobin Club, and Brissot championed a rival local group, branding the Lameth faction as aristocrats. Lameth retaliated with a smear campaign, according to the attack on him that Brissot published in *Le Patriote français* of March 7, 1791: "A man whose word can be trusted assures me that you said *that I was paid by M. La Fayette and that I was a police spy and that you have proof of it.*" Having challenged Lameth to produce his evidence and having received no reply, Brissot continued, "I therefore give him a formal denial; I defy him to publish his proof; and if he fails to do so, the public must consider him a vile slanderer."[36] In this case, too, Brissot had aroused the hostility of the right wing, for he was on the verge of preaching republicanism while the Lameth brothers, with Barnave, Duport, and the occasional collaboration of Lafayette, were laying the basis of the conservative Feuillant coalition.

The charges of spying, attached arbitrarily to a succession of unrelated issues, dogged Brissot throughout his revolutionary career. They appeared whenever he became entangled in polemics, first when he fought the efforts of conservatives to stop the progress of the Revolution, later when he himself tried to stop it. The course of the Revolution seemed always to be at stake in the accusations and counteraccusations, yet the debate itself rarely rose above the level of personal vituperation. It does not provide much information about Brissot's past, but it illustrates the character of revolutionary polemics: as before the Revolution, the French debated about personalities and scandals more readily than policies. The Feuillants argued for a constitutional monarchy and the Montagnards for an egalitarian republic by accusing Brissot of having been a police spy. They decorated their speeches with abstractions drawn from Rousseau, Montesquieu, and classical authors, but they seemed really to be getting down to the business of politics when they began hurling denunciations about the relations of Brissot and Lenoir, Pétion and Mme. de Genlis, Marie Antoinette and the Cardinal de Rohan, or Orléans and anybody. One can't even find the origin of the spying charge in the undergrowth of *libelles* surrounding Brissot's reputation. What seems to be the earliest reference to it is perhaps the most typical. A letter addressed to Brissot, reprinted in *Le Patriote français* of October 7, 1790, revealed that "a well known writer" had said that "certain people . . . claim to have seen your wife going to receive a pension from M. Lenoir under the Old Regime." Brissot replied indignantly, "That pension is a fable. Never has my wife requested or received one. My imprisonment in the Bastille cost me 20,000 to 25,000 livres. I never had a penny in damages for it."[37] Thus, by October 1790, the rumor was in the air, available to whomever needed a weapon against Brissot and the sort of revolution he represented. But *was* Brissot a police spy?

The rumormongering gave Brissot a dubious reputation and may provoke some smoke-to-fire inferences; but the rumors reveal the natural inconsistencies of the Parisian *on dit,* and they cannot be squared with some reliable facts. Lenoir was lieutenant general of police from August 1774 to May 1775 and from June 1776 to August 1785. Marat must have been wrong, then, in stating that Brissot asked to spy for Lenoir after leaving the Palais Royal (around August 1787) and after returning from the United States (January 1789); and there is no evidence for Marat's charge that Bailly won Brissot's support by threatening to reveal his connections with Lenoir. According to the *Vie privée,* Brissot began spying as soon as he first settled in Paris (May-August 1774), but Brissot, then a twenty-year-old law clerk, had neither the financial need nor the contacts to make a spy at that time. Pange made Brissot a spy in 1780, an equally unlikely time, because Brissot had then recently inherited enough money to have hopes of building a respectable literary reputation for himself. Hébert added another variation to the charge by suggesting to the Revolutionary Tribunal that Brissot had done his spying for the English, evidently after 1789, but Hébert's testimony is convincing only as a crude call for the guillotine.[38] Desmoulins, Rivarol, and Brissot's other enemies did not attach dates or many details to their accusations, which read like a succession of slanders passed from anti-Brissotin to anti-Brissotin as the Revolution progressed. The revolutionaries' habit of dealing in denunciations ("The law punishes counterfeiters; the nation rewards denunciators," said a slogan printed on the assignats) makes the attacks on Brissot seem almost natural; in fact it is surprising to find the spy reference mising in the denunciations of Saint-Just and Théveneau de Morande, an old enemy who produced a violent pamphleteering campaign against Brissot during the elections to the Legislative Assembly.[39] When one considers the confident tone of Brissot's denials of the charge and his reputation for integrity, at least among some discriminating observers,[40] one feels inclined to agree with Aulard and Brissot's biographers: the accusation of spying seems a fantasy of Brissot's enemies, used for polemical purposes.

How disturbing, then, to find the following remarks in the manuscripts of Jean-Pierre Lenoir, the lieutenant general of police who knew more about the secret activities of Paris than anyone else: "Brissot remained in Paris [after his release from the Bastille]; he came to offer his services to the police. I refused them, but for about a year he was connected as a spy with one of the secretaries of this department, who presented his reports to me, and he was paid for those reports. Shortly before my retirement [August 1785], Brissot was still retained as a spy by the police."[41] Lenoir's statement should be accepted with caution, for it was written in exile, when he had no love for revolutionaries, and it described events that had occurred at least fifteen years earlier. It is to be found among the scraps of notes that Lenoir intended to assemble into memoirs, memoirs that might have been just as biased as Brissot's. Lenoir evidently had original documents to assist his memory, but he also had resentments to distort it, and he had a case to defend: he wanted to show that the old system of policing Paris was far more effective and far less despotic than the revolutionaries maintained. Whether Lenoir had any personal resentments against Brissot seems doubtful. As already mentioned, Brissot's enemies impugned his patriotism in 1791 because he had praised Lenoir in one of his earliest pamphlets. By this time, however, Brissot had offset this praise with some suitably revolutionary descriptions of Lenoir. One pictured the head of the police and his lackies "when in their fancy suppers, while swilling champagne with pretty wives whom they abducted from their husbands, they mocked the philosophical works of those exalted spirits whom they kept in the bowels of the Bastille and mocked the stupidity of the common people, whose voice they stifled and whose blood and sweat they drank."[42] Such slander, if it ever penetrated his place of exile, might have provoked Lenoir to slander Brissot in return; but Brissot's remarks were restrained in comparison with those of other journalists, who made Lenoir into a leading villain of revolutionary folklore. Brissot's friend Jean-Louis Carra, for example, outdid him by far in publicizing the Lenoir of chains and *cachots* as a symbol of the Ancien Régime's despotism. Actually, the lieutenant general of police seems to have been an honest, quite undespotic civil servant—too honest, in fact, to have lied about Brissot in the unlikely event that he had a motive to do so.

Brissot's denials of the spying charges seem strong, but how could he have ignored them or denied them weakly? He may have felt safe in challenging his accusors to produce evidence of his spying, for he knew that his police record had disappeared from the ruins of the Bastille. His close friend Pierre Louis Manuel had given it to him, "while telling me that nothing concerning me should remain in the dung heap of the police."[43] The Bastille archives in the Arsénal contain a suggestive gap where Brissot's dossier would have been; and where they do mention his name—in scattered, routine reports—they contradict the *larmoyant* account of his imprisonment that he published during the Revolution. "I was perishing in an underground cell, me, innocent! . . . cut off from all mankind, from my wife, my child! They would not even let my letters reach my family, while swearing to me that the letters had got through . . . The barbarians amused themselves at my tears and torments."[44] Not only did the barbarians not refuse Brissot's requests to communicate with his family, but Lenoir wrote to the Marquis de Launay, the Bastille's governor, on August 23, 1784, "I pray the governor to permit M. de Warville to see Mme. de Warville his wife, while taking the usual precautions." A note by de Launay shows that the couple's first meeting took place "on the 24th [of August 1784] from 9:30 to 10:30." Other notes indicate that Brissot was well supplied with food, laundry, and opportunities to take walks within the prison walls.[45]

Brissot had good reasons during the Revolution to exploit the myth of the Bastille by picturing himself as martyr of royal despotism. When Manuel and his colleagues were preparing the publication of *La Bastille dévoilée,* a carefully edited selection of the papers they had collected from the Bastille, they asked Brissot to write his own article, instead of surrendering the documents concerning him; and he wrote, predictably, that "the true cause of my detention was the zeal with which at all times and in all my writings I have defended the principles that are triumphing today."[46] Manuel must have doctored the article about his own *embastillement,* for it stated that he had been imprisoned in 1786 for having distributed an innocent pamphlet about the Affaire du Collier and some others by Mirabeau. The records of his interrogations survive, because they were captured from him in 1793; and they show that he had been arrested for peddling pornography.[47] Did he want to hide the nature of his existence as a hack writer before the Revolution and to do the same for a friend who had shared it with him? The hypothesis seems credible, for Lenoir revealed that Manuel, too, had spied for the police. In a note about clandestine publishing in Paris, Lenoir wrote, "Manuel, a writer and book peddler who was then hired as a spy by a police inspector, revealed that he had seen some obscenities coming from a secret printing shop that Sauson had mounted in an area by the Hôtel du Contrôle des finances."[48] No amount of editing could erase all the marks made on a man by the hard life of Grub Street.

There is no getting around it: unless Lenoir was lying, Brissot was a spy and a liar, too. Brissot's publications, especially his memoirs, do not offer much evidence of his truthfulness. They misconstrue, to say the least, his relations with Lafayette, Dumouriez, and Orléans; his role during the Varennes crisis and the insurrection of August 10, 1792; the purpose of his trip to the United States; the nature of his Lycée; and his interest in the Bourse and in pamphleteering. His treatise on truth belonged to the beginning of his career; by 1789 truth had become entangled in polemics, and by 1793 it lay hidden in the shadow of the guillotine. However much one sympathizes with his circumstances, it is difficult to deny that they made him more likely than Lenoir to falsify the past.

In defense of Brissot, it should be remembered that "spying" for the police could take the form of reporting on the mood of certain sections or milieux of the city rather than betraying friends. Spies, often called *mouches* (a term apparently derived from the name of the notorious sixteenth-century agent Antoine Mouchy), buzzed like flies around the cafés and public places where gossip was to be gathered.

They often made reports on individuals known for corrupt morals or radical religious and political opinions. Lenoir possessed a report on Brissot, for example, which typifies the genre:

> BRISSOT, writer, is more dangerous than one may think. He hides a villainous soul under a seemingly gentle demeanor. His wife, if she is his wife, seems honest. He associated in Geneva with some men who have been banished from that city [a reference to Clavière and other members of the Représentant party, who were exiled after the aborted uprising of 1782]. He went around with an Englishman named Pigot, a wicked, extraordinary man who is very rich and has houses everywhere except in his native land, which he has abandoned. It is said that Brissot served him in Geneva as friend, writer, and secretary.[49]

Brissot had enough contacts among the down-and-out writers and salon radicals in Paris to have written many reports like this, but it may be that his spying consisted in reporting and manipulating rumors, as is indicated by a fragment of Lenoir's papers that Jacques Peuchet, a police archivist, claimed to publish. "The notorious Count Mirabeau and Brissot de Warville had been employed separately by the police in writing bulletins and other works and in spreading them throughout the public in order to contradict false stories and anecdotes."[50] Brissot may have supplied the police with reports on the blackmailers and smut peddlers known as *libellistes* and *sommateurs* who made up the colony of French expatriates in London before 1789. Brissot knew this colony well; he had recived his training in journalism from it, and he blamed his *embastillement* on its leader, Charles Théveneau de Morande, a literary buccaneer, political pornographer, and sometime police agent–diplomat, who backed Desforges in his quarrel with Brissot about the Lycée. During his interrogation in the Bastille,

Brissot must have been able to tell Lenoir a good deal more than he admitted in his memoirs about the *Naissance du Dauphin,* the *Petits soupers de l'hôtel de Bouillon,* the *Rois de France dégénérés,* the *Passe-temps d'Antoinette et du vizir de Vergennes,* the *Diable dans un bénitier,* and other such pamphlets that the London *libellistes* smuggled into France or surrendered for a ransom to the Parisian police.[51] A letter from Brissot's agent in Ostend exposed the falsehood of his claim that he had nothing to do, "neither directly nor indirectly," with the last-named pamphlet,[52] and a letter in the manuscripts of the Société typographique de Neuchâtel proves, as Marat maintained, that Brissot was involved in the production of much stronger pornography than *Les liaisons dangereuses,* which outraged his moral sensitivity, according to reviews that he published in two of his journals.[53] Moral sensitivity was a standard attribute of a prerevolutionary pamphleteer and so was a need for money.

Like his fellow pamphleteers, Brissot learned to work within the baroque bureaucracy that attempted to control and at times to exploit the printed word in France. His book dealer and a police agent called Goupil de Pallières gave him his first lesson in 1777, during a ceremony that they staged for the announcement of his first *lettre de cachet.* Goupil played his part delicately: Brissot should prepare himself for some bad news; he had foolishly insulted the wife of an attorney in his brochure *Le pot-pourri,* a mere "folly" to be sure, but one that would take him to the Bastille if he did not disappear before the next morning, when Goupil would arrive with the *lettre de cachet* and expect to collect, as evidence of zealous law enforcement, some pages of the manuscript that Monsieur would be pleased to leave behind. Goupil later asked to be compensated in forbidden pamphlets, which he evidently planned to peddle, because he was thrown in the Bastille himself during the next year for giving his wife pamphlets to hawk from his collections of confiscated works.[54] Owing to the nature of the place, police and pamphleteers lived symbiotically in Grub Street. Of course Brissot claimed in his memoirs that this environment never infected him, but he sounded less innocent in his letters to his publishers.

These read as if they were written from inside the Hôtel de la Police. On July 26, 1781, for example, Brissot warned the Société typographique de Neuchâtel to take care with its shipments of Raynal's recently condemned *Histoire philosophique et politique des établissements des européens dans les deux Indes:*

> The interest that I take in everything that concerns you leads me to send you this warning. The strictest orders have been issued to prevent the arrival of the Raynal in France. It is known that the book is being produced in four places [outside the kingdom]. Disguised agents have been sent to inspect the printing and to discover what route the books will take. I cannot tell you any more, but what I tell you I know from good authority. You will be kept under close watch.[55]

Six months later he put the publishers on guard against spies who were after their edition of Mercier's prohibited *Tableau de Paris:* "Be on your guard about the *Tableau de Paris.* You will be kept under close watch. I warn you, and I know this from a good source."[56] Brissot made a less guarded reference to his source in a letter informing the Society of the race to publish editions of Rousseau's works, as it was viewed by the authorities responsible for suppressing them. "About the Rousseau, I forgot to tell you that M. Martin of the police told me the other day that nine editions were under way, enough to inundate France. Yours will find favor, if you can get it across the border quickly."[57] Martin was the secretary of police in charge of "everything that concerns the Bastille, Vincennes, and other castles where prisoners of state are incarcerated, the trade in prohibited books, etc.," as his job was defined in the *Almanach royal*. He was the key official whom anyone involved with the clandestine book trade would want to know, for he could provide information about competitors, warning of repressive measures, and assistance when books got caught in the machinery for keeping prohibited works outside France and for protecting the monopoly of the booksellers' guild. Martin's friendship could be a powerful weapon in the rugged world of eighteenth-century publishing, as an agent of the Société typographique de Neuchâtel, Quandet de Lachenal, informed it in 1781:

> I am about to be introduced to M. Martin, the head officer in the section of the book trade at the police. Several friends of his whom I have the honor to know have promised to do me this favor. This officer is intimately connected with M. Boucherot [secretary to the Keeper of the Seals], and M. Boucherot is well disposed toward you. It was by his [Martin's] means that he [Boucherot] got the confiscated crates of the *Description des arts* released and delivered to M. Perre, who turned them over to me.[58]

Brissot knew Martin well. He wrote to the Society, not without a touch of pride, that "M. Martin, who seems to esteem me, to be attached to me, has assured me of his good will."[59] This friendship apparently came to full bloom in the Bastille and had to be eradicated, like the Bastille, after July 14, 1789. For July 14 metamorphosed Martin into a villain, snatched away his job, and replaced him with none other than Manuel. (The Revolution, to the populace of Grub Street, meant not only freedom from *embastillement* but employment—in the new journals bursting out all over Paris and in the new state bureaucracy.) As inspector of the book trade, Manuel did little more than gather material for his own works, and so he was hailed as a defender of the freedom of the press by Brissot, editor of the successful new journal *Le Patriote français:* "Our friend Manuel sets a very different style in the police department from that of his predecessor Martin, who used to distribute *lettres de cachet* and who tortured him, like me, in the depths of the Bastille. M. Manuel is worthy of being a republican; he does the least that he can."[60] Brissot used a different style himself before these happy transformations. Having taken care to work his way into Martin's favor, he sent his "torturer" a bread and butter letter soon after his release from the Bastille:

> I am taking advantage of my first moment of quiet to reiterate all my thanks for the interest you have taken in my misfortune . . .
> Please be good enough to give my respects to M. Lenoir and to assure him of the gratitude that his generous and delicate treatment has inspired in me and in my wife. And please accept yourself her thanks and her best wishes.
> I am, with all possible consideration, Monsieur, your most humble and obedient servant.[61]

What kind of a "servant" of Martin's was Brissot? Certainly one who had access to inside information. After the police confiscated some of the Society's illegal books, Brissot wrote,

> Although I have not been able to see M. Quandet, I know nonetheless that he submitted a good memorandum to the lieutenant of police and that he has behaved very well. I know that he is well thought of. I shall see M. M——tomorrow in order to sound him.[62]

By February 1785, Quandet had fallen from grace both with the police and with the Société typographique, having got himself exiled by *lettre de cachet*. But Brissot remained well established within the circle of Martin's confidants, according to Quandet's successor as the Parisian agent of the Société typographique:

> M. de Warville told me that at the last conversation he had with M. Martin, first secretary of the lieutenant general of police, he [Martin] said that no matter what route we should take to smuggle our books into Paris, he would find a way to discover it and to enforce his orders along the Swiss border. He would only permit M. de Warville to import 200 copies of volumes six through nine of the *Bibliothèque philosophique* into Paris.[63]

Thus the police were cracking down on smuggling from Neuchâtel but were willing to let a limited number of Brissot's prohibited books slip through their fingers, and Brissot was meeting, probably regularly, with the police officer in charge of the book trade in early 1785, exactly as Lenoir claimed.

By comparing Lenoir's claims and Brissot's correspondence with his publishers, it seems reasonable to conclude much more. Brissot sent inside information to Neuchâtel because he really was an insider among the secret police of Paris, as his enemies charged. He probably was a spy, and his spying probably concerned the *libelle* style of pamphleteering that contributed to his support before the Revolution and his downfall during it. This conclusion fits the picture of his desperation in the last half of 1784 that emerges from his and Clavière's correspondence with the Société typographique de Neuchâtel quoted above. Agonizing over the collapse of his ambitions, the welfare of his sick wife and infant, the perfidy of his enemies, the gloom of the Bastille, and the imminence of backruptcy, he evidently offered his services to Lenoir, perhaps for the 150 livres a month mentioned by Marat, Rivarol, and Desmoulins, because spying opened up a way out of his distress, maybe even a way out of the Bastille. Brissot eventually found a more important out in the financial patronage of Clavière, but that is another story. The story of his spying deserves emphasis, not in order to pass judgment on Brissot, but in order to understand him. His *embastillement* did not prove the purity of his patriotism, as he argued later. It corrupted him, and in the corrupting it confirmed his hatred of the Old Regime. How he must have hated it! How he must have raged inwardly against the system of arbitrary power that first struck him down and then enlisted him in its service. How he must have reviled the men in control of the system, who first blocked his attempts to win honor for himself and then dishonored him by making him their agent. No wonder that his rage broke out during the Revolution in declamations against the debauchery of Lenoir and the other men at the top of the Ancien Régime: they had deflowered the earnest young bourgeois who had left Chartres to pursue the dream of becoming a philosophe.

There was consolation in the thought that "they"—the aristocratic *gens en place*—had also corrupted Rousseau, whose inner self nonetheless remained pure, as Brissot knew in 1784 from his third reading of the *Confessions*. Brissot had more reason than most to identify himself with Rousseau—"I suffer myself when I read him. I enter into his suffering, and I say to myself: why was I not fortunate enough to have known him? How I would have opened up my soul to him!"[64]—because, like Jean-Jacques, he invented a fictional self to compensate for the failings of his real self. Brissot called this other self Phédor. "Phédor has an upright soul and a profound love of justice; benevolence is the basis of his character . . . When he dies, he will bring before the sovereign judge a soul that is pure and that loves virtue."[65]

Phédor was the young philosopher of Chartres who had preserved his virginity; he was the hero of Brissot's memoirs, which Brissot wrote after reading the *Confessions* for the sixth time and before presenting his case to the Revolutionary Tribunal, from which he could only appeal to posterity.

To expose the fictional Brissot of the memoirs is not to rob the real Brissot of the typicality that historians have attributed to him. Brissot's Rousseauistic ideals do typify those of his contemporaries, but idealism did not take a provincial bourgeois far in prerevolutionary France. When Brissot found his way blocked, he had to compromise with the system. When it imprisoned him and confiscated his works, he came to an understanding with its police. When it failed to provide him with a living as a philosophe, he became a hack pamphleteer and a *mouche*. And when the Revolution arrived, he threw himself into it, not as the disinterested idealist of the memoirs, but as a failure from the old system who was determined to redeem himself in the new. The Revolution made Brissot the prominent and fairly prosperous editor of *Le Patriote français,* the powerful leader of the Girondins. Is it surprising, then, that the *sans-culotte* "anarchy" of 1793 threatened everything that, after years of struggle and humiliation, he had finally won, everything that, for him, *was* the Revolution? Brissot's fellow pamphleteers in the 1780s probably hated the social system and made necessary compromises with it as he did. They were men of flesh and blood who needed to support families, satisfy ambitions, and pursue pleasures. Their failures and frustrations in the old order may serve as a measure of their dedication to the new, and the Revolution may be understood, from their point of view, as a career. The study of careers, old-fashioned and merely biographical as it seems, may provide a needed corrective to the more abstract study of ideas and ideologies. The intellectual origins of the Revolution and the character of its policies may be understood better if one descends from the level of the *Encyclopédie* and reenters Grub Street, where men like Brissot produced the newspapers and pamphlets, the posters and cartoons, the songs, rumors, and *libelles* that transformed personal quarrels and factional rivalries into an ideological struggle over the destiny of France.

A Pamphleteer
on the Run

 HIS NAME PROBABLY WAS LE SENNE, though he used so many aliases that one can't be sure. His works came to a dozen or more volumes, though none of them can be found. His life turned into a confidence game, though he had dedicated it to the cause of Enlightenment. So why exhume the case of the abbé Le Senne? He was merely a hack writer. But he was such a hack, such an unalloyed, irredeemable "poor devil," as his kind was called in eighteenth-century France, that he deserves to be rescued from oblivion. Le Senne did not merely churn out literature. He was the stuff that literature was made of. He seemed to be the incarnation of the themes developed by Voltaire in "Le Pauvre Diable" and by Diderot in *Le Neveu de Rameau*. And he illustrates one of the most elusive aspects of literature under the Old Regime: the process by which unorthodox ideas passed from the speculations of philosophers and into the hands of readers. Le Senne compiled, condensed, popularized, and peddled Enlightenment as if his life depended on it—and indeed it did, because Enlightenment was his bread and butter. The Enlightenment also was a campaign to spread light (*Lumières*)—that is, an attempt to propagate ideas among the general public and not merely to refine them among philosophers. The poor devils did the propagating. They produced far more copy than the philosophes and probably had a more direct effect

on public opinion. Without middlemen like Le Senne, the Enlightenment might have been contained within the salons, and its great voices could have called for the crushing of *l'infâme* ("the infamous thing," tyrannical orthodoxy) without raising an echo.

Nothing can be learned about Le Senne's origins, but at some stage he evidently contracted the fever for becoming a man of letters that had spread throughout France in the mid-century and nearly proved fatal for the antihero of Voltaire's satirical poem "Le Pauvre Diable."[1]

> J'étais sans bien, sans métier, sans génie,
> Et j'avais lu quelques méchants auteurs;
> Je croyais même avoir des protecteurs.
> Mordu du chien de la métromanie,
> Le mal me prit, je fus auteur aussi.
>
> I was without possessions, without a trade, without genius,
> And I had read some wicked authors;
> I even thought to have protectors.
> Infected by the craze for life in the great city,
> The disease overcame me, and I became an author, too.

Like most poor devils, Le Senne wrote anonymously, lived obscurely, and left almost no trace of his existence after he died.[2] Had he not become entangled in the business of the Société typographique de Neuchâtel (STN), he would have vanished completely in the past. But his entanglement produced a series of letters, which for a period of four years (1780–1784) provides an unusually rich view of the life of a hack philosophe.

The Swiss publishers ran across Le Senne while pursuing a plan to market their literary review, the *Journal helvétique,* in France. The plan had been suggested to them by Laus de Boissy, a minor man of letters, who hoped to take over the review and to turn it into a party organ of the philosophes.[3] The STN encouraged Laus; but when its directors, Abraham Bosset de Luze and Frédéric-Samuel Ostervald, arrived in Paris in January 1780, they went over his head, to d'Alembert; and there they met Le Senne, who somehow had won the philosophe's "protection." The Swiss tried to persuade d'Alembert to accept them as the publisher of his books and to use their review as an outlet for his essays. But he merely expressed sympathy with their plan and pointed them to Le Senne.[4]

Given his cue, Le Senne rushed into the role of journalist-philosophe. He dogged the heels of Ostervald and Bosset, bombarded them with letters, and came up with a magnificent prospectus for the journal, which began: "To avenge the great men of the century from the outrages that expiring fanaticism still dares to publish about them in those journals whose success is due only to the malignity of their authors; to expose in broad daylight the truths that philosophers have announced in writings that prejudice keeps buried in obscurity; to demonstrate the superiority of modern philosophy over the pretended wisdom of the partisans of credulity and intolerance ... such are the goals that this journal will pursue."[5] At this time, d'Alembert was being pilloried by Fréron in *L'Année littéraire* and especially by Linguet in the widely read *Annales politiques, civiles et littéraires,* and he wanted to establish a journal that would counteract the growing influence of the antiphilosophe press. Far from being above the rough and tumble of journalism, d'Alembert and his allies planned to use the press to win public opinion over to their side. But they were happy to delegate their polemics to Le Senne, while leaving the financing and the production of his operation to the STN. In his first letter to the Swiss, Le Senne explained that he would model himself on Pierre Rousseau, the hack writer who had founded the *Journal encyclopédique* and had made a fortune by defending the philosophes. But Le Senne's journal would be far more militant than Rousseau's. It would beat Linguet and Fréron at their own game, by attacking the antiphilosophes mercilessly.[6]

Ostervald and Bosset did not quite see the project that way. Although they sympathized with the philosophes, their primary aim was to break into the French market for periodicals. They wanted to get famous writers to contribute to their journal, not to leave it in the hands of a nonentity like Le Senne and not to get it banned by the French government. They also found that Le Senne put a rather high price on his services. He asked the STN to bring him to Neuchâtel at its expense and to support him for a trial period of five years. As editor in chief, he would supply all copy for a sum of 24 livres per printed sheet and 1 livre per subscription. Since he expected to produce two issues of six octavo sheets each month, he was asking for a guaranteed income of 3,456 livres a year—princely wages for a journalist, and they did not include his share in the income from subscriptions, which was to double if the subscriptions surpassed 4,000.[7]

The Swiss rejected those terms. But still hoping to snare d'Alembert, who still supported his abbé, they left an opening for new propositions; and Le Senne leaped into it. He would settle for smaller wages, he said, provided he received adequate compensation for the articles he would collect from the most eminent writers in Paris. His collaborators insisted on remaining anonymous, however, and so did he, "for fear that the clergymen who know me should seek vengeance by blocking the circulation of the journal." The abbé seemed to be in bad odor in the church. He had renounced all hope of obtaining a benefice, he explained, and desired nothing more than to establish himself in "a country that fanatics like to call heretical . . . I ask only one grace of God: to live without the temporal help of the Church." He required only a small chalet with some fields around it and the certainty of remaining as an employee of the STN in case the journal failed (not that he believed for a moment that failure was a serious possibility). He was ready to drop everything in order to come to Neuchâtel—but he evidently had nothing: "I resemble those untilled fields that do not produce anything until some resources are invested in them."[8]

This proposal did not appeal to Ostervald and Bosset, so Le Senne came back with another, still humbler plan. He would take any salary that the STN would give him and asked only that it commit itself to him for one year. But if the Swiss then decided to let him go, they would have to help him find a new job "either in the same region or elsewhere, but outside France."[9] The abbé seemed anxious to get out of the kingdom, but he was held back by obligations to two dependents, a widow named Bauprais, whom he described as his sister-in-law, and her son. Le Senne hoped the STN would make some provision for them.

At this point Ostervald and Bosset suspended their negotiations with Le Senne, in order to attend to the more pressing problem of getting permission for the journal to circulate in France. Such permissions did not come easily in the Old Regime. They required lobbying in the Direction de la librairie, the government agency in charge of the book trade; finding a censor to answer for the content of every issue; winning the good will of the lieutenant general of police, the Keeper of the Seals, and the foreign minister; bribing their secretaries; and paying an indemnity to a

French journal—for domestic journals owned *privilèges,* which gave them monopolies over certain kinds of news, such as literary items in the case of the *Mercure* and foreign affairs in the case of *Gazette de France.* After some arduous intriguing, Ostervald and Bosset found it impossible to get their journals through this obstacle course. They informed Le Senne that the project had become snagged somewhere in the French bureaucracy and that they could not hire him until it was pried loose. Le Senne's first impulse was to appeal to his protectors: "I shall write immediately to M. d'Alembert, as I can't see him until Monday. He can overcome plenty of obstacles. The antiphilosophic party is powerful, but it has adversaries who have a great deal of credit."[10] D'Alembert was willing to help. In fact, he considered asking Frederick II to apply pressure on the French officials, although he later backed away from that proposal, because he feared that Frederick would consider it beneath his dignity.[11] But the obstacles blocking the path of the new journal proved to be insurmountable. They were economic as well as ideological in character, for the greatest enemy of the project turned out to be Charles-Joseph Panckoucke, the publishing tycoon who had bought up the *Mercure* and several other journals and did not want to allow competitors into a field that he was beginning to monopolize.[12]

Despite this setback, Le Senne continued to search for a way onto the payroll of a journal, exactly as Voltaire's poor devil had done.

> Rimant une ode, et n'ayant point dîné,
> Je m'accostai d'un homme à lourde mine,
> Qui sur sa plume a fondé sa cuisine . . .
> Je m'engageai, sous l'espoir d'un salaire,
> A travailler à son hebdomadaire.

> Rhyming an ode, and not having dined,
> I accosted a man with a heavy countenance,
> Who had founded his kitchen on his pen . . .
> I agreed in the hope of having a salary
> To work on his weekly.

At first he tried to persuade the STN to buy out the privilege of the *Journal de littérature, des sciences et des arts* owned by one of his Grub Street friends, the chevalier Paulet. But Paulet wanted 3,000 livres, and the Swiss would not bite.[13] So Le Senne scrapped the plan for a philosophic review and argued for an expanded version of the current *Journal helvétique,* which he would edit from his retreat in Neuchâtel. The French language had become fashionable everywhere in Europe, he wrote. If the STN could collect only 1,000 subscriptions from French readers outside France, it could cover its costs and then could rely on smuggling to wring a profit from the rich market inside the kingdom.

Ostervald and Bosset did not respond to this line of argument, but Le Senne had become too attached to his vision of a Swiss cottage and a stable income to let it drop. "Establishing a journal is rather like buying a lottery ticket," he conceded. But the stakes made the risks worth taking. The *Mercure* had begun with only 600 subscribers and now had 5,000, he claimed, so the STN should not be discouraged about beginning from its small base of Swiss subscribers. The *Journal helvétique* had not benefited from adequate publicity in France. It would quickly take root there, especially if the STN moved into the French market before the settlement of the American war, which would cause "the most abundant source of news" to dry up.[14] But the directors of the STN knew that a periodical could not succeed in France unless it reached its readers regularly. To provide uninterrupted service, they would have to contract with the postal system for its distribution, to have it censored or at least formally permitted by the government, and above all to appease its natural enemies, the privileged domestic journalists who had enough influence in Versailles to destroy foreign competitors. At the end of May, they informed Le Senne that the project was dead.

Le Senne's journalistic projects had not been very feasible from the beginning, but at least they had put him in contact with the STN. To have a foot inside the door of a wealthy Swiss publisher was no small advantage for an unemployed writer. Indigent men of letters were forever throwing themselves at the STN's directors during their Paris trip. After they returned to Neuchâtel, Ostervald and Bosset hired an agent named Quandet de Lachenal to handle their affairs in Paris, and he reported that he was besieged by "a crowd of authors." "Do you know that I have to have days set aside for my audiences? All kinds of them pour into my apartment. I think they have formed a pact to make me go to the poor house with them."[15] These Grub Street characters lived by their wits. They were *hommes à projets* (idea men), who could dash off a prospectus or pull a manuscript out of their sleeve when the slightest opportunity arose for making a few sous. Le Senne behaved like everyone in this milieu. As soon as he met Ostervald and Bosset, he began feeding typographical propositions to them, and he continued the flow of proposals by mail after they left Paris in June 1780.

Le Senne accompanied his first proposal for the philosophic journal with an offer to bring five manuscripts to Neuchâtel, including a five-volume treatise on "the physical and moral administration of France."[16] Six weeks later, he wrote that he had lost a small pension, which had been his main source of support, and so had been forced to sell two of his best manuscripts, which were then being printed in London, presumably because they could not pass the censorship in France. But he had reserved the treatise for the STN; and it was an especially valuable work, because he had prepared it "by a tacit order of Monsieur Necker."[17] When Ostervald and Bosset failed to nibble at this offer, Le Senne sent them a memorandum.

MANUSCRIPTS FOR SALE

1. History of the peoples of Europe since the foundation of Rome, with notes.
2. History of Germany, to serve as a supplement to the history by M. Heiss.
3. Impartial account of the causes and the motives of the wars of religion in the different European states.
4. A complete course of study in agronomy.
5. A new edition of Deslandes's critical history of philosophy, with notes.
6. Analytical refutation of the *Annales littéraires et politiques* by the sieur Linguet, with an impartial appreciation of the genius of that writer.
7. Voltaire examined, praised, censured before the tribunal of letters.[18]

The memorandum explained that these were only projects, which Le Senne would complete if the STN wanted to commission them. He also offered a whole repertory of finished manuscripts: a new edition of the works of Charron; translations of two Italian works; new, enlarged editions of Hume's history of England, Langier's history of Venice, and Solignac's history of Poland; and a novel, *Les aventures d'un fou devenu sage*.

Le Senne wanted to sell these works outright or to barter them in exchange for being hired as the STN's resident journalist. When the journal's fate began to cloud over, he came forth with more projects for sale. He especially pushed the idea of "interesting compilations"—anthologies, which could be assembled with scissors and paste and which were excellent moneymakers. An abridged and updated version of Hénault's *Abrégé chronologique de l'histoire de France* would sell well, he argued, and an anthology of travel literature would do even better. He could sew together selections from a great many works, purging the boring and unphilo-sophic passages and introducing each section with a sketch of the major countries, "their customs, their government, their religion, their revolutions, their present situation. A work of this kind would be interesting and piquant; and I think that, proposed by subscription, it would sell rapidly, especially if one gives it a philosophical tone."[19]

When that project failed, Le Senne tried to launch a plan for publishing an abridged and philosophical version of a Jesuit history of the Gallican church. The work was sure to sell, he promised, but the STN would have to produce it quickly, for he had learned that it was being proposed around publishing houses by someone who sounded like a Doppelgänger, "a certain abbé Lanvin, not well known in the world of letters, but enterprising." Or, if the STN pre-ferred, he could provide it with an anthology of the best French plays or a selection of the choicest morsels by Vol-taire or a reader on fanaticism and religious wars, which had been assembled by a Protestant friend of his. The friend was desperately ill and had accumulated a large stock of philo-sophical manuscripts, since he lived by translating and com-piling. "If he dies, everything will fall into the hands of a sister, who is Catholic and intolerant, who doesn't like him and has sworn to burn his papers. I will manage to save some manuscripts from them."[20]

These proposals did not interest the STN, so Le Senne came back with more.

> *Analysis of the treatise on wisdom by Charron,* which will form a pretty large duodecimo volume of 18 printed sheets in pica
>
>   ...300 livres
>
> *Letters on the operations of the human mind and on the usage of philosophical knowledge;* calculated on the basis of the above type, this work would come to two large duodecimo volumes
>
>   ... 500 livres
>
> *Letters of a Russian philosopher on different subjects of literature and criticism;* it could make one duodecimo volume   ... 150 livres
>
> *Imaginary journey, a critical novel*   ... 120 livres[21]

Le Senne did not claim to have written all these works himself. One man could hardly have produced so much on so many different subjects. He functioned informally as an agent for other authors, who fed him manuscripts as he marketed them; for he evidently had a great many colleagues in Grub Street who would have leapt at the chance of opening up a conduit to the presses of a prosperous Swiss publisher. Le Senne's proposals also could have been mere projects for books that he planned to write or farm out to others, if the STN offered to buy them. To present a project as a finished product was one of the milder frauds in an industry where authors and publishers constantly duped one another and collaborated to deceive the public. In a later proposal, Le Senne suggested that the STN print *Observations philosophiques sur le Japon* under the new title *Les moeurs japonaises,* so that it could be marketed as a new work.[22] Although none of his books appear in standard library catalogues and the STN never printed any of them, his work probably was published under other titles, for his letters often mentioned other publishers who were willing to take his copy, and he cranked out compilations as assiduously as a character in "Le Pauvre Diable."

> Il entassait adage sur adage;
> Il compilait, compilait, compilait;
> On le voyait sans cesse écrire, écrire.
>
> He piled up adage on adage;
> He compiled, compiled, compiled;
> One saw him always writing, writing.

When he first met Ostervald and Bosset, Le Senne set a high price on his wares, boldly evaluating the copy at 24 livres per printed sheet and haggling over typographical details with considerable expertise. He knew the publishing industry intimately and referred to transactions he had had with printers in London, Holland, and Bouillon.[23] But the STN had dealt with dozens of obscure writers like him, who invariably argued that their works were certain to be best-sellers. Instead of risking capital on copy with an unpredictable selling power, it preferred to print on commission, to buy manuscripts from celebrated writers, or to pirate books whose market value had been proven. It therefore turned down every one of Le Senne's propositions. After a long string of refusals, he began to sound desperate. By April he was begging the STN to sell the manuscripts to other publishers for him, if it would not buy them itself. The buyer could even publish them under his own name, for Le Senne would sacrifice all rights to them. All that he asked was to sell them quickly, even at drastically reduced prices. He, his widowed sister-in-law, and her son depended on his "meager literary work" to survive, and they were running out of money.[24] In June, he reduced his terms still further: he would barter the manuscripts for a certain number of free copies or for a position in the STN's printing shop. "Living from my pen like many others," he explained, he could correct copy, read proof, translate, and compile or write any kind of book the STN desired, working at piece rates of 24 livres for every sheet of fresh prose and 18 livres for every sheet of a text that already existed but that required additional notes and the translation of passages in Latin.[25]

Le Senne increasingly stressed his ability to do such odd jobs as it became more and more apparent that the STN would only pay for the prose of a d'Alembert. He had picked up many useful skills in the course of his literary career, he wrote, and he could be particularly helpful to the STN in its dealings with the smugglers and peddlers who spread its books throughout the literary underground. He clearly belonged to this milieu. In late May 1780, shortly before Bosset's departure from Paris, he had introduced the STN's codirector to a typical underworld character: a *colporteur* named Cugnet, who had collaborated on the *Journal encyclopédique* and had sung bit parts in the opera before going into the "under-the-cloak" book trade. A strapping, handsome fellow, Cugnet impressed Bosset as "an honest man, though without fortune, and very enterprising."[26] After running a few errands and selling a few illegal books for Bosset, Cugnet proposed that the STN make him its main distributor in Paris. With the help of Le Senne, he had rented a tiny boutique in the Louvre "under the portal of the Cul du sac du Coq, entering from the rue Saint Honoré" and was beginning to stock it with books. If the Neuchâtelois would help him build up his inventory, he would push their books, taking care to keep exact accounts and to pay them as his sales progressed. Most important, he had a way of getting their shipments past the customs, police, and booksellers' guild of Paris. A certain abbé Bretin, "aumônier de Monsieur à Brunoy," had promised to store the crates in the estate of the Comte de Provence at Brunoy and then to sneak them into the count's wagons, which regularly made the trip from Brunoy to Paris without being inspected.[27]

Le Senne, who had some kind of interest in Cugnet's project, recommended it enthusiastically. "By helping him to make an honest profit, you will find that he will sell a prodigious number of books for you under the very nose of the Parisian bookdealers, who are almost all scoundrels." Le Senne himself would oversee the whole operation to make sure that the STN did not lose a sou. He could even provide a second clandestine route into Paris. His sister-in-law lived just outside the Barrière de Montmartre in a house where she could store shipments from the STN and even have them stitched or bound (the books were sent in unsewn sheets). Le Senne could get the books past the city gates "in a thousand ways" and then would stock them in the Collège des Bernardins, near the Place Maubert, where he rented an apartment. Other dealers stored books in the college, but Le Senne would prevent them from learning about the STN's secret stock: "One enters here only by lettre de cachet." He and Cugnet could open up a lucrative underground market for the STN in Paris. "In a word, M. Cugnet will do all he can to sell your books, especially those persecuted by fanaticism—and you should give him as well as me a list of them—for books that are a little naughty and books that attack prejudices sell with astonishing speed, if their price is not excessive. If you have two or three hundred copies of the works of Helvétius, of those of J. J. Rousseau, of the *Histoire d'Asie, d'Afrique et d'Amérique* [i.e.

Raynal's recently condemned *Histoire philosophique*], they will be sold immediately."[28]

Le Senne hoped to peddle a great many of the STN's books on his own. He wrote that he would act as a purchasing agent for the Comte du Châtelet, who was forming a library, and he sent in an order that he had placed for a teacher in the Bernardins called Giroux, one of the many anticlerical clergymen of his acquaintance, who wanted to buy *L'Intolérance ecclésiastique* and *Essai philosophique sur le monialisme*. On June 4 he ordered a substantial shipment of books whose sale, he said, had been arranged in advance. The book that had sold best (twenty copies) was the radical and obscene attack on the French monarchy entitled *Anecdotes sur Madame Du Barry*. A week later he wrote that he dared not establish a secret entrepôt in the Bernardins, because of the opposition of an official of the college who feared the ill will of the Parisian booksellers. But a Monsieur le Grand, who ran the Café de l'Opéra, rue Saint Nicaise, had agreed to stock the STN's shipments in his establishment; and the STN could always rely on Cugnet: "If you help the sieur Cugnet, you can be certain of having an outlet that will always exist for the distribution of your books in Paris. He is poor, very poor, but an honest man, who is incapable of abusing the trust of those who put bread in his hand."[29]

This recommendation did not quite square with that of the abbé Bretin, who came to see Bosset in late June in order to back out of the smuggling operation and to warn the STN against placing too much "confidence" in Cugnet.[30] But the STN already had sent off a shipment for Cugnet and another for Le Senne. While the crates were making their way through the clandestine routes between Neuchâtel and Paris, Bosset finally finished the last round of the STN's business in Paris and departed, leaving the distribution of the company's books in Paris to Cugnet and the impecunious abbé.

In July Le Senne wrote that he had had to move out of his rooms in the Collège des Bernardins and was now lodging with a friend, a former gendarme de la garde du roi called Quiquincourt, "à la gerbe d'or, rue St. Honoré," where he was waiting for word of his shipment.[31] At last, in mid-September, his crates arrived safely in the entrepôt outside the gates of Paris. But Cugnet's crate was captured by the police after it had been smuggled past the customs. Cugnet had been "sold" to the police, Le Senne reported. Far from being a disaster, however, his arrest had opened up an even better channel to the illegal market in Paris, for somehow Cugnet had persuaded Jean-Pierre Lenoir, the lieutenant general of police, to protect his business. Lenoir had been feuding with the booksellers' guild over the government's attempts to reform the book trade in 1777. The government had restricted the booksellers' hold on *privilèges*—the permanent and exclusive right to publish certain texts—and the booksellers had retaliated by protests, demonstrations, and lobbying for the repeal of the reforms in Versailles and in the Parlement of Paris. Their agitation had brought them into conflict with Lenoir, who evidently meant to retaliate by favoring nonguild bookdealers like Cugnet. To be sure, Lenoir insisted that Cugnet refuse to handle any prohibited books (irreligious, seditious, or pornographic books); but he agreed to permit Cugnet's trade in pirated works (counterfeit editions of books with privileges). "M. Lenoir will only give the permission tacitly," Le Senne explained. "He is on bad terms with the guild, that is what is behind it all. But on this matter we must be extremely circumspect and guard the secret as if our lives depended on it."[32]

Cugnet himself confirmed this version of his lucky mishap in a letter reporting the release of his shipment. He now could get any pirated book into Paris, he announced triumphantly. The police would even let him sell the works of Voltaire and Rousseau, but they would not tolerate anything that openly attacked religion, the state, or morality. Here was the perfect opportunity for the STN to open up its much desired outlet in Paris. If it sent him a limited number of crates at regular intervals, he could quietly build up a large stock without tipping off the guild. He would pay for the books as he sold them. "But secrecy is necessary in all of this, because it would not be desirable for the guild to find out that I am favored by the lieutenant of police."[33] In a later letter he claimed that Lenoir even had permitted him to have the books shipped to Lenoir's own residence, where Cugnet could pick them up and transfer them to a safe stockroom in a "royal house" like the Louvre or the Palais Royal.[34]

Just when this magnificent plot seemed certain to succeed, the roof fell in on Le Senne. "I have enough confidence in you to open my heart and to speak to you in complete frankness," he wrote to the STN on September 20. "My bishop is making my life miserable because of a letter on the clergy, which he insists I wrote. Furthermore, he has discovered, I don't know how, that I was the editor of a collection of selected pieces by Voltaire, which I only undertook at the repeated urging of M. d'Alembert. You can imagine my embarrassment." Now he had to seek refuge in a "free country." Couldn't Ostervald find him a thatched cottage with a little land near Neuchâtel? He would undertake any work that the STN could provide and soon would pay back the money that he was forced to request for the expenses of his journey. He would live frugally like a true philosopher: "Provided that I have bread earned by the sweat of my brow, I do not expect any side-dishes. Happy is he who, in philosophical independence, knows how to live on little and to be contented." If the STN could not come to his rescue, he would have to take the less philosophic course of fleeing to a monastery outside France. Although that idea repelled him, he remembered that Ostervald had mentioned a Swiss abbey, which might take him in. He was desperate and had to get out of the country.[35]

When Ostervald replied that he would recommend Le Senne to a monastery of Blancs Manteaux in nearby Belle-lay, the abbé revealed that there were further complications. As a "regular canon," he would have to ask permission from the bishop who was persecuting him. And he would find it almost impossible to shut himself up for the year of proba-tion, because he had to support the widow and her son, "who sheltered me during a time of misfortune, supported me in distress, consoled me in affliction, and who now have suffered with me from the persecution that is forcing me to flee from this ungrateful country." Le Senne did not go into details about the tribulations of his earlier life, but his "sis-ter-in-law" evidently had shared them as his mistress. In any case, he could not bear to be separated from her. So he asked Ostervald to find out whether she and her son could live with him and he could move into the monastery as a teacher instead of as a monk, although he also announced that he would gladly change religious orders if he could pick up "a little benefice" by doing so. The main thing was to find "a refuge where I can live peacefully and devote my-self entirely to philosophy."[36]

By now Le Senne was sounding like an incarnation of Voltaire's "Pauvre Diable":

A tous les emplois on me ferme la porte.
Rebut du monde, errant, privé d'espoir,
Je me fais moine, ou gris, ou blanc, ou noir,
Rasé, barbu, chaussé, déchaux, n'importe.

I am shut out of every job.
Cast off by society, wandering, deprived of hope,
I'll make myself a monk, whether gray, or white, or black,
Shaven, bearded, sandaled, or discalced, it does not matter.

He could not wait to learn whether the abbot would accept his conditions, he informed the STN on October 12, because he had to leave Paris immediately: "May God bless my enemies and put me out of reach of their teeth! . . . I will be on the road until I can find a refuge." He included a forwarding address so that the STN could reach him in case the Blancs Manteaux job came through; and fulminating as usual against "fanaticism and unreason," he said that he was heading for a small border town, where there was some possibility of work in a new printing company. Because he did not have time to settle his financial affairs or to sell the shipment he had received from the STN, he had ceded the books to Cugnet. Cugnet had paid for them in two notes worth 462 livres in all, which Le Senne had endorsed to the STN and included in his letter. He still owed 202 livres and 1 sou for the shipment, but he promised that he would pay it faithfully, as soon as he got his hands on some money.[37]

In short, Le Senne was attempting to shift two-thirds of his debt onto Cugnet without providing any assurance of his ability to pay the rest—though he spoke vaguely of "a rich and reliable man,"[38] who was to help him scrape up the final 202 livres. The STN had watched too many poor devils go under to be taken in by this maneuver, and it began to feel uneasy after five weeks went by without a letter from Le Senne, who usually wrote at least once a week. On November 19, Ostervald tried to find out what had become of him by writing to him at the forwarding address. The STN was continuing its efforts "to make you a drinking companion of our monks," Ostervald said, but it could not take on Cugnet as its debtor in Le Senne's place; for Cugnet, too, had disappeared. The Paris agents of the STN had been unable to locate him or his boutique.[39]

Two weeks later, the STN received a reply dated from a chateau "where I have found a shelter from the ecclesiastical inquisition," somewhere near Luzarches, about sixteen miles north of Paris. Le Senne could not understand why Cugnet and his wife—who, incidentally, was the real manager of the business—were not operating openly from their boutique. Lenoir's protection had been assured, the requisite capital collected, and the lease signed for the shop. Le Senne himself had invested in the enterprise, though he did not explain where he had found the money and avoided the subject of the 462 livres in Cugnet's notes. He would make inquiries as best he could by mail, since he dared not return to Paris. He had had to flee from the capital, he now revealed, because he was suspected of being the author of an anticlerical tract called *Nouveau cadastre ecclésiastique*. Despite "the most arduous pursuit," he had escaped and had sought work in the printing shop he had mentioned earlier. It was to be established by the president of a provincial parlement (that is, it could have been a clandestine press for the production of parlementary propaganda), but the president had died suddenly. Somehow Le Senne had found sanctuary in the chateau, but he needed a secure job, well beyond the reach of the French government, which had received "a horrible memorandum" denouncing him. His only hope was the STN or the teaching job it might arrange for him with the Blancs Manteaux.[40] Ostervald replied that he and Bosset would put in a good word with the abbot, who might be tractable, as Bosset, who owned some of Neuchâtel's choicest vineyards, supplied the monastery with wine. In return, they expected Le Senne to see that Cugnet paid his notes. If Cugnet proved honorable, the STN would do business with him, and "we can furnish him with material that will make his trade turn into gold; but he must be active, orderly, and exact in his payments."[41] The possibility of tapping the Parisian market and the need to get 462 livres out of Cugnet were reason enough for the STN to string Le Senne along, enticing him with the hope of employment instead of threatening him with legal action, as it usually did when it suspected a debtor of defaulting.

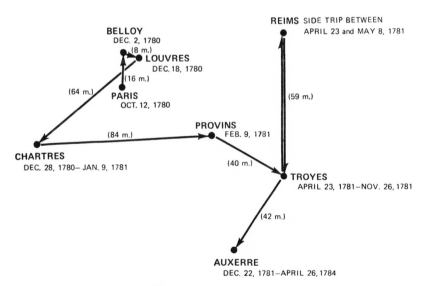

The peregrinations of the abbé Le Senne (in miles)

Le Senne provided the STN with another incentive for leniency in his next letter, dated December 18 from Louvres,
a small town about eight miles southeast of his last stop. He
announced that he had been in touch with d'Alembert, who
had more or less promised to let the STN publish his complete works, if it would hire Le Senne to edit them.
D'Alembert seemed genuinely willing to bargain with the
STN in this manner, for two weeks later he wrote to Ostervald, asking the STN to persevere in its attempt to arrange
the teaching position for Le Senne and to give him some
work in its printing shop: "The miserable man of letters is
just now in a predicament that makes a job more necessary
than ever for him. I would especially hope that he could
settle in Neuchâtel in that if I print something with you, as
will perhaps happen soon, he could be useful to you as well
as to me in the correcting of the proofs."[42] D'Alembert evidently felt real concern for his protégé. He had supported
and coached Le Senne throughout the abbé's negotiations
with the STN over the *Journal helvétique* in the spring, and
he had even attempted to get Frederick II to help "this poor
devil of a priest" in July.[43]

Le Senne needed all the help he could get. He was in a
critical situation, he assured the STN in December. "Far
from diminishing, the persecution is beginning again, or
rather is continuing with more fury than ever. They say
there is a lettre de cachet out against me; but although that
is not certain, I can clearly see that for the moment I must
fight against too many enemies to hope for victory. M.
d'Alembert is the first one to advise me to flee and to accept
the asylum that you propose." Le Senne now lifted another
corner of the secret hiding the explanation of the campaign
against him. He had had to flee from his rooms in the
Collége des Bernardins, he wrote, because the police had

broken into them and had confiscated all his manuscripts, including some precious "Observations patriotiques," a political pamphlet, which, he claimed, had the backing of Lamoignon de Malesherbes, the former Directeur de la Librairie and Secrétaire de la Maison du Roi. Also, he had learned that Mme. Cugnet had been summoned to the police in order to explain her connections with him, evidently because the authorities held the Cugnets and Le Senne responsible for the production and distribution of a pamphlet entitled *Lettre contre le premier ordre du clergé en faveur du second.* Mme. Cugnet had promised to have nothing more to do with Le Senne and had closed the boutique temporarily—that was why she had seemed so elusive. But a friend of his had tracked her down and had been assured that she would continue her business, wanted to maintain good relations with the STN, and would honor the notes for 462 livres.

Skirting around the subject of his own indebtedness, Le Senne tried to tempt the STN with a surefire, moneymaking proposition for another book. He had discovered that there was tremendous demand among the curés of France for a new edition of their "code"—a polemical work that would bring together all the lower clergy's complaints about their superiors, especially "the bishops and tithe-collecting monks." Le Senne knew the book would sell spectacularly because he and his collaborators had already received 1,720 letters from underprivileged clerics, many of whom had provided material for it. "The new edition will be devoured, because of the questions about their [the upper clergy's] divine mission, their competence, the use and destination of tithes," he assured the STN. "The speculation will be lucrative." If the STN was interested, it should write to him in care of Father Du Fossé, the bursar of the Jacobin monastery in Chartres, who had offered to hide him until word came through about the possibility of employment in Switzerland.[44]

The proposal was indeed attractive, Ostervald replied, but what work did Le Senne have in mind? The *Traité du gouvernement de l'Eglise telle que J. C. l'a ordonnée, ouvrage très utile à MM. les curés pour la défense de leurs droits,* three duodecimo volumes? Ostervald was more interested, however, in publishing the works of d'Alembert, and he asked Le Senne to send the philosophe a reminder about "the desire which he expressed to me of for once being printed in a free country." As to the teaching position, the abbot of the monastery in Bellelay had not yet answered the STN's letters recommending Le Senne.[45] That job was his last remaining hope, but he could not hold out much longer, Le Senne answered on December 28, soon after his arrival in Chartres. "My departure from France is now more necessary than ever. My pursuers are hard on my heels, the storm is about to break ... One day you will know the complete story. M. d'Alembert himself, who is to write to you, is indignant over it. I cannot go on being a burden to my friends, useless to myself, and every day exposed to the danger of becoming a victim to a cabale, which is implacable in its hatred, atrocious in its vengeance, and unfortunately powerful in its influence." He no longer asked that any provision be made for the widow and her son, whom he had left behind in Paris. He only wanted a job for himself, anything that would keep him alive. He would travel to Neuchâtel by foot, if the abbot did not want to advance his coach fare. But he could not remain with the Jacobins in Chartres much longer. "They aren't all reliable in this house," he wrote fearfully, adding that the mail was watched (he also asked the STN to write to him under Du

Fossé's name and to pay the postage, as he did not have enough money for the usual COD payments on letters). His proposed attack on the upper clergy made his situation all the more precarious, but it also could provide the STN with a sensational best-seller for it treated an inflammable subject. "Outraged at the unjust distribution of the ecclesiastical tithe (*décime*), the uselessness of its protests in the last assembly [the General Assembly of the French Clergy, which met in May and June 1780], and the despotism of the bishops, the second order of the clergy wants finally to bring out into the open the rights of the curés, the question of tithes, the distribution of the ecclesiastical tithe . . . There is not a curé in the country who won't buy it as soon as it appears and not a bishop who won't proscribe it. It was the idea for this work that exposed me to the hatred of the upper clergy." Le Senne explained that he had in mind a radical revision of a work that had appeared earlier under the title *Code des curés*. He could produce a prospectus for it in three days and the text in a year. It would have to be printed outside France by a publisher like the STN, which could send agents to gather subscriptions secretly within the kingdom and could count on making a fortune by tapping the discontent of the lower clergy.[46]

A week later, Ostervald sent some bad news: the abbot had reported that the Blancs Manteaux did not have any more teaching positions, although they would consider Le Senne for the first vacancy to arise.[47] Le Senne immediately shot back a letter imploring help and explaining in full the reasons for his need to escape from France. "The first order of the clergy got the authorities to confiscate the 'Mémoire des curés' attacking episcopal taxes, the abuse of the tithes, and the distribution of benefices. In the raid, they found four of my letters along with those of the printer and my collaborator. Since then, they have been pursuing us very actively. Those who are most sincerely attached to me, M. d'Alembert first of all, have advised me to go to a foreign country so that the storm may blow over."[48]

Now the full story behind Le Senne's flight was out. He had been caught producing propaganda against the wealth and privileges of the upper clergy during the sensitive period when the General Assembly of the Clergy held its meetings. Those meetings often produced controversies about the administration and the finances of the Gallican church, and they touched off some unusually strong polemics in the spring of 1780. The *Mémoires secrets* carried several articles about the pamphleteering against despotism and decadence among the prelates, who complained about being slandered individually and collectively and got the government to confiscate a great many of the pamphlets, including 2,000 copies of Le Senne's "Mémoire des curés."[49] He had proposed it to the STN in a letter of May 24: "As the Assembly of the clergy opens next Monday the 29th, I would like to have printed during its session a fairly short pamphlet, which could be distributed in Paris before the bishops adjourn." But the Swiss had paid no more attention to it than to his other projects, and so he had had it printed clandestinely in France. Someone had denounced him to the authorities, who had seized almost every copy of the "Mémoire" along with all his manuscripts and papers; and now, armed with a lettre de cachet, they were trying to seize him.

In January 1781, Le Senne thought he could feel the police breathing down his neck. "Despite my disguise, I am being forced to leave Chartres . . . You see, Monsieur, I can no longer live without a place of refuge, a burden to my friends and in a constant state of alarm." He planned to go to Provins next, but he could not predict when or how he would get there, because the route was fraught with danger and he had to cover it on foot. Father Du Fossé would forward the STN's letters, and Le Senne fervently hoped that they would bring an offer of at least part-time employment in Neuchâtel. He would write articles for the *Journal helvétique*. He could reproduce the *Nouveau code des curés* from memory. And he also could put together again his *Pensées choisies de M. Voltaire rangées par ordre alphabétique,* an anthology that he had prepared at d'Alembert's suggestion and that the police had confiscated. "M. d'Alembert outlined it for me and noted the subjects that it was important to stress . . . He formally promised me that he would see to its sale. With such a guide, the choice is bound to be good." Playing up his only "protection" for all it was worth, Le Senne emphasized that d'Alembert was acting as his "mentor" and had promised to let him produce the definitive edition of d'Alembert's works. If that inducement were not sufficient, perhaps Ostervald would hire him as an act of charity: "Deign for a moment to act like a father to me and to let your heart speak. I have neither the talent of Rousseau nor the genius of Voltaire . . . but I flatter myself that I have their ardor for work."[50]

A month later Le Senne had reached Provins, eighty-four miles east of Chartres, and he had hit bottom. He could not produce any articles for the *Journal helvétique,* because he could not buy books to review. He could not put up any manuscripts for sale, because the police had seized them all. He could not even send a prospectus for the *Code des curés,* because he could not afford the postage. He had been desperately ill and had imagined the lettre de cachet pursuing him as he trudged through the cold and muck of February to the Jacobin monastery in Provins. "I arrived there dead tired and covered with mud after having had alarms all along the route," Le Senne wrote. The prior, a friend called Father Fardel, could keep him hidden a little while, but Le Senne could not hold out much longer. "Because it is time at last for this wandering life to stop. I desire only to settle down and to work . . . It depends on you for my misery to cease and for me finally to get the only things I wish for—work and subsistence."[51] He had sunk as low as the *pauvre diable* in the basest stage of the life cycle described by Voltaire.

> Las! où courir dans mon destin maudit!
> N'ayant ni pain, ni gite, ni crédit,
> Je résolus de finir ma carrière.

> Weary! Where to run in the course of my accursed fate!
> Having neither bread, nor shelter, nor credit,
> I resolved to end my career.

In his reply, Ostervald removed the last straws at which Le Senne had been grasping. The abbot of Bellelay had written that there was no prospect of any future position among the Blancs Manteaux; and the STN could provide nothing, because its own business had gone into a slump, an indirect casualty of the American war. Moreover it was worried about its notes from Cugnet, who still had not opened his shop in the Louvre, according to reports from Quandet de Lachenal, the STN agent in Paris, whom it had hired on Le Senne's recommendation.[52] Soon afterwards, however, Quandet found Cugnet and his wife in their boutique, which they had just opened with the full but secret support of the police. Sounding as optimistic as ever about their prospects, they said thay they still expected to trade heavily with the STN, thanks to Lenoir's protection, and that they would honor all three of the notes totaling 662 livres, which they had given to Le Senne for the STN's books. Quandet, a veteran of the underground book trade, gave them a clean bill of health, but he had nothing good to say about Le Senne: "I call a spade a spade, and this ex-monk, shut up for ten years in St. Yon at Rouen, is a scoundrel, according to what I've heard ... He is known here as a man with no integrity and with sordid morals."[53]

The STN hardly needed to be put on its guard, however, because Quandet's reference to the three notes was a revelation in itself. Le Senne had only endorsed two of Cugnet's notes over to the STN: one for 262 livres, which was to become due in June 1781, and one for 200 livres, due in August 1781. He had kept the third, which was worth 202 livres 1 sou and had the nearest date of maturity: April 1781. On the eve of his departure from Paris, when he was desperate for cash, he had sold all of his Swiss books to Cugnet, not just two-thirds of them, as he had written to Ostervald. He had endorsed the 202-livre note to the widow Bauprais, so that she could cash it in his absence when it became due. And he had told the STN that he would send that sum as soon as he had collected it from his customers. Thus the "share" that he claimed to have in Cugnet's boutique was merely a credit for 202 livres' worth of books, which rightfully belonged to the STN, and which he wrongfully planned to collect in April through the intermediary of Mme. Bauprais. Ostervald therefore instructed Quandet to foil "the saintly man" by getting Cugnet to withhold the payment of the 202 livres.[54]

Quandet did even better. He swooped down on the widow one day as she was entering Cugnet's shop; and when she presented the note, he snatched it out of her hands, gave her a ferocious scolding, and marched off to the home of a police officer called Chesnon, where he demanded that the note be confiscated as evidence of a swindle. In fact, as Quandet wrote to the STN, he had no authority to act in that manner, and Chesnon only cooperated because he was Cugnet's liaison with the police. In strictly legal terms, the note bound Cugnet to pay 202 livres 1 sou to the widow Bauprais. As its endorsee, she could insist on the payment of that sum, leaving the ultimate settlement of the debt to the STN. The Swiss did not have any formal claim on Le Senne, because he had adroitly shifted his debt onto Cugnet without even sending any notes of his own to Neuchâtel. To be sure, they could prosecute him for fraud, but they would have to smoke him out of his hiding places, which he changed almost every week; and even if they got him arrested, he would be kept in prison as a seditious pamphleteer, without any resources to apply toward the repayment of his debt. So the Swiss had to move carefully on two fronts: first, they had to persuade Le Senne to direct the widow Bauprais to sacrifice her legal right to the 202 livres, and then they had to squeeze that sum out of Cugnet, even though his formal obligation was to the unfindable Le Senne and not to them. The two poor devils had lived long enough in Grub Street to withstand any amount of moral pressure, but the STN could rely upon Le Senne's need for a job and Cugnet's desire for pirated books to bring them around.[55]

Soon after Quandet's ambush of the widow Bauprais, the STN wrote to Le Senne, demanding that the widow abandon her claim to the money. Finding himself outflanked and foiled, Le Senne agreed to surrender the note and attempted to shift the blame for the struggle over it to Quandet and the Cugnets. They were a pack of rogues, he wrote, and the STN would be lucky to escape from them with its fortune intact. To be sure, he had introduced the STN to them in the first place, having himself failed to detect their iniquity; "But who is not duped every day?" He then produced a long, confused, and unconvincing explanation of his own role in the imbroglio, and passed on to the happier subject of how he could be a useful auxiliary of the STN. He had just received a letter from d'Alembert, who still planned to publish his works with the STN; and he had come upon an even more promising job in the camp of the enemy: a religious order in which he had good contacts needed new editions of several devotional works, including a breviary that would require a printing of 10,000 copies. If the STN was interested, it should write to him in Troyes. He had just arrived there, having somehow completed the forty miles from his sickbed in Provins; and he apparently expected to stay there a while, although he was about to leave on a side trip to Reims.[56]

Soon afterwards, Quandet reported that the widow Bauprais had agreed to give up her claim to the note, leaving only Cugnet for the STN to contend with. The outlook for the boutique seemed good, because on April 2, Cugnet had informed the STN that the business had got off the ground successfully. Lenoir was as willing as ever to protect it, since he knew that "my relations with the said abbé Le Senne were all the more innocent in that I did not know about and did not share in any respect the vices that are attributed to him. They are foreign to me and I don't even want to know what they are." Cugnet still had all of the STN's books in his possession and freely acknowledged his debt for them. He asked only that the STN permit him to postpone the payment of the 202-livre note, a reasonable request, considering the difficulties with Le Senne and the delay in the opening of the shop.[57] The STN granted the postponement, and so the financial element in its relations with Le Senne was liquidated. The Swiss told Cugnet that they wanted to drop the subject of the wandering abbé altogether: "We are now completely cured of our desire to find a position for him in our area."[58]

The abbé, however, would not let himself be dropped. The STN's settlement with Cugnet took the heat out of its correspondence with Le Senne, and Le Senne's reference to the breviary printing kept alive some of the STN's interest in him, which he continued to feed from his inexhaustible supply of projects and proposals. On May 8, 1781, he was back in Troyes, announcing that he had learned his lesson, viz. "that all traffickers in letters like Quandet and Cugnet deserve only the opprobrium and sovereign scorn of thinking men." He was negotiating for the printing of the breviary with the abbot of Cîteaux and thought he could get the STN preferred over two French printers, who also wanted the job. Unfortunately, in a fit of enlightened despotism, Joseph II had forbidden the importation of breviaries to monasteries in the Empire. That order would eliminate more than 100 Cistercian abbeys from the market for the new edition; so the abbot hesitated to commission it. Meanwhile, Le Senne could suggest some excellent manuscripts: a "State of France for the year 1780" and the Voltaire anthology, which surely would prove profitable, because d'Alembert had promised to arrange for the sale of at least 500 copies in France. Le Senne still yearned for "a benefice and consequently some certain bread," and concluded with an appeal for a place in a monastery anywhere in Switzerland or a teaching post in Bern or Soleure, should Porrentruy and Fribourg prove impossible.

When the STN replied that it was interested but wary about advancing any money for the printing of the breviary, Le Senne reassured it that the Cistercian order would pay all costs and that the market was enormous, because 1,500 monasteries used the Cistercian rite, not counting the 100 under the Emperor's interdict in Germany. He urged the STN to make a bid for the job and to explain its terms in a letter, which he would present to the head of the order while arguing its case in Cîteaux. The Swiss followed his advice, offering to buy a new font of type, if the abbot would subsidize a printing of 8,000 copies. But the project never came to anything, evidently because Le Senne had exaggerated his influence in Cîteaux. It seems that he merely knew a monk there who had produced a few pages of a draft for the new breviary in the hope of persuading the abbot to authorize the composition of the new work, while Le Senne was trying to arrange its printing.[59] The enterprise collapsed at both ends, but it was a significant scheme; for it reveals the rawness of the profit motive in late-eighteenth-century publishing. The presses of Neuchâtel had turned out violent Protestant propaganda throughout the sixteenth century. In the seventeenth century one of Ostervald's ancestors had produced an annotated edition of the Bible, which was condemned and confiscated throughout France. Ostervald knew a great many philosophes and shared their views. Yet, if he had been paid enough, this enlightened Protestant publisher would have gladly printed a breviary for the Cistercians at the suggestion of an anticlerical abbé.

Le Senne was full of other suggestions. He continued to push his plan for a "State of France," which would consist of "a systematic survey of everything written during the last twenty years on the moral and physical aspects of public administration ... M. Malesherbes [C. G. de Lamoignon de Malesherbes, the former Directeur de la Librairie and Secrétaire de la Maison du Roi] has seen it and thinks well of it."[60] It was a compilation of physiocratic writing—more than 500 volumes distilled down to two under the guidance

of Malesherbes himself, Le Senne wrote triumphantly, adding that he could also produce a preface for an "Historical,
Critical, and Philosophical Account of Modern Europe,
from Charles V to Joseph II," if the STN was interested.
And finally, he still could be useful in the smuggling side of
the STN's business, for he had discovered a foolproof
method of getting its books into Paris through the intermediary of a grocer in Saint Denis.[61] The Swiss did not even
reply to these proposals, but Le Senne sent them the "State
of France" anyway, in the hope that they would buy the
manuscript if only he could get them to read it. Although
he did not even have enough money to pay for its postage
(he sent it with a friend who was traveling to Switzerland),
he calculated that it would be profitabe enough for him to
finance the printing of a work on education, which he was
preparing. But he was worried by the onset of autumn. In
order to avoid another winter of illness and vagabondage,
he had to quickly find "some means, at least temporary, to
subsist, even though in a state of perpetual anxiety." Perhaps the STN would let him try to peddle some of its books
in Troyes, or alternatively could it find him a job in Prussia?
He knew that it had contacts there and that there might be
a position as the second or third librarian of the "philosopher king."[62]

The STN did not answer that appeal, or the next one. In
late November Le Senne tried once again to learn the fate of
his manuscript, requesting the STN to write to him as "M.
l'abbé Hubert chez M. Richard, maître de pension, vis-à-vis
la collégiale de St. Etienne à Troyes."[63] He apparently had
adopted "Hubert" as an alias and had found a temporary
teaching job. Ostervald finally replied that the STN would
print the work, but only if Le Senne could pay for it entirely
in advance with funds collected from any Troyens whom he
could persuade to back him.[64] If, as he claimed, Le Senne

had found backers in Troyes, he had lost their support by December 22, when he wrote to the STN from Auxerre, forty-two miles away, imploring it to print the work at its own expense, or to sell it to another publisher for him, or to buy a manuscript "Treatise on Morality for the Use of Young People," or to help him set up a small school in Neuchâtel. He clearly was desperate again and evidently had got into some trouble in Troyes. As he was only in Auxerre "in passing," he asked the STN to write to him "quite simply . . . as M. Bauprais chez M. Charton, rue de Poncelot, Auxerre, without letting my name appear."[65]

Ten weeks later, however, Le Senne was still in Auxerre, living as "Bauprais, instructor of young people," and things were looking up. "Bauprais is the maternal name," he explained. "I thought its use necessary to keep away the envious and persecuting sort. I have found a feeble means of subsistence in this town by teaching mathematics and belles-lettres. To be sure, I often feel more dead than alive, but I am working and making myself useful . . . I don't expect any favors from fortune. Everything makes me expect the opposite. But as one can't scrutinize the implacable decrees of the Eternal, one must float between hope and despair. I think that that is a good article of philosophy."[66] It was a philosophy of helplessness and resignation, a philosophy of the *pauvre diable:*

Quel parti prendre? où suis-je et qui dois-je être?
Né dépourvu, dans la foule jeté,
Germe naissant par le vent emporté,
Sur quel terrain puis-je espérer de craître?

What course to take? Where am I, and what will become of me?
Born destitute, thrown in the crowd,
A seed carried off by the wind,
In what soil can I hope to grow?

Le Senne still kept in touch with events in Paris through his old friend Quiquincourt, who tipped him off whenever a possibility arose of speculating on the literary marketplace. The best speculation in the spring of 1782 still seemed to be on anticlerical subjects, and Le Senne still came up with proposals for attacks against the wealth, malfeasance, and despotism of the upper clergy. But the Swiss no longer bothered to answer many of his letters, much as he chided them for being "terribly indifferent to the lot of writers" and for failing to appreciate the selling power of topical pamphlets: "These kinds of works sell far better than the best books."[67] Nonetheless, he continued to offer up manuscripts, including two works on ecclesiastical history and a "course of study" with a "catechism of morality" adapted from d'Alembert's works with d'Alembert's blessing.[68] The STN agreed that any book would gain luster and lucre from so great a name, but it backed away from the project after doing some informal market research through Quandet de Lachenal. Quandet sounded his contacts among the writers and booksellers of Paris and reported that d'Alembert's star had set: "Despite the sort of celebrity that surrounds M. d'Alembert, Messieurs, I would make bold to advise you to offer him only half the price that he asks for his works. Aside from his essays (*mélanges*), which no one would buy here even for scrap paper, I know by testimony other than my own that his writings on geometry, which are supposed to be the best he has done, are very far from demonstrating the profundity of genius that distinguishes a Kepler, a Newton, etc."[69] Having cooled to the idea of publishing d'Alembert's writings, the STN could not warm up to Le Senne's proposal to filter them through his own prose.

But, as always, the abbé bounced back with another project. He had filled the ear of a local young *littérateur* with talk about the pleasures and profits of the book trade. The lad was eager to establish a book store with capital to be supplied by a rich, aged, and childless relative, who doted on him and intended to leave him a fortune. Le Senne would act as guardian angel to the business and would make sure that it became an important outlet for the STN's books, if the Swiss were willing to stock the shop. "This is no Cugnet business," he wrote enticingly.[70] But the STN had learned at last to beware of *hommes à projets*. It ignored this proposition and tried to discourage others by ceasing to answer Le Senne's letters.

This strategy finally succeeded in shutting off the abbé's endless flow of proposals—or at least in diverting them to his contacts among other publishers in Switzerland, Avignon, the Low Countries, and England. But in April 1784 Le Senne made another try at arousing the STN's speculative instincts. He was still in Auxerre and had ingratiated himself with a bookseller called Fournier fils, "rich, active, and knowledgeable." Fournier had established a *cabinet littéraire,* a book club of the kind that was sprouting up all over France, and he could stock and distribute the STN's books on a large scale. Le Senne also asked whether the Swiss had ever been tempted by some manuscripts that he had sent to Neuchâtel two years earlier. He would abandon all rights to them in exchange for a few free books. But he no longer sounded desperate for cash. He still had a teaching job and somehow had snared an ecclesiastical pension of 1,000 livres a year. The pension may have produced the new note of piety which crept into Le Senne's letters, for he now sounded almost devout on the subject of d'Alembert, who had died on October 29, 1783, and had been buried as an unbeliever in an unmarked grave. Six weeks before his death, the philosophe had written about his plan to publish his works with the STN, Le Senne said. Although d'Alembert was then too ill to revise his manuscripts, he intended to go ahead with the project and wanted Le Senne to travel to Neuchâtel in order to arrange it. But before he could make the trip, Le Senne had learned of his patron's death—"a death that saddened the truly faithful, so they say, because he showed no sign of repentance, of retracting [his non-Christian philosophy]. God alone can judge him. But M. d'Alembert would have been no less great if he had shown less veneration for the infamous Voltaire."[71] The abbé seemed to have forgotten his attempt to produce an anthology of Voltairiana under d'Alembert's direction during his earlier days in Grub Street.

Five months later, however, he reverted to his Voltairian style. He was on the road and on the run again. Writing from the village of Monetau near Auxerre, he said that the chapter of his order in Auxerre had been suppressed and that his pension and his teaching position had been snuffed out. Once again he begged the STN to find him a job in Fribourg and proposed to print an old tract under a new title: " 'Revenues of the French clergy' . . . The introductory discourse is intended to give the public a correct idea of the clergy's wealth."[72] He asked the Swiss to send their reply to a new forwarding address, but they never answered and never heard from him again.

LE SENNE PERSONIFIED the moral that Voltaire himself attached to "Le Pauvre Diable": "We are informed that the author amused himself by composing this work in 1758 in order to deter a young man, who took his passion for scribbling verse to be genius, from the dangerous career of letters. The number of those who ruin themselves by this unhappy passion is prodigious ... They live off rhymes and hopes, and die in destitution."[73] The abbé also could have been one of the table companions of Rameau's nephew: "a heap of disreputable beggars, dull parasites, timid troops of whom I have the honor to be the brave commander. We appear gay; but at bottom we are all resentful and especially hungry. Wolves are not more famished; tigers are not more cruel."[74] In fact, Le Senne embodied the theme of the poor devil so perfectly that his career may shed new light on it. For just as one can understand the satire of Pope and Swift more fully by relating it to the context of Grub Street, London,[75] so one should be able to put the work of Voltaire and Diderot in perspective by exploring the milieux behind their motifs. They made the hack writer into an object of ridicule, an intellectual pantaloon, and then cast their enemies in this role. But they had plenty of hacks in their own camp. The Republic of Letters was crowded with poor devils, real men of flesh and blood, who struggled to sustain their miserable lives by doing whatever odd jobs fell their way—compiling anthologies, writing for journals, peddling manuscripts, smuggling forbidden books, and spying for the police. Poor deviltry was a way of life but one that is difficult to reconstruct, because most literary hacks lived in an obscurity that has become increasingly impenetrable with the passage of time. Hence the importance of the case of Le Senne, a representative specimen of this species. Despite his enormous output of articles, pamphlets, and books, he would have disappeared irretrievably into the past had his dossier not survived in the papers of the STN. To go through that dossier is to get a sense of life at the bottom of *la basse littérature* (low literature), as Voltaire scornfully called it.

As Le Senne's unending flow of proposals to the STN indicates, he was an idea merchant, an *homme à projets.* He turned out projects of all shapes and sizes—novels, histories, treatises, travel books, pamphlets, anything that he thought would sell. But in his sales talk, he stressed that the most profitable books were "those that attack prejudices,"[76] and most of his proposals expressed some theme of the Enlightenment. He popularized the work of the philosophes, both implicitly, as in his suggestion for a philosophical history of religious warfare, and explicitly, as in his plans to produce a collection of Physiocratic writing, an anthology of Voltairiana, a work on public administration, which had the blessing of Malesherbes, and a tract on education and morality, which had been inspired by d'Alembert.

Within his repertory of philosophic projects, the theme that stood out was desecration of the church. Le Senne was an anticlerical cleric, one of the abbés who appeared in such profusion among the partisans of the Enlightenment, and he concentrated his fire on "episcopal despotism" and the wealth of the upper clergy. His pamphleteering on this subject during the general assembly of the French clergy in 1780 earned him a lettre de cachet and made him flee around the countryside like a hunted animal for the next two years. He found shelter with sympathetic priests like Father Du Fossé of Chartres and Father Fardel of Provins, and in fact he seems to have had contacts with disenchanted curés and abbés throughout France: hence his remark about the hundreds of letters he had received from clergymen while preparing his antiepiscopal "Code des curés," a work, he said, that would be devoured by every curé and prosecuted by every bishop in France. He often referred to obscure clergymen like himself who peddled or purchased anticlerical pamphlets: the abbé Bretin who stocked shipments for Cugnet, the abbé from Chez-le-Roi who also had some connection with the Cugnet shop, the abbé Lanvin who secretly sold propaganda against the bishops, and Giroux of the Bernardins who bought works like *L'Intolérance ecclésiastique* and *Essai philosophique sur le monialisme.* These men illustrate the existence of an "ecclesiastical underground,"[77] which may have been more important than is generally realized. For Le Senne and his collaborators did not merely express the frustrations of those at the bottom of the ecclesiastical hierarchy. They represented an ideology that had gone beyond Richerism to Voltairianism, and they spoke for an alienated intelligentsia of poor devils within the ranks of the Church itself. Although his remarks about a network of 1,720 curés were probably exaggerated, Le Senne contributed to a wave of propaganda that helped to split the First Estate in 1789.

But Le Senne appeared before the STN primarily in the role of a minor philosophe, a hanger-on of d'Alembert's circle, not as a dissident clergyman. Although he probably exaggerated his closeness to d'Alembert, Le Senne certainly received patronage and protection from the philosophe and performed all sorts of tasks in return. The reciprocity in their relationship deserves to be emphasized, because the philosophes needed auxiliaries in their fight against *l'infâme.* The philosophic manuscripts that Le Senne kept proposing to the STN may not have originated from d'Alembert's atelier, although Le Senne sometimes mentioned that a particular manuscript had been corrected by d'Alembert or represented his views. But d'Alembert evidently wanted anonymous pens to popularize his ideas. His correspondence with Voltaire showed that the two philosophes worked hard at placing protégés in strategic positions, at discrediting ideological enemies, and at disseminating philosophic propaganda.[78] By helping d'Alembert in this enterprise, Le Senne earned his patronage, which he then tried to exploit for all it was worth.

But d'Alembert had no reason to feel exploited himself. If he had persuaded the STN to hire his abbé, he would have placed a propagandist for his cause in a powerful publishing house. And if he had got the Swiss to transform the *Journal helvétique* into a party organ for the philosophes with Le Senne as its editor, he could have done a great deal to counteract the antiphilosophe press, which had developed enormous popular appeal, thanks largely to the journalistic genius of Linguet, a sworn enemy of Voltaire and d'Alembert. It was no accident that Le Senne's first projects included a survey of philosophy from the ancients to d'Alembert, a defense of Voltaire, and an attack on Linguet; nor that journalism was so important in his dealings with the STN. The philosophes sought to seize command of public opinion. They wanted to do battle—to change minds, reform institutions, and avenge slurs—not merely to philosophize in peace. For them, the Enlightenment was a struggle to spread light. And so they needed literary agents, popularizers, polemicists, journalists, and ideological "carriers" like Le Senne.

Le Senne's role also shows that communicating *Lumières* to the French public was a difficult business. The directors of the STN would not purchase a manuscript until they had made an estimate of its printing cost, had checked on its market value with booksellers and literary agents, and had driven the hardest possible bargain. They were as eager to print the Cistercian breviary as the work of d'Alembert. In fact, they ultimately decided that d'Alembert overvalued his writing and never reached an agreement with him. They would not consider buying a manuscript from an obscure writer like Le Senne, nor would they print one on commission, unless he could guarantee to cover their costs, either by arranging for sales in advance or by finding speculators to back him. He seems to have supplied a good deal of copy to less cautious and less reputable publishers but not to have derived much income from them. That was one of the hack writer's dilemmas: he could not get his work accepted by publishers who would pay a decent price for it and could not get a decent price from the publishers who would accept it. The STN had its own problems. It could not reach the French market without fighting its way through the bureaucracy that protected the French publishers, who were its natural enemies. It probably would have hired Le Senne to produce a French edition of the *Journal helvétique* if it had been able to pacify the censors, bribe the officials, and buy off the owners of the rival French journals. But it could not overcome the opposition of the bureaucratic and vested interests. Its failure indicates how badly the growth of journalism had been stunted under the Old Regime and provides some perspective to the journalistic explosion of 1789.

The book police, the censors, and the whole apparatus of the Direction de la Librairie were intended to suppress irreligious, seditious, and immoral books; and they frequently did so. But they also stifled innovative literature and subjected the publishing industry to a monopoly dominated by the members of the Parisian booksellers' guild. The STN ran into the opposition of the guild whenever it tried to sell its books in Paris, and therefore it relied on the services of men like Le Senne and Cugnet, who operated around the fringe of the law. This strategy seemed promising, because Cugnet had the support of the police; and the police supported him—provided he dealt in pirated and not in prohibited books—because they had come into conflict with the guild while attempting to implement the government's reforms of the book trade. But one should not attribute too much importance to Cugnet's boutique: Lenoir's tolerance of it did not mean that the police had an extensive alliance with the literary underground. It merely exemplified the contradictions and limitations of the government's attempt at reform. In trying to trim back the privileges of the established bookdealers, the French authorities occasionally made pacts with the poor devils, but they never permitted large-scale smuggling and never allowed the illegal dealers to sell prohibited books.

Those were the kind that sold best of all, according to Le Senne, who asked the STN to supply atheistic and seditious material like the works of d'Holbach and the *Anecdotes secrètes sur Madame Du Barry.* He and his friends could not abide by any implicit contracts or ad hoc arrangements with the police, because they derived their living from the illegal activities of the literary underground. The illegal book trade had developed into a major industry, thanks to the restrictions of legitimate publishing in France. It needed hands to process its merchandise, so it recruited hacks from the undernourished literary population of Paris. To ask a poor devil to keep his fingers off the forbidden fruit of his trade was like asking a jackal to renounce meat. Le Senne pounced on any sustenance he could find. Not only did he write illegal literature, he acted as an agent for other writers who produced it. Clandestine manuscripts seem to have circulated widely in Grub Street. Le Senne's letters indicate that fellow scribblers provided him with much of the material that he peddled to publishers outside France. Once these works were printed, he helped distribute them by setting up smuggling routes, secret stockrooms, and clandestine retailers. The Cugnet operation was only one of his many efforts to open up underground channels by employing characters like the grocer who smuggled books from Saint Denis and the cafe manager who stored them in his shop on the rue Saint Nicaise. Le Senne imported books himself and probably went around Paris selling them under his cloak. He lived by his wits and turned his hand to whatever would bring a few sous. As a pamphleteer, a journalist, a literary agent, a smuggler, and a peddler, he personified the multifarious activities of the literary underground.

This existence took its toll on the soul. When he began to bargain for a job with the STN, Le Senne put up a bold front, demanding 24 livres per sheet of prose, guaranteed employment for five years, travel expenses, and help in finding a chalet for himself and his dependents. But he soon dropped his charitable talk about the widow Bauprais and groveled, begging for any work that the Swiss would give him. He offered to come to Neuchâtel on foot, to correct copy and read proof, and to accept any wages he could get. When the STN said it could not hire him, he implored it to find him employment elsewhere, in Bellelay, Soleure, Fribourg, or Bern, as a writer, a teacher, a monk—anything, anywhere, to keep him alive and out of prison. While pleading for a place in a monastery and a benefice, he ignored his earlier attacks on monasticism and the unjust allotment of the church's wealth. While enjoying a brief respite and an ecclesiastical pension in Auxerre as the abbé Bauprais, he denounced Voltaire's impieties as if he had never planned to edit an anthology of them. And after his position in Auxerre collapsed, he returned to his pamphleteering against the upper clergy. Poor devils could not afford to be consistent. They put themselves up for hire and wrote whatever was ordered by the highest bidder, when they were fortunate enough to sell themselves. They therefore produced propaganda on opposite sides of controversial issues and, like most camp followers, belonged to the camp that fed them.

Nevertheless, they do not seem to have been evenly divided. Voltaire and Diderot made the poor devils in their writing appear as the hatchet men of their enemies, Fréron, Palissot, and the other antiphilosophes; but Le Senne belonged to their friend d'Alembert, and Le Senne's experience suggests that his comrades tended to be *frondeurs* rather than partisans of the Old Regime. Of course, he may not have been typical of his milieu. Most of the men in it were too obscure to have left behind any evidence of their existence; so one can hardly know how the majority of them thought and behaved. When their names have survived, however, they appear most often in police reports and in the archives of the Bastille, which contain a high proportion of book peddlers and pamphleteers. Lettres de cachet were a hazard of the trade and did not make hack writers and clandestine book dealers look favorably on the government. The government certainly was suspicious of them: it hired spies and police inspectors to keep track of their activities. And those activities tended to be illegal if not downright seditious, because the poor devils specialized in the production and distribution of outlawed literature. They would write for the government if given a chance—Le Senne probably did produce propaganda for Necker, as he claimed—but their main chance lay on the other side of the law. The literary underground drew them irresistibly into illegal activities and made them into natural enemies of the state.

It also attracted deviant and even criminal characters. The men in Le Senne's milieu knew how to present themselves as upright citizens of the republic of letters when they first established contact with Neuchâtel. They vouched for each other's virtue in letters of recommendation to the STN and maintained a united front of integrity as long as they collaborated in their efforts to exploit the Swiss. But they soon divided over the spoils and gave a different account of each other's morals in their later letters to Neuchâtel. Quandet revealed that the Cugnets rented out their daughter just as Rameau's nephew tried to solicit for his wife. The Cugnets and Quandet wrote that Le Senne was a depraved creature who had spent years in prison. And he described them as rogues and thieves. They did in fact outdo him in defrauding the Swiss, but that is another story. Suffice it to say that Quandet eventually swindled the STN of 10,145 livres and was forced out of Paris by lettre de cachet and that Cugnet embezzled 830 livres before disappearing into the provinces.

Le Senne's embezzlement involved relatively petty cash, but it demonstrated the contradiction between the elevation of his pretensions and the baseness of his actions. After every defeat and every humiliation, he had to come back and beg for more. After failing to break into respectability, he had to live by dirty work and petty crime. Literary scavenging made him sick—he often complained about ill health and lameness—and it also wounded his sense of self. Of course one can only read his letters, not his soul. But the letters show what it was to hit bottom, to be ill, famished, and afraid. Although one must discount their calculated, stylized appeal to the sensibility of the Swiss, they have an unmistakable note of anguish. They show the philosophe as a broken man, down and out in Paris and on the road in the provinces, driven from place to place by hunger and fear. With more talent, money, and luck, Le Senne might have become a respectable philosophe-abbé like Condillac, Morellet, or Raynal. But his life seemed to bear out the bitter reflection of Rameau's nephew: "We are driven by accursed

circumstances, and driven very cruelly."[79] He degenerated
into an outlaw and an outcast, stumbling about the countryside on foot in the dead of winter, living off charity, hiding under an alias, fleeing from a lettre de cachet, and sus-
tained only by the hope of escape to a Swiss cottage, which
was as remote as a castle in Spain. What happened to him
after he disappeared down the road? Did he play a part in
the Revolution? One cannot say, because he vanished in
1784 without leaving a trace. But one can easily imagine
him among the followers of Jacques Roux. His experience
shows where the rage of the enragés came from: it was a
deep, visceral hatred of a regime whose corruption had
spread into their own inner beings.

To penetrate the inner world of the poor devils, one must
turn from Voltaire, who felt nothing but scorn for them, to
Diderot, who had lived as a hack writer for many years, who
understood the degradation caused by poverty, and who
could write sympathetically about frustrated ambition,
déclassement, and marginal characters. *Le Neveu de Rameau*—a dialogue between a decent, successful philosophe
and a deviant, Grub Street genius—is Diderot's answer to
"Le Pauvre Diable," which was also written as a dialogue
between an implicit "Moi" and "Lui." But where Voltaire
merely used his stooge to score points off his enemies, Diderot penetrated into a deeper psychological reality. In fact,
Le Neveu de Rameau can be read as a gloss on Le Senne's letters and vice versa; for the life of Le Senne and the literature
of Diderot mirror one another in ways that are mutually revealing.

Rameau's nephew was no happy Bohemian but a tor-
mented man, who suffered from the psychology of the *raté*
as well as the pangs of hunger. Hunger made him debase
himself as a professional sponger, and debasement drove

him beyond the bounds of police society into a dangerous state of marginality: "But if it is natural to have an appetite—because I keep coming back to appetite, to the sensation that is always present within me—I find it a poor order of things when we don't have enough to eat. What a miserable economy—on the one hand, men gorged with everything; on the other, men with stomachs that are just as demanding and with hunger that is just as alive but who don't have a thing to sink their teeth into." The thought took a revolutionary turn under Diderot's fast moving pen. But the Revolution remained unthinkable under Louis XV, and the thought turned inward again. "The worst thing is the constrained posture forced upon us by our need. The needy man doesn't walk like others. He jumps, he grovels, he squirms, he crawls. He passes his life in striking poses."[80] This cringing and groveling wounded his dignity, the nephew (Lui) confessed.

> MOI: Your dignity makes me laugh.
>
> LUI: Every person has his own. I am quite willing to forget mine, but at my discretion and not at someone else's orders. Is it necessary that someone should be able to say to me: grovel, and that I should then have to grovel? It is the gait of a worm; it is my gait. We both adopt it when we are left alone. But we rise up when someone steps on our tails.[81]

An uprising of worms was an absurdity. But if worms could not overthrow, they could undermine. Rameau's nephew explained that they took their revenge in a "beggars' pantomime," which parodied everything decent and respectable in police society (*le monde*). By ridiculing his patrons, he salvaged some of his pride; and he got away with metaphorical murder, because he had perfected a role in which misbehavior was accepted as part of the game. He had made himself into the supreme clown of *le monde*. Like the court jester, the salon buffoon could inflict wounds and plead innocent by reason of zaniness. But he also wounded himself. His self-imposed eccentricity put him outside the limits of politeness, outside society, in a Hobbesian state of nature, where the appetite ruled supreme. Rameau's nephew and his cohorts inhabited a moral wilderness, so they behaved like animals when they gathered around their patron's table: "When someone takes us up, doesn't he know us for what we are—corrupt, vile, and perfidious? If he knows us, all is well. There is a tacit pact that he will do good to us and that sooner or later we will return evil for the good he has done. Doesn't such a pact exist between a man and his monkey or his parakeet? . . . What would you think of us if with our depraved morals we pretended to enjoy the public's esteem? That we were mad. Is it reasonable to expect upright behavior from people born vicious, from low and vile characters? Everything has its price in this world. There are two prosecuting attorneys: one at your doorstep, which punishes crimes against society; nature is the other. The latter is well acquainted with all the vices that escape from the law."[82] By perceiving his degeneration with such merciless clarity, and by accepting it, Rameau's nephew renounced his humanity. He sacrificed his soul for his stomach. And the sacrifice hurt, because he knew that he had destroyed the most essential part of his self. That self-inflicted wound may have been what pained Le Senne the most when he fought off vagabondage by posing as "Bauprais, instructor of young people," and by alternately peddling and denouncing the impieties of his dead protector, d'Alembert.

Le Neveu de Rameau belongs to an underworld current in French literature that stretches from Villon to Genet. But it also expresses something peculiar to the world of Le Senne. In propounding his antisocial ethics, Rameau's nephew articulated the unwritten code of Grub Street. In placing himself beyond the fringe of respectability, he defined the situation of the literary hacks. And in exposing the hypocrisy of *le monde,* he vented the hatred of the hacks for the system that had corrupted them. Extravagant as he was, Rameau's nephew represented an important aspect of literary life in the eighteenth century, when the distinction between literature and life had begun to blur. In order to create him, Diderot had to distill the essence out of many lives, including his own. But the raw material does not show through the text. By watching a real poor devil stagger through the pitfalls of an actual career, one can see why poor deviltry developed into such an important literary theme. It represented the human condition as a great many writers had experienced it. Conversely, one can read Diderot's text in order to imagine the inner life of a man like Le Senne. Of course it is impossible to know whether the abbé thought and felt as Rameau's nephew did. One can only assert that in a heightened, fictionalized form *Le Neveu de Rameau* expressed the poor-devil mentality. But to dismiss Diderot's fiction as irrelevant to the understanding of a real historical character would be to deprive history of a rich source of insight. With some suspension of disbelief, literature and history should be able to come to each other's aid. *Le Neveu de Rameau* suggests the psychological dimensions of Le Senne's life, and Le Senne's life reveals the social context of *Le Neveu de Rameau.* Taken together, they help one to understand the struggle to survive in Grub Street and the tensions that tore through the Republic of Letters on the eve of the French Revolution.

A Clandestine Bookseller
in the Provinces

 ALTHOUGH THE CLANDESTINE BOOK TRADE of the Old Regime has aroused the interest of a few scholars, no one has been able to discover very much about the actual books that circulated "under the cloak" or the shady characters who handled them. The literary underground has been studied only from the perspective of the state—inevitably so, because the documentation has come almost entirely from the bureaucracy charged with suppressing illegal books. But in the papers of the Société typographique de Neuchâtel, the clandestine bookdealers emerge as full-blown personalities, grappling with very human problems—disease, debt, loneliness, failure, and above all the frustrations of a difficult trade. By exploring the world of one of them, we can see how the underground operated and what material it conveyed to ordinary readers in an ordinary town.

THE STN was one of many publishing houses that grew up around the borders of France in order to supply Frenchmen with books that could not be produced legally or safely within the kingdom. Some of these publishers specialized in *livres philosophiques,* as they were known in the trade—obscene, irreligious, or seditious works. Others printed cheap, pirated editions of books that French publishers had marketed with a *privilège,* a kind of copyright. The STN did a little of each, and it often received manuscripts from obscure authors who wanted a book printed cheaply and safely and smuggled to them through underground channels. One such proposal arrived in a letter from Tonnerre dated April 14, 1781, and signed "De Mauvelain, écuyer." Mauvelain wanted to print "a little brochure about monks."[1] The STN had been recommended to him by a friend, Jacques-Pierre Brissot de Warville, the future leader of the Girondists, who was then struggling to establish himself as a man of letters and had hired the STN to print his first philosophic works. The STN accepted and Mauvelain wrote back that he was delighted to establish relations with them. He would expand his pamphlet with a "letter about houses of detention in France"[2] and that was only the beginning of his plans for publishing: he rattled off proposals and projects in a constant stream of letters and presented himself as an assiduous scholar-philosophe. So assiduous, in fact, that he had ruined his health pouring over old manuscripts and pondering eternal truths. His ailments were another theme of his correspondence: "To remain seated too long causes the humors to stagnate; the body's corridors clog, causing headaches, upsetting the stomach, and throwing the whole body out of order."[3]

But Mauvelain was no hermit. He wrote like a man of the world. In 1782 he announced that he had moved to Troyes, where he frequented the finest company. He had dropped his earlier projects and wrote to recommend a local lawyer named Millon, who wanted to print a philosophical treatise. "I am told that he is no great genius and has no manners or sense of how to behave in society, which is not surprising, since he is the son of an innkeeper . . . But he has money, and there is no danger in dealing with him financially."[4] So Mauvelain was a snob, too: his letters made his superior status perfectly clear. But such letters were common in the correspondence of eighteenth-century publishers who relied on them for protection against confidence men. The clandestine book trade suffered more from the debtors and swindlers within its own ranks than from the police, and so the term *confiance* recurs like a leitmotiv in the correspondence of bookdealers. They extended and withdrew confidence like credit, in carefully measured doses according to the reliability of their clients.

Mauvelain returned to the role of a recommender in his next letter, which he wrote in favor of a certain Bouvet, whom he described as one of the region's most important booksellers. He was renting part of Bouvet's house, he explained, and the bookseller, who was eager to increase his stock, had asked to be recommended to the STN. "I do so with pleasure," Mauvelain wrote, "because he is a decent chap who will pay you well, very well indeed. I promise to see to that."[5] Mauvelain made it clear that he was only a gentleman author doing a favor for a plebeian friend and that he would make sure that the Swiss had not misplaced their confidence. He would watch his landlord like a hawk and even would withold the rent if Bouvet failed to pay the STN on time. So ardently did he desire to be of service that he would handle all the STN's affairs with Bouvet: he would communicate Bouvet's orders (it turned out that Bouvet was barely able to write anyhow), would see to their payment, and even would receive the shipments of books, because crates addressed to a respectable gentleman would not arouse the suspicions of the police.

As a favor to some friends, Mauvelain occasionally would order some books himself. In fact, he wanted thirty-eight works right away. They concerned a variety of subjects—

belles-lettres, history, natural history; and they included a half-dozen prohibited books, like *Les Fastes de Louis XV* and *L'Espion dévalisé,* which Mauvelain slipped casually into his order, as if he were testing the STN's willingness and ability to provide them. Bouvet's order, which Mauvelain wrote out in an accompanying letter, contained a larger proportion of illegal literature: *Anecdotes sur Mme Du Barry, Vénus dans le cloître, La Fille de joie, Les trois imposteurs,* and many others. Bouvet needed the books in time for the fair that would open in Troyes on March 15; and if this first shipment could be slipped past the authorities successfully, Mauvelain announced, "We will be able to do a handsome business together later."[6]

Everything went beautifully: the crate left Neuchâtel on February 6 and arrived at Troyes on March 12, which was good time for a clandestine shipment of 210 miles, much of it through mountainous terrain. Encouraged by this first experience, Mauvelain began to pile order on order, gradually increasing the proportion of prohibited works, and neglecting each time to send a bill of exchange in payment. By April 9, when he sent in his fourth order, he could avoid the subject of payment no longer. The most convenient way of paying for him, he explained, was to let his debts accumulate until he could discharge them all by a single bill of exchange on Paris. "Please do not worry: everything will work out fine . . . and *please* procure the forbidden books for me."[7]

"De Mauvelain, écuyer" treated financial affairs with aristocratic casualness. Instead of supplying the promised bill of exchange, he sent the STN a boar's head, "still hot" from the hunt, on May 3 with elaborate instructions on how to prepare and eat it. It traveled by coach (Mauvelain explained that such things kept for three months in winter and for six weeks in summer), and it weathered the trip as well as the books had done. Having received it "in good health," the Neuchâtelois ate it "in good company."[8] So it served Mauvelain's purpose, which, he said, his tone becoming constantly more intimate, was to cement his friendship with the publishers.

It is a colorful correspondence, full of gossip and surprising anecdotes (Mauvelain reported a rumor that the Lake of Geneva was boiling as a result of an earthquake in Burgundy and that Louis Sébastien Mercier had died in the arms of the abbé Raynal). Mauvelain's letters gave a vivid picture of the eighteenth-century bon vivant. They present him as an enormous, fat man in his early forties, who took a Rabelaisian approach to the pleasures of the table and the bed. They contain a delightful stream of comments on boars' heads, tongues, pigs' feet, women, and priests. But they never went beyond the boundaries of good taste. Mauvelain indulged in Voltairian irreverence, but he put himself across as a gentleman and a scholar. It is not surprising, therefore, that he amused, charmed, and captivated the STN ... which was exactly what he intended to do.

Mauvelain's letter-writing was really a campaign to capture the STN's confidence. Interspersed among his witticisms were requests for books. Gradually and almost imperceptibly, Mauvelain kept piling up his orders, increasing their volume, and avoiding the subject of payment. Thus, after receiving a shipment in May 1784, he did not send a bill of exchange, as was customary and as he had promised, but offered to send another hot boar's head and some tongues, and he sounded increasingly intimate: "Let us be friends, sir, I pray you." He announced that he would travel to Neuchâtel "to embrace you. It is a violent desire, which torments me."[9] He would come bearing charcuterie—and money; for he attached the payment of his bills to the Neuchâtel trip, which he kept postponing in subsequent letters.

This confidence game worked. By the summer of 1784, Mauvelain had charmed the Swiss so successfully that they were willing to supply him regularly and on a large scale with prohibited books. At that point, Mauvelain dropped his pose as a man of letters and began to sound and act like a professional, under-the-cloak bookdealer. The transformation became apparent in three ways.

First, the manuscripts that he proposed ceased to be philosophical or historical treatises, which he would pay to have printed; instead they contained underground literature, which he put up for sale. Thus he offered a polemical work about French finances, which was designed to capitalize on the controversy aroused by Necker's ministry: "It will be spicy and will sell well."[10] Next he came up with "a small novel and an [anticlerical] farce written in the name of a capuchin friar."[11] Then an irreligious manuscript supplied by one of his Grub Street contacts: "The book is good, really an excellent work: it saps everything that the Bible, that the Book of Genesis, teaches about creation. It will sell well, I promise you."[12] And finally an anthology of erotic poetry prepared by another hack-writer friend: "It has some charming things; it will sell . . . yes, it will sell, believe me. That kind of book is a sure seller."[13]

Secondly, Mauvelain cut the other booksellers of Troyes out of the STN's business. In contradiction to his earlier letters, he now wrote that Bouvet was a marginal type, who was teetering on the brink of bankruptcy, had failed to pay his bills, and was expected to flee town at any moment. Mauvelain offered to act as the STN's bill collector and persuaded the Swiss to give him their power of attorney, so that he could negotiate a settlement or take Bouvet to court. At the same time, he became the STN's agent in its dealings with the other two booksellers of the town, André and Sainton, who also owed it small sums. He denigrated them as *coquins* and *fripons* in his letters: "The Bouvets, Andrés, and Saintons of the world are rogues with whom nothing can be done without forcing them into court."[14] The STN completely accepted his view of "the twisted and perverted breed of booksellers in Troyes"[15] and empowered him to collect all its bills.

Thirdly, Mauvelain began to hassle like a professional over the transportation of his books. This point brings up the subject of book smuggling, which warrants a digression, for Mauvelain's dealings with the STN give one a rare opportunity to see how smugglers actually operated.

In the eighteenth century, smugglers considered themselves businessmen—*assureurs*—and they referred to their trade as *assurance* or insurance. On August 16, 1783, one of these insurance entrepreneurs, a man from Pontarlier named Faivre, signed a contract with the STN. It committed him to get the STN's crates of books across the Swiss-French border for 15 livres per quintal (hundredweight), which was to be paid by the STN's customers upon receipt of the merchandise. Faivre bound himself to reimburse the customers for the wholesale price of the books, if the crates were seized by the French customs agents. He hired teams of "porters," commanded by "captains," to do the actual labor. After nightfall and a free drink in a tavern of Les Verrières on the Swiss side of the border, they picked up the books in a secret warehouse and loaded them on their backs in fifty-pound packs. Then they carried them in the dark over tortuous mountain trails to a secret entrepôt in Pontarlier, France, and received a few sous for their work. If captured, they could be condemned to the galleys, for life.

Faivre's system, which was exactly like the insurance operations mounted by other border agents, worked quite well until August 1784, when the French seized five crates of Mirabeau's pornographic tract *Le libertin de qualité,* which were being smuggled across the border for another Neuchâtel publisher by another insurer. This major "bust" produced consternation up and down the Pontarlier route, which was one of the most important circuits for supplying France with prohibited books. Although his porters were not implicated, Faivre reported that they now refused to take the slightest risk, and rightly so: "The customs officials are on the alert, day and night."[16] "And there are spies and scoundrels in Les Verrières who sell [my men to the police]."[17] He ordered Michaut, his warehousekeeper in Les Verrières to hide seven crates, which were destined for Mauvelain, on top of a nearby mountain, and then slowly he began to rebuild his route. That turned out to be only a matter of time. After the dust had settled, Faivre managed to bribe some customs officials (he also gave them free copies of a pornographic book), raised the wages of his porters, and found fresh trails for them to follow at night. So it is possible to trace Mauvelain's seven crates, step-by-step and week-by-week, as they moved from Neuchâtel to Troyes. In fact, the information is so rich that one can attempt some economic analysis of this insurance business (see the map).

It is evident, first of all, that far from being a romantic adventure, smuggling was a complicated business. It called for considerable shrewdness in coordinating a complex organization and avoiding foul-ups. And it required the insurer to be particularly acute in gauging his profit margin and his risks. Mauvelain's seven crates had a wholesale value of 1,019 livres 11 sous. They weighed 440 pounds (*poids de marc*). And their total handling and transport cost came to

The Underground Route from Neuchâtel to Troyes

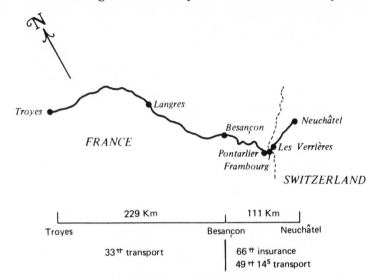

The Evolution of an Order

1. March–June 1784, Mauvelain sends in his orders in a series of four letters.
2. July 26 (approximately), the STN sends off the seven crates numbered BM 107-110, BT 120, and BM 121-122.
3. October 4, Faivre reports that all of the crates have been stalled at Michaut's storehouse in Les Verrières, owing to the critical new conditions at the border.
4. October 14, Faivre writes that he has reconstructed his smuggling system: the customs agents at Frambourg have been won over, and his porters will resume work soon.
5. November 12, the first five of Mauvelain's crates cross the border.
6. November 18, the other crates arrive safely in Pontarlier and will be forwarded by Faivre to Péchy in Besançon to-morrow.
7. Early December, Péchey's wagoner, Claude Carteret, loads the seven crates on his cart in Besançon and sets off for Troyes.
8. December 31, Mauvelain acknowledges reception of the crates, which arrived at some previous date, probably soon after December 13.

148 livres 14 sous or 14.7 percent of their wholesale value. Those costs included 66 livres for insurance—only 6½ percent of their value, which was inexpensive, considering the risks involved for Faivre.

But Mauvelain found the overall costs excessive and complained bitterly about being gouged by middlemen. He estimated that the transport and handling costs increased the price of each volume by about 6 sous: "Here is an example. You charge 25 sous for *Barjac* [*Le Vicomte de Barjac*, an erotic libel by Luchet]; 6 sous handling charges makes 31 sous; 3 sous for stitching makes 34 sous; at least 1 or 2 sous in expenses and postage makes 36. It already sells here for that price."[18] He added that he expected to make a 33 percent profit on each book, which would have made his *Barjac* cost 44 sous, 8 sous more than those being sold by other dealers in the area and almost twice as much as the book's wholesale price.

Mauvelain's figures were slightly exaggerated, because he was trying to get the STN to give him a reduction and because he was haggling over costs in order to avoid making payments—a classic ploy of marginal, underground book-dealers. Nonetheless, his experience with these seven crates shows that the system for distributing clandestine books could be as expensive as the system for producing them. A book could double in price between the time it left the manufacturer and reached the consumer. Why?

The insurance charges were not really excessive, as Mauvelain tacitly conceded by continuing to subscribe to Faivre's service. In this case, the culprit was not the smuggler but the other middlemen. A breakdown of the charges from the bill of lading shows that Mauvelain paid half again as much in transport costs for the Neuchâtel-Besançon leg of the journey as for the Besançon-Troyes leg—even though the latter was twice as long (but less mountainous, it is true). Mauvelain had been swindled by Péchey, the forwarding agent in Besançon, or by Carteret, the wagoner: that was the STN's explanation. There were ways to protect oneself from being overcharged in this manner, and the STN suggested some to Mauvelain. But the middlemen had still other techniques of duping their customers. Mauvelain's experience was typical of the clandestine retailers, and it illustrates one of the greatest weaknesses of the underground book trade, namely, that the system operated on the ineffective principle of honor among thieves.

The STN was to learn that lesson itself in the course of the rest of its dealings with Mauvelain. For while he was being fleeced by the wagon drivers and entrepôt keepers, he was robbing the STN. By the beginning of 1785 he had received shipment upon shipment of books for two years, and he had sent nothing in return except five dozen letters and a boar's head. Mauvelain's palaver had lulled the Swiss into a foolish commitment of confidence. When they came to their senses in the spring of 1785, they discovered that Mauvelain owed them 2,405 livres (the equivalent of three years' wages for a skilled laborer like one of the STN's printers). They wrote him a stiff note demanding payment and in return received a vehement declaration of outraged innocence. Mauvelain wrote indignantly that he could not pay just then because he was a sick man. He had undergone several costly and ghastly operations on his genital area and had been confined to bed for five months. To try to squeeze money out of him at this critical moment was the height of inhumanity. "One does not hold a pistol to a man's head ... I do not like incivility ... I'm beginning to believe that you are avaricious and selfish and treat everyone vilely ... I can see that you are not accustomed to dealing with well-bred persons. I am piqued at what you have done to me. I am piqued, I tell you. That is my last word."[19]

This bold attempt to seize the offense did not work, because the Swiss had also unraveled two subplots in their dealings with Mauvelain. First, they discovered that he had collected 194 livres of the old debt owed to them by Bouvet and had secretly kept the money. Then they learned that he had embezzled 168 livres for a small printing job that he had arranged for them to do for a local nobleman. So they sent Mauvelain a stiff note saying that they had instructed a lawyer from Troyes to collect everything he owed them or to take him to court. There was little Mauvelain could say by way of reply: he had reached the end of a confidence game that he had kept going with a good deal of wit and bravura for two years.

He therefore dropped his disguise and sent the STN an extraordinary letter telling the story of his life. He was Burgundian, he said, and belonged to a distinguished family from the nobility of the robe. His career in the law had been cut short by a fight he had had with a nobleman of the sword. He had been condemned by a court, had had to flee, and now lived on a meager pension given to him by his family. He was penniless, deadly sick, and tired of living. But his situation was not hopeless because he had a father-in-law and a bachelor brother who were even more ill than he; and if they died, he would inherit 300,000 livres. The STN would be wise to leave him alone until he could collect his inheritances. If it brought him to court, it would win its case; but he had no assets for it to seize and the scandal would cause his family to disinherit him. Moreover, "I have been a man of the law: I know all its ins and outs ... And I warn you, if you force me to the bar, I will tie the case up in court until the glorious resurrection of our bodies ... Finally, Messieurs, permit me to remind you of the proverb that says, 'One does not comb a devil who has no hair.' That happens, for the moment, to be my case."[20]

The lawyer in Troyes confirmed Mauvelain's indigence, his illness, and the futility of resorting to the courts, so there was little that the STN could do but let him wait for a windfall. With their concurrence, he sent them an undated IOU for 2,405 livres and left for Paris. After that, he disappeared. The STN sent several agents and friends in search of him but they came up with only one discovery, "the dishonorable nature of his disease and the depravation of his morals."[21] They kept him on their account books until 1792 under the heading "bad debtors" for the uncollected debit of 2,405 livres, but by that time he probably had died of venereal disease.

It is an extraordinary story, but it does not differ in essentials from other histories of downward mobility and marginality in the republic of letters. Mauvelain's life ran parallel, on an obscure level, to the lives of the hack writers whose books he peddled. Indeed, there was an affinity between authors and book distributors at the bottom of the literary underworld: they undermined the Old Regime together in their common struggle to survive. And there were more of them than has been realized, although they usually disappeared into the fathomless depths of history, leaving behind only a signature on a police report, an entry in the registers of the Bastille, or nothing at all. What makes Mauvelain's case so fascinating is the fact that it can be known in such detail. To open his dossier is to come into contact with a colorful cross section of vanished humanity, to enjoy the first close-up view of a world in which men's business was to stay invisible.

So much for one man's story of publishing and perishing

in the literary underground. More important is the story of Mauvelain's books.

EVERY TIME Mauvelain ordered a book, a clerk of the STN recorded the title and the number of copies in a register called a *Livre de Commissions*. By systematically tracing his orders through this register, it is possible to watch the unfolding of the demand for prohibited books in Troyes, week-by-week, for a period of two years. Two years, one town, 1,000 books—of course it would be absurd to claim that the pattern of Mauvelain's business represents France as a whole. But one must begin somewhere. And all previous attempts to discover the reading habits of eighteenth-century Frenchmen have floundered because they have been based on sources like publishers' requests for *privilèges* (copyrights), which exclude all unorthodox literature. Mauvelain specialized in forbidden books. So the study of his trade should reveal the missing element in a research tradition that goes back to the beginning of this century. Of course this is only a preliminary case study, a microscopic analysis of a small segment of the illegal book trade, and we must hope that we have chosen a fairly representative specimen. But the *Livres de Commissions* are extraordinary documents: they show the raw demand for prohibited literature—the taste for the taboo—in a small provincial city.

Unfortunately, they do not reveal who bought Mauvelain's books; and even if they did, we cannot know what went on in the minds of their readers. Mauvelain did not mention his clients in his letters, except for a few references to army officers who were garrisoned in Troyes and who had a strong preference for obscene and irreligious works.

Troyes was a great center for colportage; so Mauvelain probably sold some books to peddlers, who stocked up at the town's fairs and spread their wares throughout central France. But Mauvelain's letters indicate that he concentrated on the local market. His entire stock apparently did not amount to more than a few thousand volumes, which he kept in an attic and parceled out when clients stopped by or when he went on his rounds.

The prices of the books would have put them beyond the purchasing power of the working classes but not the bourgeoisie of Troyes. Mirabeau's *Errotika biblion,* one volume in octavo, is a typical example. It cost Mauvelain 1 livre 10 sous, in addition to which he paid 10 sous to cover transport, insurance, and other costs—and then added another third or 13 sous for his profit, making a selling price of 2 livres 13 (or, more probably, 2 livres 15) sous. That was the equivalent of half a week's supply of bread—which was the main source of nourishment—for a working class family with three children—or a day's wages of a skilled carpenter. But the expenditure of 2 or 3 livres for a book could have been managed easily by the lawyers and magistrates of the presidial and bailliage courts of Troyes, who made 2,000 or 3,000 livres a year.

Troyes's courts made it a provincial legal center. As the see of a bishopric and the site of a dozen monasteries, it was also an ecclesiastical center. But most important, it was a center for the trade and manufacture of textiles. Its population of 22,000 included 360 master weavers in the 1780s, and it also had a great many artisans, who manufactured pins, paper, and leather goods. The town's cultural life seems to have been less active than that of the rival champenois towns of Châlons and Reims. But Troyes had a theater, an important library, and a masonic lodge; and its educational institutions included four primary schools, a seminary, and an Oratorian college with 300–400 students. The rate of literacy seems to have been relatively low for northern France, because only 40–49% of the adults in the Troyes region could sign their names on marriage certificates. Local historians have searched in vain for evidence of intellectual ferment in the town during the eighteenth century. They have found only one *very* minor philosophe, P.-J. Grosley, "le Voltaire champenois." Yet the cahier of the Third Estate in Troyes was quite outspoken in 1789. All in all, the town probably epitomized what the Parisians mean by "provincial": it was a cultural backwater.

If that were the case, Mauvelain's book business seems particularly significant, for one would not expect much demand for radical literature in a small and sleepy corner of the provinces. The quantitative analysis of his orders shows that this demand did, in fact, exist.

The graphs show the main pattern of Mauvelain's orders according to subject matter. As the orders accumulated, week-by-week, in the STN's registers, it became clear that the demand for certain books remained strong. Mauvelain's customers kept coming back, asking for more of them; and Mauvelain passed their requests on to Neuchâtel according to the incidence of his sales, which he frequently concluded in advance. The bottom graph measures this incidence by depicting the number of orders placed for each title. The top graph shows the volume of Mauvelain's orders by indicating the number of copies requested for each title. The pattern is pretty much the same on each graph, but it is necessarily abstract. So that one can see the importance of each book within the general pattern, I have listed all the titles under the appropriate categories, giving the total number of copies ordered and the number of orders.

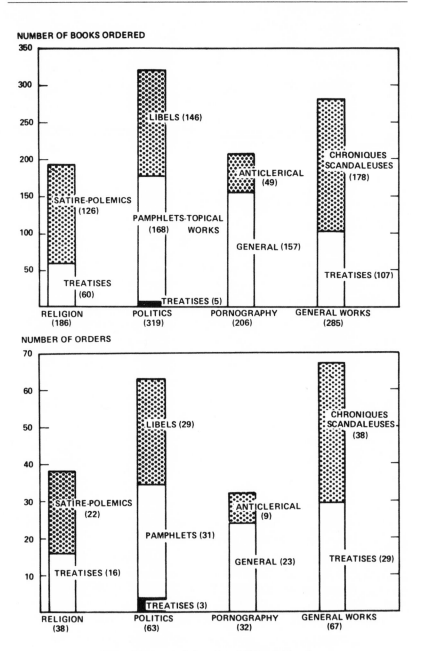

NUMBER OF BOOKS ORDERED

350

300

LIBELS (146)

250

CHRONIQUES
SCANDALEUSES
(178)

200

SATIRE-POLEMICS
(126)

ANTICLERICAL
(49)

150

PAMPHLETS-TOPICAL
(168)   WORKS

GENERAL (157)

100

50

TREATISES
(60)

TREATISES (107)

TREATISES (5)

RELIGION
(186)

POLITICS
(319)

PORNOGRAPHY
(206)

GENERAL WORKS
(285)

NUMBER OF ORDERS

70

60

LIBELS (29)

50

CHRONIQUES
SCANDALEUSES
(38)

40

SATIRE-POLEMICS
(22)

30

ANTICLERICAL
(9)

PAMPHLETS (31)

GENERAL (23)

TREATISES (29)

20

TREATISES (16)

10

TREATISES (3)

RELIGION
(38)

POLITICS
(63)

PORNOGRAPHY
(32)

GENERAL WORKS
(67)

The Demand for Prohibited Books

BEST-SELLERS BY GENRE

I. Religion

   A. Satire and polemics

L'Intolérance ecclésiastique	10/4	
La Papesse Jeanne	44/6	
Le Gazetier monastique	18/3	
La Mule du pape	18/3	
Histoire des voyages des papes	18/3	
Requête pour la suppression des moines	18/3	
Total		126/22

   B. Treatises

Le Christianisme dévoilé	3/3	
Histoire critique de Jésus Christ	19/6	
Le Ciel ouvert à tous les hommes	11/3	
Théologie portative	27/4	
Total		60/16
Total		186/38

II. Politics

   A. Libels

Les Fastes de Louis XV	84/11	
L'Espion dévalisé	37/10	
Vie privée de Louis XV	7/5	
Vie privée . . . de Mgr. le duc de Chartres	18/3	
Total		146/29

   B. Pamphlets and topical works

Mémoires sur la Bastille, Linguet	30/7	
Des Lettres de cachet, Mirabeau	21/5	
Lettres sur la liberté politique	18/3	
Dialogue des morts	31/4	
Remarques historiques sur la Bastille	18/3	
Anecdotes du Marquis de Pombal	18/3	
Mémoire sur les maisons de force	18/3	
L'Horoscope de la Pologne	14/3	
Total		168/31

C. Treatises

Système social	5/3
Total	319/63

III. Pornography

A. Anticlerical

Aventures de la marquise de xxx et St.	
François	13/3
Le Chien après les moines	18/3
Les Moines après les chiens	18/3
Total	49/9

B. General

Muses du foyer de l'Opéra	46/5
Errotika Biblion	18/3
Le Vicomte de Barjac	24/4
Le Portefeuille de Madame Gourdan	31/4
L'Art de rendre les femmes fidèles	24/4
Le Désoeuvré	14/3
Total	157/23
Total	206/32

VI. General Works

A. *Chroniques scandaleuses*

Suite de l'Espion anglois	16/5
Vie privée des françois	9/3
Mémoires secrets, Bachaumont	16/9
La Chronique scandaleuse	45/5
Correspondance politique, civile et	
littéraire	18/3
Essais historiques, critiques, littéraires	20/4
Le Journal des gens du monde	14/3
L'Observateur anglois	22/3
Anecdotes du dix-huitième siècle	18/3
Total	178/38

B. Treatises

Histoire philosophique, Raynal	18/9
L'An 2440	25/5

Tableau de Paris	27/5
Lettres Iroquoises	18/3
Oeuvres de Lamettrie	16/4
Oeuvres d'Helvétius	3/3
Total	107/29
Total	285/67

What is the place of the Enlightenment in this pattern? As the feeble subcategory of "treatises" shows, Mauvelain's clients did not want abstract or theoretical works. They did not order a single book by the four great philosophes, Montesquieu, Voltaire, Diderot, and Rousseau. Instead, they favored the popularizers and vulgarizers of the Enlightenment: Raynal, Mercier, Mirabeau fils. Some minor philosophes appeared in Mauvelain's orders: Borde, Cuppé, Maubert de Gouvest. But most of the books were anonymous tracts by obscure hacks: Imbert, Manuel, Luchet, Buffonidor, Mayeur de Saint-Paul, Baudouin de Guémadeuc, Mouffle d'Angerville, Pidansat de Mairobert, Théveneau de Morande. These were the men who apparently produced the clandestine bestsellers of the 1780s—yet they and their books have vanished from the history of literature. Some familiar names do appear among Mauvelain's authors: La Mettrie, Helvétius, and especially d'Holbach. The demand for illegal books in Troyes evidently had gone beyond Voltairean impiety to the rank atheism that horrified Voltaire himself. Of course, one cannot conclude that readers who wanted atheistic books were atheists. The point is that the trade in hard-core prohibited books favored the most extreme, Holbachean version of Enlightenment thought and that that kind of Enlightenment held a subordinate but significant place in the pattern of Mauvelain's orders.

Mauvelain wanted immoral books about as badly as he

wanted irreligious ones—that is, he wanted them in moderation, for the two categories together amounted to only two-fifths of his orders, and each of them looks rather small in comparison with the political and general works on the bar graphs. By modern standards, the pornography was restrained; and like the painting of the period, it was veiled and voyeuristic. Mauvelain's customers favored books that would give them glimpses of prostitutes at work. In a typical passage from *Le Portefeuille de Madame Gourdan,* the bishop of M * * * complains to Madame Gourdan, who runs a high-class brothel: "I ought to have you shut up in the Hôpital [a prison for prostitutes]. I received in your establishment a powerful *coup de pied de Vénus* [venereal disease], which has forced me to leave the capital in order to restore my health in my diocese. It's true what they say: there is no more uprightness in the world, and you don't know who to trust anymore."[22] Not very flattering to the upper clergy. The themes of Mauvelain's pornographic and anticlerical books often overlapped—the result, no doubt, of a literary tradition that went back to the Middle Ages. Perhaps this old-fashioned, gaulois anticlericalism reinforced the austere, modern atheism of the books in the subcategory "treatises" of Mauvelain's irreligious works. His books certainly gave the Church a beating.

The books in Mauvelain's orders that did not have a dominant motif and that contained something to offend almost everyone in authority in France belong to the category labeled "general works." About a third of them were treatises like Raynal's *Histoire philosophique,* which expressed Enlightenment thought on a wide variety of subjects. The rest can best be described as *chroniques scandaleuses*—journalistic accounts of love affairs, crimes, and sensational events. Most of these consisted of a series of short stories, written in a gossipy spirit, as if the author had uncovered some spectacular secret. They were not particularly political in character, but they specialized in anecdotes about the misbehavior of *les grands*—great courtiers, the analogues of the "beautiful people" featured in the popular press today—and so they made the aristocracy look bad. Thus a typical, two-sentence vignette from the publication that epitomizes the genre, Imbert's *La Chronique scandaleuse:* "One day the Duke of * * * surprised his chaste spouse in the arms of his son's tutor. The worthy lady said to him with ducal impudence, 'Why weren't you there, Monsieur? When I don't have my knight, I take the arm of my lackey.' "[23]

The *chroniques scandaleuses* seem to have been written according to the principle that names make news, but "news" as we know it did not exist in the Old Regime. At that time the French had no "news" papers, only journals that circulated by virtue of royal privileges, which were restricted by censors to nonpolitical subjects, and which therefore could not afford to mention anything that would give offense in Versailles. The French got their uncensored news or *nouvelles* from rumor. Specialists called *nouvellistes* gathered in certain parts of Paris—under the "tree of Cracow" in the gardens of the Palais Royal, for example—to communicate *nouvelles.* When they consigned their gossip to writing, they produced *nouvelles à la main.* And when these manuscript gazettes were printed, they became *chroniques scandaleuses*—a genre that stands halfway in the process by which archaic rumor-mongering developed into popular journalism. Because this news was utterly illegal, it showed no self-restraint in recounting the events of the day. Thus Bachaumont's *Mémoires secrets* and Mairobert's *L'Espion anglois* contain some very barbed remarks about affairs of state. But their tone differs completely from that of the political pamphlets. Essentially, they informed a news-starved public about what was going on in the world of *les grands.* Like most provincials, Mauvelain's clients were cut off from the nerve centers of gossip in Paris. That must be why they asked for more *chroniques scandaleuses* than for any of the other types of literature. The prevalence of these crude chronicles among Mauvelain's orders suggests the importance of a variety of underground journalism that has been forgotten today.

The most important general category of works ordered by Mauvelain, however, was political. Of course "political" is a tricky term when applied to a premodern society in which the public did not participate in the political process. The politics of the Old Regime were court politics; and so its political literature—which was also inherently illegal—tended to be of three kinds: political theory, topical pamphleteering, and libel.

Mauvelain's clients had virtually no interest in theory: they ordered only five copies of d'Holbach's *Système social.* But they wanted polemical tracts and pamphlets like Linguet's *Mémoires sur la Bastille* (30 copies) and Mirabeau's *Des Lettres de cachet et des prisons d'Etat* (21 copies). These two writers recounted their own imprisonment in a sensationalist manner as if it were a parable about French despotism. Promising to reveal the deepest, darkest secrets of state, they took their readers on a tour of the dungeons where the king kept his political prisoners. They "told all" about how prisoners were frisked, thrown into fetid cells, cut off from all contact with the outside world, and denied the right not only to be tried but even to know what they had been accused of. Their own innocence demonstrated the defenselessness of any Frenchman who might fall victim to the machinations of Versailles, Linguet and Mirabeau argued. And they drove the point home by dwelling on lurid details: the worm-eaten mattresses, the thick, clammy walls, the villainous turnkeys, and the repulsive food. All this inside information came with rhetorical outbursts against the unlimited power of "them," the unseen men at the top of the government who could reach into the life of any man, no matter how innocent, and bury him forever in an impenetrable *cachot*. These were powerful pamphlets and best-sellers in Mauvelain's area, according to his letters. They helped create a political mythology that made many Frenchmen feel they were slaves—even though the Bastille was almost empty by 1789.

The works that sold best of all in Mauvelain's repertory were the libels (*libelles*). These were violent attacks on individuals who commanded positions of prestige and power as ministers, courtiers, or members of the royal family. They resembled *chroniques scandaleuses* in their emphasis on scandal, but they also had political "bite." They probed the sensitive area where private decadence became a public issue, and by slandering eminent individuals, they desecrated the whole regime.

The genre is epitomized by the supreme best-seller among Mauvelain's books, *Les Fastes de Louis XV,* which Mauvelain ordered on eleven occasions for a total of 84 copies. Although the book presented itself as an objective history of Louis's reign, it treated the reader to a scabrous inside account of his sex life. The king's agents procured girls for his "harem" from the farthest corners of the kingdom, it explained, and he consumed two a week, pensioning them off after they ceased to arouse his jaded appetite. That came to 1,000 girls in ten years, the libeler calculated, and a cost of a billion livres; so Louis's depravity was "one of the main sources of the depredation of the state's finances."[24] The real villain of the book and the true despot of France was Madame Du Barry, who played the same role in other bestsellers like *Anecdotes secrètes sur Madame Du Barry, Correspondance de Madame Du Barry,* and *Vie privée de Louis XV,* which were liberally plagiarized in *Les Fastes.* The royal mistress always appeared in some extravagant pose: caressing her Negro servant boy Zamore, flagellating a lady-in-waiting, mocking the Dauphin (that is, the future Louis XVI) for his impotence, making a fool of the king while seducing his ministers behind his back, and all the while milking the treasury of millions—18 million, according to the libeler's best estimate. And he made his political point perfectly explicit: "Louis XV remained always the same, that is always up to his neck in filth and voluptuousness. Despite the desperation of his starving peoples and the public calamities, his mistress grew so wild in her prodigality and pillaging, that in a few more years she would have brought the kingdom down, had not the death of the despot put an end to her extravagance."[25] And how did Louis die? The libeler revealed the awful secret: having ceased to satisfy Louis's libido, Madame Du Barry turned procuress and swept the streets for girls who could excite him. One day she found a luscious peasant who was suffering from an undetected case of smallpox. The girl's father protested and was removed by *lettre de cachet.* Then the girl submitted to her royal master, gave him her disease, and sent him to his grave, causing a sigh of relief throughout the nation.

Perhaps the most important and unexpected conclusion to be drawn from this analysis of Mauvelain's orders is not that he called for a fair number of irreligious and obscene books but that the great bulk of his orders went for political material—not Enlightenment treatises but hard-hitting underground journalism and political pamphlets. The graph of political works towers above the others, and its dominance is strengthened by the fact that the pamphlets, libels, and *chroniques scandaleuses* all fulfilled the same function of communicating news. Far from being neutral, this news made the regime look rotten. It served as radical propaganda, even in the *chroniques,* where political matters took second place to crime and sex. Of course, "radical" does not mean revolutionary. The political tracts worked a dozen variations on a single theme: the monarchy had degenerated into despotism. They did not call for a revolution or foresee 1789 or even provide much discussion of the deeper social and political issues that were to make the destruction of the monarchy possible. Inadvertently, however, they prepared for that event by desanctifying the symbols and deflating the myths that had made the monarchy appear legitimate in the eyes of its subjects.

Having failed to rise to the level of at least minor classics, most of Mauvelain's books have dropped out of French literature, just as Mauvelain himself dropped out of French history. No one reads or remembers them today, because by a process of cultural evolution they have become extinct; they do not live in the repertory of reading that constitutes literary culture in the present. Unfortunately, one cannot follow the evolutionary path backward in order to discover the culture actually experienced in the past. Too much has fallen by the wayside, and it is too easy to assume that the French of the eighteenth century read what passes today for eighteenth-century French literature. But by studying the business of a clandestine bookdealer in the 1780s, one can catch a glimpse of that literature as it actually existed, at its most explosive, in its real context. Mauvelain's books and his life reveal a lost world of literary experience, waiting to be explored.

A Printing Shop
across the Border

THE FORBIDDEN BOOKS MAY HAVE SPREAD sedition when they traveled through the underground of eighteenth-century France, but since then they have settled into rare book rooms, where they sit in state, surrounded by vaulted ceilings and paneled walls. They have become antiques. The books looked very different when they first came off the press; but it is difficult to picture them in their original condition, because the printing shop is as poorly known as the distribution system of eighteenth-century publishing. To form some idea of the world in which the books came into being, we need to go back to the papers of the Société typographique de Neuchâtel, where we can watch the printers at work and listen to the bosses talking about them.

As the STN drew labor from printing centers scattered through France, Switzerland, and the Rhineland, its directors developed a network of recruiting agents, who dispatched journeymen and discussed the labor market in a stream of letters that reveal some basic assumptions about work and workers under the Old Regime. The most revealing exchange of letters occurred in 1777, when the STN doubled the size of its shop in order to print the quarto edition of the *Encyclopédie* and when an *Encyclopédie* boom strained resources throughout the printing industry. The workers took advantage of this temporary labor shortage by moving from job to job, whenever they could find better pay or working conditions: hence the theme of journeying, which recurs throughout the letters. The STN's greatest inducement in hiring workers was probably *le voyage,* a sum of money that corresponded roughly to the amount a man would have made during the time it took him to walk to his new job. Workers preferred to spend ten or twelve hours on the road, with stops at country inns, to heaving at the bar of a press or bending over type cases for an equal amount of time. Their journeys became a kind of paid vacation and journeying a way of life, at least during the journeyman's early years.

Sometimes one can follow the men by the dates on letters. They commonly took two days to cover the 70 kilometers to Neuchâtel from Lausanne, three days for the 120 kilometers from Basel, a week for the 300 kilometers from Lyons, and two weeks for the 500 kilometers from Paris. For example, on June 16, 1777, at the height of the *Encyclopédie* boom, a Parisian recruiter sent off six workers to Neuchâtel, promising that they would receive 24 livres in *voyage* upon their arrival. They reported to the STN exactly two weeks later, having averaged 36 kilometers a day. As they made about 10–15 livres a week, their travel money covered two weeks' wages—good compensation for a cross-country hike in the early summer. But the STN refused to pay the *voyage* until the men had worked for at least one month. The recruiter had neglected to inform them of this proviso; and in case they refused to accept it, he had kept their belongings (*hardes*) as a kind of security deposit, which he later shipped to the STN. The men had no choice but to set to work, composing and printing the *Encyclopédie.* Their names appeared regularly in the foreman's wage book for eight weeks, long enough for them to collect their *voyage* and their *hardes*—and then they disappeared. Some of them turned up a few weeks later in Genevan shops that were also printing the *Encyclopédie*. At least one went to the shop of Barthélemy de Félice, who was producing a rival, "Protestant" version of the *Encyclopédie* in Yverdon. Others probably worked on the octavo edition of the *Encyclopédie* in Bern and Lausanne, for a traveling salesman of the STN reported that he had found several "deserters" from Neuchâtel in the other Swiss printing houses. And at least one pressman, Gaillard, surfaced in Paris a year later, asking to be rehired by the STN. He repented for "all the faults he committed," according to a letter written for him by a Parisian leather merchant, and he was ready to set out for Switzerland once more—for the third time.[1]

What were Gaillard's "faults"? His letter does not say, but the STN's correspondence shows that men often "deserted" after getting in trouble. Sometimes they ran off after piling up debts or collecting *salé,* a small advance on the next week's wages. They rarely accumulated capital and were often tempted to leave one town in order to escape debts and to collect some *voyage* in another. As a result of these incidents, the employers' letters struck a note of basic mistrust whenever they referred to workers. Workers were unreliable. If they did not make off with their *voyage* or their *salé,* they would fail to show up because they were drunk; and at worst they would act as spies, either for the French police or for rival publishers. A kind of characterology transpires through the letters of recommendation from the recruiting agents, leaving one with the impression of an ideal type. He had three qualities: he showed up regularly for work, he did not get drunk, and he was reasonably skillful. Thus the perfect compositor, according to a recruiter in Geneva: "He is a good worker and able to do whatever job you should give him, not at all dissolute, and assiduous at his work."[2]

Similar comments suggest some unspoken premises about what moved workers. In a typical, offhand remark to a recruiter in Paris, the STN said, "You may now continue on occasion to send us those who are curious about life in this region, but don't advance any more money."[3] It went without saying that "curiosity" could impel a man to walk to a job in a foreign country, 500 kilometers away. Occasionally the letters allude to other motives, but these seem equally flighty to the modern reader. For example, the STN instructed an agent who was dispatching some workers from Lyons: "We promise to pay them, after their arrival, twelve livres for their *voyage,* provided they remain with us at least three months . . . and you may assure them that they will be satisfied with us and with this country, where good wine grows."[4] The assumption was that work was mixed up with wine—and that employment would be short.

The remarks about wine and *Wanderlust* should not be construed to mean that the cash nexus did not exist in the eighteenth century. On the contrary, the recruiters often mentioned the workers' concern for wages, the amount of work available, and specific provisions such as the formats favored in type-setting and payment by time (*conscience*) as well as by piece-rates. "It is precisely on the question of wages that they insist," one recruiter explained, "because they don't want to leave one place, where they are well off, unless they can be better off elsewhere."[5] The STN even slipped a secret agent into some Genevan shops that were also printing the *Encyclopédie* in order to woo away workers by promising higher wages. The workers responded with a *cabale* to force up the rates in Geneva; the Genevan masters got wind of the STN's maneuver; and eventually the masters made peace among themselves by conspiring to hold the workers' wages down at a common level.

In the course of the hiring and firing, the employers seemed to treat workers as things. They ordered them in batches, like paper and ink. As the STN explained to an agent in Lyons, "They should come assorted, that is, so many compositors, so many pressmen."[6] It sometimes rejected these "assortments," if the goods were shoddy, precisely as it did in its purchases of paper. Thus it explained to a fellow publisher that it had been badly served by a recruiter in Lyons: "He sent us a couple in such a bad state that we were obliged to ship them off."[7] And it reprimanded the recruiter for failing to inspect the men before dispatching them: "Two of those whom you have sent to us have arrived all right, but so sick that they could infect all the rest; so we haven't been able to hire them. No one in town wanted to give them lodging. They have therefore left again and took the route for Besançon, in order to turn themselves in at the *hôpital*."[8] As the *hôpital* usually meant death for the disease-ridden poor, the STN must have known that it was probably sending those men on the last leg of their last tour de France—and it was no easy road across the Jura Mountains from Neuchâtel to Besançon.

The STN did dispense some old-fashioned charity. The wage book of its foreman contains several entries like "Alms to a German worker, 7 batz [1 livre tournois]."[9] And occasionally the incoming letters showed some sympathy for the men. For example, a master printer in Bern recommended an old compositor as follows: "He is a good worker, who worked quite a while in Neuchâtel some time ago, but I must tell you that his sight and his hearing are beginning to go and that his old age means that he no longer has the speed in composing of a robust young man.

Still, as you will only be paying him piece-rates, I beg you to keep him as long as you can; for he is reduced by his indigence to a pitiful state."[10] The fact remains that the Bernois had fired him and that the Neuchâtelois refused to hire him. Indeed, the STN fired two-thirds of its workers as soon as it completed the *Encyclopédie*, despite the protests of one of the director's daughters, who wrote to him while he was on a business trip and she was tending the shop, "One can hardly turn out on the street, from one day to the next, people who have wives and children."[11] That objection had not occurred to the director, who brushed it off with a lecture about profitability. It would be wrong, therefore, to think of life on the tour de France as a period of happy, youthful *Wanderjahre* or to imagine that workers and employers felt much affection for each other.

But how did the workers themselves represent their condition? It has been impossible to say, up to now, because historians have failed to make direct contact with eighteenth-century artisans, despite the research of specialists like E. P. Thompson, Maurice Garden, and Rudolf Braun. But printers were an unusually literate group. Some of them exchanged letters; some of their letters were intercepted by the masters; and some of the intercepted letters have survived in the papers of the STN. One of those precious specimens of worker-to-worker communication is a note by an Avignonese compositor named Offray to a Savoyard named Ducret, who was working at the *casse* (composing crew) of the STN. Offray had recently quit the STN in order to join the shop of Barthélemy de Félice at Yverdon, where, he assured Ducret, conditions were much better. To be sure, employment with Félice had its disadvantages: the "professor," as the men called him, never loaned his employees a penny, and the German workers did not get on

well with the French. But life was cheaper and the shop
better run than in Neuchâtel. And above all, there was
plenty of work: "Work here is sufficient . . . You will not
need to worry about work."[12]

Work could be a source of worry because the masters
hired by the job. When they finished printing one book,
they often fired the hands who had worked on it and then
hired new ones when they were ready to begin another.
Thus Offray passed on reports about the availability of jobs
in other shops in the area. Heubach of Lausanne needed a
compositor and maybe even a foreman; there was room for
at least two pressmen in Yverdon and also for three compositors, because three of Offray's comrades were secretly plan-
ning to walk out on Félice next Sunday. "It's not that there
is any lack of work, but only because of the caprice of the
workers—and me first of all—to change jobs all the time."
Finally, Offray sent news about mutual friends in other
shops and sent his regards to his former mates in Neuchâtel:
"I wrote to M. Gorin, and when I hear from him, as I hope
I will, I'll let you know. Please say hello to M. Cloches, M.
Borrel, M. Poncillon, M. Patin, M. Ango and don't forget
my old mate Gaillé . . . My wife also sends her greeting to all
these Messieurs. I had forgotten M. Lancy, whom I greet
also, as well as Madame pot-au-lait."[13] The nicknames, the
allusion to other exchanges of letters, and the sense of a
shared network of friends all suggest that the workers had
developed their own information system and exchanged letters of recommendation about their bosses—or *bourgeois* as
they called them—just as the masters and recruiting agents
exchanged letters about them.

Most of the information in the workers' grapevine circulated by word of mouth, whenever printers crossed paths on
the road or exchanged drinks in taverns frequented by their

trade. The currents and the content are difficult to trace. But scattered references suggest that the workers discussed work with savvy and realism. They wanted to know where the pay was good, the work plentiful, the companions sympathetic, the wine cheap, and the foreman a soft touch.[14] The messages circulating through the information system of the employers showed a different set of concerns. Labor had to be supplied like paper and type, as cheaply and efficiently as possible. It had to be made tractable, by bonuses, fines, and firing. And when it was no longer needed in the production process, it could be discarded.

Workers and bourgeois did not live together in the familial coziness imagined by some historians of preindustrial Europe. They probably hated each other as much as they did in the nineteenth and twentieth centuries. But they shared common assumptions about the relationships between them—that is, about the fundamental character of employment: they expected it to be erratic and irregular, possibly stormy and probably short, but nothing that would remotely resemble such modern phenomena as the forty-hour, nine-to-five work week, with time-and-a-half for overtime, clocking in and clocking out, inputs and outputs, production schedules, contracts, unions, automation, inflation, "real" wages, retirement pensions, "leisure," boredom, alienation, and sociologists attempting to make sense of it all.

Such were the attitudes toward work among eighteenth-century printers and their masters, but what was work in and of itself? Its subjective reality may always elude the historian, but one can measure its productivity by analyzing the wage book kept by Barthélemy Spineux, the STN's shop foreman. Every Saturday evening, Spineux noted how much work each man had done during the preceding week and how much pay he had received for it. Spineux tallied the compositors' output according to the signatures on the bottom of the sheets they had composed and reckoned the output of pressmen by thousands of impressions. By counting the ens in the actual texts, one can use Spineux's record to calculate the number of motions made by each compositor each week as he transferred type from the case to the composing stick. One can also calculate the number of times each pressman pulled on the bar of his press. Unfortunately, these calculations involve some strenuous exercises in analytical bibliography, a rather recondite discipline, which seems so abstruse to the French that they usually append the adjective "Anglo-Saxon" to it. But the historiographical stakes make the effort worthwhile, for a bibliographical analysis of Spineux's wage book provides the first precise record of output and income among preindustrial workers.

Without wandering into bibliographical complexities and presenting a full set of charts and graphs, I would like to mention the main conclusions that I have drawn from my statistics.[15] First, it is clear that the personnel changed at a tremendous pace. Almost half the work force was new every six months, and the shop as a whole was rarely the same from one week to the next, because the men came and went pell-mell, according to the irregular availability of jobs and their own "caprice," as Offray put it. It would be misleading to extract averages from such an erratic pattern, but it seems that the men fell into two main groups: transients, who usually stayed with the STN for less than six months, and regulars, who remained for a year or more. The regulars tended to be older, married men, although they included some youths. And in the case of compositors, they were identified with particular jobs: for example, one veteran,

Bertho, handled most of the typesetting on the *Encyclopédie* for eighty-eight weeks and left the STN as soon as it had printed its last volume. Thus the statistics bear out the emphasis on jobs—*ouvrage* or *labeur* in the printer's jargon—which shows up so strongly in the letters of the workers.

Second, by tracing the composition and presswork done by every man on every sheet for a period of five months in 1778, it is possible to see how the foreman coped with the irregular supply of labor. Pressmen worked downstream of compositors in the flow of work. So if several compositors quit the STN, a proportionate number of pressmen had to be fired. Thus in the week of October 10, three compositors left the STN, reducing the size of the *casse* from thirteen to ten workers, and the foreman cut the work force at the *presse* from twenty to twelve, while total output declined by half. A new job and a fresh infusion of compositors would reverse the process, as in the period from September 5 to 19, when the *casse* grew from nine to twelve workers and the *presse* from thirteen to eighteen, while output doubled. The graph of manpower and productivity is extraordinarily jagged; it soars and plunges dramatically from week to week, suggesting that labor management was a balancing act, performed at a heavy cost, both economic and human.

Third, it is possible to trace the output and income of individual workers, and here, too, the pattern shows enormous variety, both from worker to worker and in the behavior of the same workers from week to week. Typographers belonged to what is often called, rather misleadingly, the "labor aristocracy"—that is, they were skilled craftsmen, who made twice as much money as common laborers. As long as their work held out, they could bring home about 100 Neuchâtel batz or 15 livres tournois a week—enough to support a family and a good deal more than the earnings of textile workers, masons, and carpenters in France. But they frequently earned far less than they were capable of earning, not because the work gave out but because they chose to do less of it.

In the week of October 3, for example, the output of one compositor, Tef, dropped by half (from 92 to 46 batz), while that of another, Maley, increased by a third (from 70 to 105 batz). Each man had plenty of copy to set but preferred to work at his own pace, in erratic spurts. The irregularities were even more pronounced among the press crews. Chambrault and his companion earned 258 batz and ran off 18,000 impressions in the week of June 13; and in the next two weeks their output plummeted to 12,000 and then 7,000 impressions, while their combined income dropped to 172 to 101 batz. During another three-week period, the productivity of Yonicle and his companion soared from 12,525 to 18,000 to 24,000 impressions and their earnings from 182 to 258 to 344 batz. At their peak they made almost twice as much as in their off-weeks and well over three times as much as the slower crews. Most crews worked well below their full capacity most of the time. Only rarely can the drops in their productivity be attributed to holidays or a decline in the supply of work. The men slowed down or stopped completely in order to enjoy *débauche*, an old tradition in the printing trade, as is suggested by the following entry in the records of the Plantinian Press of Antwerp, dated June 11, 1564: "The said Michel went to the brothel and remained there Sunday, Monday, Tuesday, and Wednesday; then on Thursday morning came back to sleep on a trunk in the room where he normally abode."[16]

Although the papers of the STN do not provide such generous details about how the men spent their free time, they show that there was time and money to be spent. The *conscience* workers or time hands were considered to be the most reliable in the shop, as their name indicates. But records of their attendance show that they frequently failed to put in a full, six-day week. Pataud, for example, worked *en conscience* for five weeks in the summer of 1778. In the first week he worked five days, in the second five, in the third six, in the fourth six, and in the fifth three. The examples could be multiplied indefinitely; but no matter how one works up the data in the wage book, one finds erratic patterns of labor—in its duration, rhythm, organization, productivity, and remuneration.

If one compares the statistical data with the attitudes expressed in the letters, the pattern begins to look significant. The two types of evidence complement one another, suggesting the basic character of work as it was experienced and understood by the workers themselves. But before jumping to conclusions, I would like to take account of a third variety of evidence, one which can be called "cultural" in the anthropological sense of the term: I mean information about the traditions, folkways, and lore of the printing craft. There is a great deal of it, scattered through sources like printers' manuals and memoirs, notably those of Benjamin Franklin and Nicolas Restif de la Bretonne. The richest source of all is the *Anecdotes typographiques* of Nicolas Contat, a Parisian compositor who described his rise from apprentice to foreman in a shop of the rue Saint-Séverin in the 1730s and 1740s. Contat's account of how workers were hired, managed, and paid conforms in dozens of details to the picture that emerges from the papers of the STN. But it also adds a new dimension to that picture, because it is full of information about the culture of the printing shop and especially about three key subjects: rituals, slang, and jokes.

Attributing his experience to a fictional lad named

Jerome, Contat describes a great many ceremonies, mainly feast days like those of St. Martin and St. John the Evangelist; but he puts special emphasis on the rituals that marked an apprentice's progress through the shop. For example, when Jerome joined the work force, he underwent a rite called *la prise de tablier,* or taking of the apron. He had to pay 6 livres (about three days' wages for a good journeyman) to the *chapelle* or shop organization. The journeymen also taxed themselves slightly (*la reconnaissance,* their payments were called), and the whole work force repaired to Le Panier Fleury, one of the bistros patronized by printers in the rue de la Huchette. There the journeymen gathered around Jerome and the foreman in the center of the room with their glasses filled. The subforeman approached carrying the printer's apron, followed by two *anciens,* one from each of the two "estates" of the shop—the *casse* and the *presse.* The foreman made a short speech and placed the apron over the boy, tying the strings behind him. Then the journeymen applauded, drank to his health, and he, too, received a glass and joined in the drinking.

To complete the ceremony, the workers tucked into a gargantuan spread, which was waiting for them at the end of the room. While cramming meat and bread into their mouths, they talked . . . and the *Anecdotes* gives us snatches of their conversation: "Isn't it true, says one of them, that printers know how to shovel it in? I am sure that if someone presented us with a roast mutton, as big as you like, we would leave nothing but the bones behind . . . They don't talk about theology nor philosophy and still less of politics. Each one speaks of his job: one will talk to you about the *casse,* another the *presse,* this one of the tympan, another of the inkball leathers. They all speak at the same time, whether they can be heard or not." At last, early in the morning, they separate—sotted but ceremonial to the end: "Bonsoir, M. notre prote; bonsoir Messieurs les compositeurs; bonsoir Messieurs les imprimeurs; bonsoir Jérôme." The text then explains that Jerome will be called by his first name until he is received as a journeyman.[17]

That moment comes four years later, after a good deal of hazing and two intermediary ceremonies called "Admission à l'ouvrage" and "Admission à la Banque." The form is the same—a celebration over food and drink after taxing the initiate—but this time the *Anecdotes* provides a précis of the speech directed at Jerome: "The newcomer is indoctrinated. He is told never to betray his colleagues and to maintain the wage rate. If a worker doesn't accept a price [for a job] and leaves the shop, no one in the house should do the job for a smaller price. Those are the laws among the workers. Faithfulness and probity are recommended to him. Any worker who betrays the others when something forbidden, called *marron* [chestnut], is being printed must be expelled ignominiously from the shop. The workers [blacklist] him by circular letters sent around all the shops of Paris and the provinces ... Aside from that, anything is permitted: excessive drinking is considered a good quality, gallantry and debauchery as follies of youth, indebtedness as a sign of wit, irreligion as sincerity; it's a free and republican territory in which everything is permitted; live as you like but be an *honnête homme,* no hypocrisy." In short, Jerome assimilates a clearly articulated ethos, which seems several light years away from the worldly asceticism of Max Weber and the work discipline of the modern factory. And at this point he receives a new name: he drops Jerome and becomes a "Monsieur"—that is he occupies a new *état* or social estate. He has gone through a rite of passage in the strict, anthropological sense of the term.[18]

Meanwhile, of course, he has learned a trade. Much of the *Anecdotes* concerns the way an apprentice picks up the skills of setting type and imposing formes. It even contains a glossary to help the reader through the technicalities. On close inspection, however, the language of the craft turns out to be less a matter of technology than of slang, and it suggests the atmosphere in which the work was done as well as the ways of doing it. The slang clusters around six subjects.

1. Ceremonies: In addition to the *bienvenue, banque,* and *reconnaissance* already mentioned, the workers celebrated *la conduite* (a feast to see off a comrade leaving on the tour de France) and *le chevet* (a payment that a journeyman made to the chapel when he married).

2. Horseplay: The workers often knocked off to enjoy a *copie* (a burlesque imitation of an incident in the life of the shop), *joberie* (joking, mockery), a *pio* (a tall tale), or *une bonne huée* (hell-raising).

3. Eating and drinking: Terms like *fripper* (to eat), *prendre la barbe* (to get drunk), *une manche* (half-drunkenness), and *faire la déroute* (to cut up in the cabaret) suggest a heavy flow of traffic between the printing shop and the pub.

4. Violence: Judging from specialized terms like *prendre la chèvre* (to lose your temper), *chèvre capitale* (a violent tantrum), and *se donner la gratte* (to brawl), the shop often erupted in fights.

5. Trouble: A worker might *promener sa chape* (knock off), *emporter son Saint Jean* (quit, walk off with his tools, which were named after the patron saint of printing), *faire des loups* (pile up debts), or *prendre à symbole* (buy on credit); but he always seemed to be getting in trouble. If he went to *la petite porte* (the ear of the boss), he was a toady or a traitor, and the trouble would come from his mates.

6. The character of work: The printers naturally used many expressions for foul-ups and errors: *pâté, coquille, moine, bourdon.* They acknowledged the main divisions of the shop by distinguishing between *singes* (monkeys or compositors) and *ours* (bears or pressmen, an apprentice at the press being an *oursin*) and by referring to *la casse* and *la presse* as separate estates. And they used *labeur* or *ouvrage* to convey the fundamental notion of being hired by the job, which contrasts with the modern concept of joining a firm.[19]

The workers also developed a special repertory of gestures and jokes. At their most elaborate, the jokes took the form of *copies,* or burlesque skits designed to bring the house down in gales of laughter and rough music (*bais* and *huées*). The supreme *copie* during Jerome's years in the shop was staged by his fellow apprentice Léveillé, who had an unusual talent for mimicry. Forced to get up early and work late before retiring to a miserable room in the attic, the boys thought they were being treated like animals—worse, in fact, than the favorite animal of the household, a pet cat called *la grise.* It seems that something of a fashion for cats had spread among the master printers of Paris. One master kept twenty-five of them. He had their portraits painted and fed them on roast fowl. Jerome and Léveillé ate nothing but slops, while *la grise* received the choicest morsels from the plate of the master's wife. Early one morning, Léveillé decided he had had enough of this injustice. He crawled out on the roof near the master's bedroom window and began to howl and meow so loudly that he woke up the *bourgeois* and the *bourgeoise.* After a week of this treatment, the master decided he was being bewitched by a pack of satanic alley cats. He commissioned the boys to get rid of the cats; and they gladly complied because "The masters love cats, so [the workers] as a consequence hate them."

Gleefully the two apprentices organized a cat massacre. Armed with tools from the shop, they clubbed every cat they could find, beginning with *la grise.* They collected the half-dead creatures in sacks and piled them up in the court-yard, where they staged a mock execution. They stationed guards, named a confessor, and pronounced the sentence, then stood back and roared with laughter as a burlesque hangman dispatched the cats on an improvised gallows. The master's wife arrived in the midst of the fun and thinking she had seen *la grise* dangling from the noose, let out a scream. The master came running. But there was little he could do, aside from scolding the men for slacking off work, because he had provided the occasion for the slaughter in the first place. The scene ended with the *bourgeois* retreating before a fresh chorus of laughter, and then it passed into the lore of the shop. For months afterwards, Léveillé reenacted the entire episode in a kind of vaudeville routine, a *copie* of a *copie,* which provided the shop with comic relief whenever work began to drag. After he finished his number, the work-ers would express their delight by running composing sticks over the type cases, banging hammers against chases, and bleating like goats. They had got the master's goat, had made him *prendre la chèvre.* Not only did the workers love noise and jokes, they hated the masters: "The workers are in league against the masters; it is enough to speak badly of them to be esteemed by the entire assembly of typogra-phers."[20]

Of course jokes are not innocent, and this seems to be a case of especially meaningful joking. Léveillé's *copie* shows how intensely the workers hated the *bourgeois* and their alien way of life—a matter not just of wealth and power but of incompatible sensitivities. Pleasure in the coddling of pets was as foreign to the artisans as delight in cruelty to animals was to the masters. The ritual element in the cruelty warrants attention, because rituals abounded in the popular culture of the Old Regime, especially during periods of festivity like Mardi Gras, when the lower classes turned the world upside down in ceremonies that often ended with burlesque public executions. By condemning the cats, the journeymen printers symbolically put their masters on trial and vented their grievances in a mixture of street theater, carnival, and riotous witch-hunting.

The conclusions to be drawn from this material tend to be impresssionistic, but I sense, first, a great emphasis on the specific and the concrete—the implements of work, conversation about the job at hand, a general concern with the here and now and the everyday world of familiar objects and immediate relations. The workers decked this world out with ceremonies and enlivened it with jokes, so work itself involved collective rituals, rites of passage, and fun. There was no clear dividing line between work and play, or labor and what now passes for "leisure," a phenomenon that did not exist in the eighteenth century, when men mixed work and play indiscriminately throughout a twelve-, fourteen-, or sixteen-hour day.

At the same time, the jokes and slang emphasized the instability and irregularity of this kind of work—the violence, drunkenness, impoverishment, walking off, and being laid off. Work was *labeur*. It was job-oriented and occurred by fits and starts rather than by regular employment in a single firm. The craft lore confirms the pattern of rapid turnover that one can see in the wage books and the emphasis on *voyages* that emerges from the masters' correspondence. As the men tramped from job to job, they identified not with a class or a community or a firm, but with the craft itself. They thought of themselves as journeymen printers, not simply as workers. They spoke their own language, worshipped their own saint (at least in Catholic countries), patronized their own bistros, and followed their own tour de France. Fellow-traveling even extended to Sunday outings, when they would wander about country taverns together, sometimes divided according to estate, the *casse* in one group and the *presse* in another, and brawling with rival groups of cobblers or masons. The printers defined themselves against other crafts—and also against their masters. If the highly developed lore and ethos of their craft prevented them from feeling solidarity with workers in general, it expressed a strong hostility to the *bourgeois*. The printing shop did not function as some kind of warm and happy extended family. It was an intense and explosive little world.

In order to reconstruct that world, I have attempted to measure work statistically, to uncover the attitudes toward it among the workers and their bosses, and to see how it became embodied in a craft culture. Those three elements fit together, revealing the meaning of work for a particular group of workers, the journeymen printers of eighteenth-century France and Switzerland. Other men in other crafts, and the great mass of unskilled laborers, probably understood their work differently; for the experience of working must have varied enormously. But if this very specific material yields any generalizations, it suggests that preindustrial work tended to be irregular and unstable, craft-specific and task-oriented, collective in its organization and individual in its pace—and that all these characteristics set it apart, as a general phenomenon, from work in the industrial era. Thus in observing the operations of a printing shop, we can see how a fundamental element of the human condition has shifted, cutting us off from the forgotten collaborators of eighteenth-century literature, the men who made the books come into being.

Reading, Writing,
and Publishing

THE HISTORY OF LITERATURE TENDS INEVI-
tably to anachronism. Because each age re-
constructs literary experience in its own
terms and each historian tampers with the
canon of the classics, literature refuses to
remain fixed within interpretive schemata. Like Walter
Benjamin's library,[1] it is a state of mind, which can always
be unpacked and rearranged. Yet there is something unsat-
isfactory about the notion of literary history as an endless
reshuffling of great books. If one could take stock of a great
mass of books over a long stretch of time, would it not be
possible to find some general patterns in the experience of
exposure to the printed word? That question belongs to the
sociology or the social history of literature. It was raised sev-
enty years ago by Daniel Mornet, who asked quite simply,
what did Frenchmen read in the eighteenth century?

MORNET THOUGHT he could find an answer by counting titles in five hundred catalogues of private libraries,
which had mostly been printed for auctions in the Paris area
between 1750 and 1780. He found one lonely copy of Rousseau's *Contrat social.* Eighteenth-century libraries contained a
surprisingly small percentage of the other Enlightenment
classics, he discovered. Instead their shelves bulged with the
works of history's forgotten men and women: Thémiseul de
Saint-Hyacinthe, Mme. de Graffigny, and Mme. Riccoboni.

Eighteenth-century booklovers divided French literature into "before" and "after" Clément Marot. When they read the philosophes, it was the Voltaire of *La Henriade* and the Rousseau of *La nouvelle Héloise*.[2]

Coinciding ironically with the "great books" approach to the study of civilization, Mornet's research seemed to knock out some of the pillars of the Enlightenment. He made a gap, at least, in the view that the *Social Contract* prepared the way for Robespierre, and his followers have been trying to widen the breach ever since.[3] Meanwhile, the Rousseauists have repaired some of the damage in a counterattack on Mornet's evidence. Why should private libraries important enough to have printed catalogues be taken as an indication of a book's appeal to ordinary and impecunious readers? they ask. They point out that the message of the *Social Contract* could have reached the general reading public through the version of it in book five of Rousseau's highly popular *Emile,* through numerous editions of his collected works, or through editions that came out during the momentous last decade of the Ancien Régime, which Mornet's study did not cover.[4] Moreover, Mornet failed to note that auction catalogues had to pass the censorship before being printed.[5] So his case remains unproved, either right or wrong.

Nonetheless, Mornet raised some fundamental problems that have only begun to be faced: What was the character of literary culture under the Old Regime? Who produced books in the eighteenth century, who read them, and what were they? It will be impossible to locate the Enlightenment in any cultural and social context until those questions are answered, and they cannot be answered by traditional methods of research.

The most influential attempt to formulate a new methodology has been Robert Escarpit's *Sociologie de la littérature*

(Paris, 1958).[6] As his title suggests, Escarpit, the director of the Centre de sociologie des faits littéraires at Bordeaux, wanted to define the objects and methods of a new branch of sociology. He treated books as agents in a psychological process, the communication of writer and reader, and also as commodities, circulating through a system of production, distribution, and consumption. Since the author plays a crucial role in both the psychological and the economic circuits of exchange, Escarpit concentrated on the study of writers. They constitute a distinct segment of the population subject to normal demographic laws, he argued, and on this assumption he produced a demographic history of authorship.

In order to survey the literary population, he began with the back pages of the *Petit Larousse,* moved on to bibliographies and biographical dictionaries, and emerged with a list of 937 writers born between 1490 and 1900. He then worked this material into a two-page graph, where the *fait littéraire* appeared in terms of the rise and fall of writers under the age of forty. Escarpit observed that the proportion of young writers rose after the deaths of Louis XIV, Louis XV, and Napoleon. The Edict of Nantes also coincided with an upsurge of youth, which was cut short first after the triumph of Richelieu and then following the collapse of the Fronde. To Escarpit the conclusion was clear: political events determine literary demography. He confirmed this interpretation by reference to England, where the Armada produced a *vieillissement* (aging) among writers that was only overcome by the death of James I.

It is a stirring spectacle, this adjustment of the literary population to battles, edicts, revolutions, and the birth of sovereigns. But it leaves the reader confused. Is one to believe that a kind of intellectual contraception took hold of the republic of letters? Did writers limit their population out of loyalty to Good Queen Bess (and Victoria, too), or was *vieillissement* their curse on the queens? Did young men start writing in England in order to make life more difficult for Charles I, or did they stop in France in order to show disaffection for Louis XIV? If one should discount any conscious motivation, why did young writers decrease in numbers after the accession of Louis XIV and increase after the accession of Louis XV and Louis XVI? And why should the birth and death of rulers have such demographic importance—or so much more than the revolutions of 1789 and 1848, which do not disturb the undulations of Escarpit's graph, although 1830 appears as a great turning point?

The answers to these questions might be found among the deficiencies of Escarpit's statistics. To take 937 writers over 410 years is to spread the sampling pretty thin—an average of 2.3 writers a year. Adding or subtracting a single man could shift the graph by 5 percent or more, yet Escarpit hung some weighty conclusions on such shifts—his distinction, for example, between a youthful romantic movement and the middle-aged character of literary life under the Empire. More important, Escarpit had no idea of how many writers went uncounted. He evidently believed that a few dozen men (Lamartine and twenty-three others in the case of the early romantics) could represent, demographically, an entire literary generation. A few individuals could, to be sure, represent a new stylistic trend or cultural movement but not phenomena that can be analyzed demographically, like generational conflict and the adjustment of population to resources.

Escarpit attributed the sociological differences between eighteenth- and nineteenth-century writing to two other factors: "provincialization" and professionalization. He detected a rhythmic *alternance Paris-province* by tracing the geographical origins of his preselected authors. But the geographical argument suffers from the same statistical fallacies as the demographical, and so Escarpit fails to prove that the Paris of Balzac dominated French literature any more than the Paris of Diderot. In the case of professionalization, Escarpit's conclusions seem sounder. He produced two statistical tables to show that there were more middle-class professionals, or writers who lived entirely from their pens, in the nineteenth than in the eighteenth century. But his argument is not helped by the fact that the percentages in the table of eighteenth-century writers add up to 166 percent.[7]

In this instance, Escarpit drew his statistics from *The French Book Trade in the Ancien Régime* by David Pottinger, another example of the quantitative study of authorship. Pottinger proceeded by combing biographical dictionaries for information about 600 "writers" who lived between 1500 and 1800. He then sorted his men into five social categories—the clergy, nobility of the sword, high bourgeoisie, middle bourgeoisie, and petty bourgeosie—and apparently concluded that the authors of the Old Regime belonged predominantly to the nobility of the sword and the high bourgeosie. Again, the conclusion is more convincing than the statistics, because Pottinger destroyed the representativeness of his sample by eliminating 48.5 percent of the writers on the grounds that he could not identify their social background. That stroke of statistical surgery left an average of one author a year to support a social analysis spread out over three centuries. Moreover, Pottinger apparently misfiled many individuals like Restif de la Bretonne, who went into the category of the First Estate because he had a brother who went into the church. Most of the sixteen others in that category either had relatives or protectors who were clergymen. But who in the Old Regime, excepting peasants, did not? Pottinger's other categories are not much more solid. He placed all writers who served in the army or navy with the nobility of the sword and placed teachers, apothecaries, architects, and anyone "whom we can identify with the law or with semilegal positions in the State"[8] in the high bourgeoisie. That kind of admissions policy would put at the top of society many lowly writers who lived like the Neveu de Rameau but called themselves lawyers and even registered with the Paris bar. In any case, it is almost impossible to delimit strata of high, middle, and low bourgeois, because social historians have struggled vainly for years to reach agreement on a meaningful definition of the "bourgeoisie"; and definitions of social stratification in the sixteenth century may not be applicable to the eighteenth.

What then can one conclude from quantitative history's attempts to analyze authorship? Nothing at all. Neither Escarpit nor Pottinger produced evidence to prove that the handful of men they chose to represent the entire literary population of a given period was in fact representative—and neither could possibly do so, because it would first be necessary to have a census of all the writers of the Old Regime. No such census can be contrived, for what, after all, is a writer? Someone who has written a book, someone who depends on writing for a living, someone who claims the title, or someone on whom posterity has bestowed it? Conceptual confusion and deficient data blighted this branch of sociocultural history before it bore its first fruit. But the sociology of literature need not stand or fall on the first attempts to put it in practice. And statistics on reading should be more fruitful than those on writers—if Mornet can be modernized.

MORNET SHOWED that a primary obstacle to understanding the literary culture of the Old Regime is our inability to answer the fundamental question: What did eighteenth-century Frenchmen read? The answer eludes us because we have no best-seller lists or statistics on book "consumption" for the early modern period. Quantitative historians therefore have taken soundings in a variety of sources, hoping to tap enough information to reconstruct the general outline of eighteenth-century reading habits. Their predilection for statistics does not imply any belief that they can reduce the reader's internal experience to numbers, or measure quality quantitatively, or produce a numerical standard of literary influence. (Newton's *Principia* would score low on any crude statistical survey.) The quantifiers merely hope to get an overall view of reading in general and by genre. An enormous amount of data has already been compiled in monographic articles and books by François Furet, Jean Ehrard, Jacques Roger, Daniel Roche, François Bluche (using the work of Régine Petit), and Jean Meyer.[9] Each drew on one of three kinds of sources: catalogues of private libraries, book reviews, and applications to the state for authorization to publish. So the reading problem has been heavily attacked on three sides. If it has been cornered, if those long hours in the archives and those laborious calculations have extracted a common pattern from the data, then one can hope to watch the general contours of eighteenth-century literary culture come slowly into focus. Before seeing whether all of the monographs can be synthesized, it is necessary to explain the character of each, because each has special strengths and weaknesses.

François Furet surveyed the Bibliothèque Nationale's registers of requests for permission to publish books. The requests fell into two categories: *permissions publiques* (both *privilèges* and *permissions de Sceau*) for books processed formally through the state's censoring and bureaucratic machinery, and *permissions tacites* for books that censors would not openly certify as inoffensive to morals, religion, or the state. Furet expected that a traditional cultural pattern would show up in the first category and an innovative pattern in the second, because, thanks to Malesherbes's liberal directorship of the book trade, the *permissions tacites* became a paralegal loophole through which many Enlightenment works reached the market during the last half of the century. But what works? How many of them? And in what proportion to the total number of books that can be identified with innovation? Furet could not say. He acknowledged that an unrecorded mass of books circulated with *permissions simples, permissions de police,* and mere *tolérances* according to the Old Regime's carefully graduated scale of quasilegality. Furthermore, the French stuffed unknown quantities of completely illegal *mauvais livres* or *livres philosophiques* into their breeches, the false bottoms of their trunks, and even the coach of the Parisian lieutenant general of police. So the official list of *permissions tacites* may not take one very far in identifying innovation.

The identification problems thicken when it comes to classifying the titles entered in the registers. Furet adopted the classification scheme of eighteenth-century catalogues: five standard headings—theology, jurisprudence, history, *sciences et arts,* and belles-lettres—and a profusion of subcategories that would produce bedlam in any modern library. To rococo readers, travel books belonged under history, and *économie politique* rightly came after chemistry and medicine and before agriculture and agronomy, all happy neighbors in *sciences et arts*. But the modern reader is bewildered upon learning that early works on politics (of the *permissions publiques* variety) were "almost all technical commercial textbooks."[10] How can statistics on *économie politique* satisfy his desire to know whether French reading became increasingly political as the eighteenth century progressed? Framing twentieth-century questions within the confines of eighteenth-century categories can be misleading, especially for the researcher trying to fit the Enlightenment into the overall picture of reading in the Old Regime.

Finally, Furet faced the problem of incomplete data. The requests to print books do not indicate how many copies were printed or the number of volumes, dates, places, and social groups involved in sales. Except in the case of privilege renewals, they give best-sellers the same numerical value as failures—the value of one. They do not even indicate whether a request resulted in an actual publication. And of course they tell nothing about the connection between buying and reading books.

To compensate for these deficiencies, Furet made a broad statistical sweep of the 30,000 titles registered between 1723 and 1789. His analysis of six samplings from the data was thorough enough for him to map out some general trends without professing a detailed knowledge of the eighteenth century's literary topography. He reduced his findings to bar graphs divided into the eighteenth-century categories. The graphs reveal a decline in theological and an increase in scientific writing, which is enough to carry Furet's main conclusion about the *désacralisation* of the world. They also reinforce Mornet's belief that the traditional, classical culture inherited from the seventeenth century outweighed the enlightened elements of the eighteenth. But those elements are scattered too haphazardly throughout the graphs to provide any quantitative profile of the Enlightenment.

By quantifying book reviews, Jean Ehrard and Jacques Roger tried to measure eighteenth-century reading by a standard that could not be applied to Furet's data. They attempted to show which kinds of writing had most vogue, as indicated by the number of books reviewed and the length of the reviews in two serious, "quality" periodicals, the *Journal des savants* and the *Mémoires i'e Trévoux*. They gathered their statistics from approximately the same periods and fit them into the same categories as Furet did, and they came up with complementary conclusions about the rise of interest in science (they locate it earlier in the eighteenth century), the decline of theology, and the "persistence of traditional forms of literature."[11] Unfortunately, they made no similar effort to measure their results against Mornet's. Mornet himself had made a careful study of reviews in the *Mercure* and concluded that they bore no relation whatsoever to the real popularity of novels.[12] His findings might be corroborated by more consultation of literary evidence, because eighteenth-century journalism frequently reflected the interests of journalists rather than those of their readers. The journalists of the Old Regime scratched and clawed their way through a world of *cabales, combines,* and *pistons* (to use terms that necessity was obliged to invent in the rough-and-tumble French Republic of Letters), and their copy bore the marks of their struggle for survival. Thus the *Journal des savants* featured medical articles very heavily in the early eighteenth century, not because of any great interest among its readers—who actually ceased buying "this sad repertory of diseases"—but because the government in effect had taken it over and then surrendered it to a *cabale* of doctors, who used it to propagate their own views on medicine.[13]

Ehrard and Roger tried to cushion their statistics against the shock of such incidents by analyzing a large number of reviews—reviews of 1,800 books in the case of the *Journal des savants.* But it is difficult to winnow conclusions from such data and to coordinate them with other studies. What, for example, can be made of the fact that the *Journal des savants,* a predominantly scientific periodical, reduced its scientific reviewing by almost a third in the late eighteenth century? Its reviews showed a decline in the whole category *sciences et arts,* while the category "belles-lettres" rose spectacularly. It would be rash to conclude that the public lost interest in science, because the *permissions tacites* showed precisely the opposite trend, according to François Furet. Moreover, a study of three other journals by Jean-Louis and Maria Flandrin produced results that contradict both those of Furet and those of Ehrard and Roger.[14] Periodicals do not seem to be a good source for quarrying statistics about the tastes of the reading public.

The catalogues of private libraries, as Mornet originally indicated, might serve quantitative history better. But they present difficulties of their own. Few persons read all the books they own, and many, especially in the eighteenth century, read books they never purchased. Libraries were usually built up over several generations: far from representing reading tastes at any given time, they were automatically archaic. And eighteenth-century libraries were censored for all illegal books being put up for auction. The censoring may have been imperfect (Mornet found forty-one copies of Voltaire's forbidden *Lettres philosophiques*), but it may also have been influential enough to exclude much of the Enlightenment from the auction catalogues.

Despite these difficulties, Mornet's work remains the most important of its kind, because it covered so many (500) libraries, and because Mornet was able to trace the social position of so many of the owners. He found that they came from a variety of stations above the middle middle-class (a great many doctors, lawyers, and especially state officials, as well as clergymen and nobles of the robe and sword) and that reading tastes did not correlate closely with social status. Louis Trenard got similar results from a non-quantitative investigation of libraries in Lyons.[15] But the most successful applications of Mornet's methods have occurred in studies of a single social group. Daniel Roche's research on the library of Dortous de Mairan actually was limited to the reading of a single man. But Roche made a convincing case for Mairan's typicality as a second-rank savant of the mid-eighteenth century; so his results suggest the general character of reading habits in the influential milieu of lesser academicians. Drawing on the research of Régine Petit, François Bluche studied the libraries of thirty members of the Parlement of Paris, which were catalogued between 1734 and 1795. He worked his findings into a convincing picture of parlementary culture, but not as it evolved over time. His comparison of catalogues taken from 1734–1765 and from 1766–1780 does not reveal a declining interest in law and an increased interest in belles-lettres and *sciences et arts,* as he maintained, because the statistical differences are trivial—not more than 1 percent. Nonetheless, Bluche's conclusions correspond quite closely with those of Jean Meyer, who studied the libraries of twenty members of the Parlement of Brittany. Meyer based his statistics on posthumous inventories of property (*inventaires après décès*), which usually are more reliable than auction catalogues as sources. He found a preponderance of "traditional" literature in contrast to a small proportion of enlightened works, and he also noted a decline in the incidence of legal and religious works and an increase in contemporary literature as the century progressed. Quantitative history thus seems to have been instrumental in defining the culture of the high nobility of the robe.

But has it succeeded in measuring the reading habits of France as a whole? There is hope for success in the complementary character of the monographs. Where one is weak, another is strong. Furet surveyed the whole terrain but gave equal weight to every title and did not get near the eighteenth-century reader. Ehrard and Roger got nearer, but their measure of reading incidence seems faulty; Mornet, Roche, and Bluche entered right into eighteenth-century libraries, but only the sections of those libraries that reached public auction. If each monograph covered the exposed portions of another, the entire topic may be considered safely under wraps. Are the results mutually reinforcing or mutually contradictory? The issue seems important enough to be put graphically.[16]

No consistent pattern, unfortunately, can be extracted from this confusing mosaic of graphs. Some of the inconsistencies can be explained away: law naturally shows strongly on the graphs of the *parlementaires,* science on Dortous de Mairan's graph, and theology among the *permissions publiques* as opposed to the *permissions tacites.* But standard categories like belles-lettres, history, and science vary enormously; and the proportions are wildly different. By imagining each bar graph as a sunbather and each black stripe as part of her two-piece bathing suit, one can see what a misshapen, motley crowd of monographs we must live with.

Patterns of Reading in Mid-Eighteenth-Century France

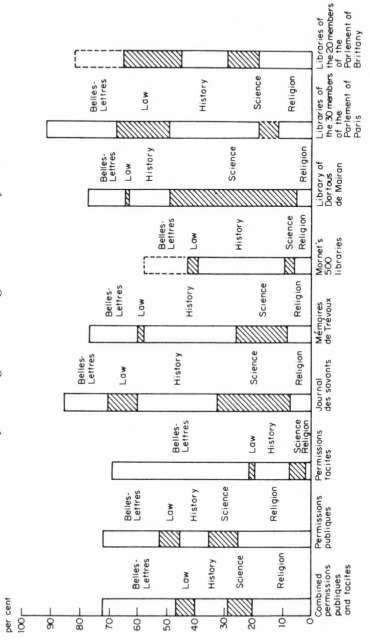

For explanation, see note 16.

There is some relief from this bikini effect in considering how the monographs spread their proportions over time. They all agree that the French read a great deal of history— so much as to make untenable the already discredited myth about an ahistorical eighteenth century—and read a consistent amount of it throughout the century. The monographs also indicate that the French read less religious literature as time went on. Scientific reading probably increased, although it may have remained constant. And, in general, some *désacralisation,* as Furet put it, took hold of the reading public. This tendency, however, might represent an acceleration of a secularizing trend that had begun in the Middle Ages; acknowledging it does not help to refine any generalizations about the Age of the Enlightenment, and no other generalizations can be extracted from the quantitative studies.

Perhaps it is impossible to generalize about the overall literary culture of eighteenth-century France because there might not have been any such thing. In a country where something like 9,600,000 people had enough instruction by the 1780s to sign their names,[17] there could have been several reading publics and several cultures. In that case, quantitative historians would do better to avoid macroanalysis of reading and to concentrate instead on studies of specific groups like the *parlementaires* of Bluche and Meyer. When used carefully, in conjunction with other kinds of evidence and in reference to clearly defined segments of the population, this kind of quantitative history has proved to be a valuable tool. But it has not provided answers to the broad questions raised by Mornet, and there is no reason to expect that those answers will emerge from the continued multiplication of monographs.[18]

But even Mornet's interpretation calls for further proof,

because none of the sources examined by him or his successors were likely to contain the most modern works, and none of the categories used for the examining could be considered commensurate with the Enlightenment. The problem of measuring "inertia" against "innovation" (to use the vocabulary of the *Annales* school) in studies of reading habits under the Old Regime always comes down to a problem of data: to sift statistics through administrative sources, censored journals, or censored library catalogues is to eliminate much of the Enlightenment. No wonder the quantitative historians found the weight of the past so heavy, when so much of the present was excluded from their balance. It may be cruel to conclude that all this laborious quantification has not advanced us far beyond Mornet, but the fact remains that we still do not know much about what eighteenth-century Frenchmen read.

IF THE HISTORICAL sociology of literature has failed to develop a coherent discipline of its own, and if its commitment to quantification has not yet produced answers to the basic questions about reading and writing in the past, nonetheless the sociologists and quantifiers have demonstrated the importance of interpreting the Old Regime's literary culture in more than merely literary terms. Books have a social life and an economic value. All the aspects of their existence—literary, social, economic, and even political— came together with the greatest force in the publishing industry of the eighteenth century. So the history and sociology of literature might gain a great deal from the study of publishing. To suggest some of the possible gains, I will draw on material in the papers of publishers and other related sources in order to develop three hypotheses: what

Frenchmen read was determined in part by the way in which their books were produced and distributed; there were basically two kinds of book production and distribution in the eighteenth century, legal and clandestine; and the differences between the two were crucial to the culture and politics of the Old Regime.[19]

The differences emerge clearly by a comparison of documents in official archives and those in the papers of clandestine publishers. The bookdealers of Lyons, for example, filled the *Direction de la librairie* with letters and memoranda about their devotion to the law,[20] while addressing the foreign publishers who supplied them with illegal books in terms like the following (A. J. Revol, a Lyonnais dealer, is arguing that he did not overcharge the Société typographique de Neuchâtel for his smuggling services):

> We have risked liberty, life, health, money and reputation.
>
> Liberty, in that without the intervention of friends, we would have been locked up by *lettre de cachet*.
>
> Life, in that we have had several encounters with customs agents and have forced them, weapons in hand, to return confiscated crates (at one point they had twelve from your firm, which otherwise would have been lost without hope of recovery).
>
> Health: how many nights have we spent, exposed to the most intemperate weather, on snow, fording flooded rivers, sometimes even on ice!
>
> Money: what sums have we not spent, on various occasions, both for smoothing the way for shipments and for avoiding prosecution and calming spirits?
>
> Reputation, in that we have come to be known as smugglers.[21]

Hundreds of men like these operated the underground system for supplying French readers with prohibited and pirated works, the kind that could never qualify for *permissions tacites*. They were colorful characters, these literary buccaneers: the obscure teams of smugglers who hauled crates of books over tortuous trails in the Jura Mountains for 12 livres the quintal and a stiff drink; the merchants on both sides of the border who paid off the drivers and cleared paths into France for them by bribing agents of the General Tax Farm;[22] the wagoners who took the crates to stockpiles in provincial clearing houses like the Auberge du Cheval Rouge outside Lyons; the provincial bookdealers who cleared the crates through their local guilds (at 5 livres a quintal in Revol's case) and relayed them to entrepôts outside Paris; the entrepôt keepers like Mme. La Noue of Versailles—to all the world a garrulous, warmhearted widow, to her customers a shrewd businesswoman, who "bargains like an Arab,"[23] full of professional pride ("I flatter myself that there is some appreciation for the care I take in handling that sort of merchandise,"[24] she wrote to a client in her semiliterate hand); the peddlers like Cugnet and wife, "bandits without morals or shame,"[25] as they were known in the trade, who smuggled the books from Versailles to Paris; and deviate Parisian distributors like Desauges père et fils, who were well acquainted with the Bastille,[26] and Poinçot "in good with the police"[27] but "the prickliest character I know,"[28] according to J. F. Bornand, one of the many literary secret agents in Paris who did odd jobs for the foreign publishers and completed the circuit by supplying them with manuscripts and best-sellers to pirate.[29] An enormous number of illegal books passed through these slippery hands, greasing palms as they went. Their importance in relation to legal and quasilegal literature cannot be calculated until the clandestine import records are compiled. But one nonquantitative conclusion seems significant at the outset: underground publishing and legal publishing operated in separate circuits, and the underground operation was a complicated affair, involving a large labor force drawn from particular milieux. Far from having been lost in the unrecorded depths of history, the individuals who processed clandestine books can be found and situated socially. They had names and faces, which show up vividly in the papers of eighteenth-century publishers. And their experience suggests that underground publishing was a world of its own.

How different was the world of legal publishing. The thirty-six master printers and one hundred or so master booksellers of Paris lived in pomp and circumstance, parading behind their beadle, dressed splendidly in velvet trimmed with gold lilies, on ceremonial occasions; celebrating solemn masses before the silver statue of their patron, Saint John the Evangelist, in the Church of the Mathurins; feasting at the sumptuous banquets held by their confraternity; initiating new members into their guild, a matter of ritualistic oaths and examinations; participating in the Tuesday and Friday inspections of legally imported books delivered to the guildhall by "forts" from the customs and city gates; and minding their own businesses. As businessmen, they kept closed shops. Elaborate regulations—at least 3,000 edicts and ordinances of all kinds in the eighteenth century alone[30]—specified the qualifications and limited the number of everyone connected with legal publishing, down to the 120 ragged colporteurs who divided up the official monopoly of hawking almanacs and proclamations in the streets and wore leather badges to prove membership in their corps. Corporateness, monopoly, and family connections tied down every corner of the trade. In fact the cornering of the market dated from a seventeenth-century crisis. In 1666 Colbert had settled a trade war between the Parisian and provincial publishers by, in effect, ruining provincial printing and placing the industry under the control of the Communauté des libraires et imprimeurs de Paris. By ruling this guild, a few families of master printer-booksellers dominated legal French publishing throughout the eighteenth century.

The guild spirit shows clearly through the major edicts on publishing issued in 1686, 1723, 1744, and 1777. The edict of 1723, which laid down the law throughout most of the eighteenth century, communicates an attitude that might be called "mercantilistic" or "Colbertist," for it codified the reorganization of the trade produced in the 1660s by Colbert himself. Condemning capitalist "hunger for profit,"[31] it stressed the importance of maintaining quality standards, which it defined in great detail. The typeface of three "l"'s must be exactly the same in width as one "m," and the "m" must conform precisely to a model "m" deposited with the syndics and deputies of the guild, who were to inspect the thirty-six printing shops once every three months in order to make sure that each contained the requisite minimum of four presses and nine fonts of type, both roman and italic, in good condition. Strict requirements regulated the advancement of apprentices to masterships, which were limited in number and tended to become family possessions—for at every point the edict favored the widows, sons, and sons-in-law of the established masters. These privileged few enjoyed an airtight monopoly of book production and marketing. Non-guild members could not even sell old paper without facing a 500 livres fine and "exemplary punishment."[32] The guild was elaborately organized and favored with "rights, liberties, immunities, prerogatives, and privileges."[33] Not only did it monopolize its trade, but as a corps within the university it benefited from special tax exemptions. Books themselves were tax-exempt. Each contained a formal *privilège* or "permission," granted by the king's "grace" and registered in the chancellery and in the guild's Chambre syndicale. By purchasing a privilege, a guild member acquired an exclusive right to sell a book, thereby transforming a "grace" into a kind of commodity, which he could divide into portions and sell to other members. So monopoly and privilege existed at three levels in the publishing industry: within the book itself, within the guild, and as an aspect of the guild's own special status within the Old Regime.

This third level deserves emphasis, because the guild's special position involved a policing as well as an economic function. The state had not often shown an enlightened attitude in its attempts to police the printed word before 1750, when Malesherbes became *Directeur de la librairie.* In 1535 it responded to the discovery that books could be seditious by deciding to hang anyone who printed them. In 1521 it had tried to tame the new industry by subjecting it to the surveillance of a medieval body, the university. And in 1618 it tried again, this time by confining publishers within the guild, another rather archaic kind of organization. In addition, the state attempted to bring books under control by developing its own apparatus—at first within the chancellery and the Parisian *lieutenance-générale de police,* later under the *Direction de la librairie*—and by holding its own against rival book-inspectors in the Parlement of Paris, the General Assembly of the Clergy, and other influential institutions. This bureaucratic entanglement did not choke the power of the guild; on the contrary, the guild continued to hunt out *mauvais livres* until the Revolution. The edicts of 1723 and 1777 reaffirmed its authority to search for illegal printing and to inspect books shipped to Paris. This policy made perfect sense: the state created a monopoly with a vested interest in law enforcement, and the monopolists maintained their interest by crushing extralegal competition. Although some guild members dabbled in underground publishing, most of them wanted to stamp it out. It robbed and undersold them, while the guild existed to protect their privileges. Well-protected privileges meant secure profits, which looked more attractive than the risky business of illegal publishing, especially since illegality exposed them to a double danger: punishment for the particular infraction and then expulsion from the magic circle of monopolists. A printer-bookseller's mastership really belonged to his family. He could not risk it lightly. Better to buy the privilege on a prayer book and to collect a certain but limited profit than to wager everything on a clandestine edition of Voltaire. Such an attitude suited a "traditional" economy, where even merchant adventurers dropped out of trade as soon as they had made enough to invest in *rentes*—or borrowed at 5 percent to buy land that yielded 1–2 percent of its purchase price in annual profits.[34]

It would be a mistake, therefore, to underestimate the economic element in the Old Regime's legislation on publishing. P. J. Blondel, an old-fashioned abbé who had no love for philosophes, fulminated against the edict of 1723, even though it tightened the restrictions on philosophic works, because he saw it as a purely economic measure: an extension of the guild's monopoly.[35] Actually, the political and economic aspects of the edict complemented each other. Strengthening the guild seemed to serve the interests of the state as well as those of the privileged publishers. But the reform movement modified the state's view of its interests, and the publishing code of 1777, promulgated soon after Turgot's attacks on the six great commercial guilds of Paris, shows a shift away from the old "Colbertism." Instead of condemning "hunger for profit," the king now repudiated any intention of favoring "monopoly," praised the effects of "competition," and relaxed the rules governing privileges in order to "increase commercial activity."[36] He did not undercut the notion of privileges; in fact he confirmed its character as a "grace founded in justice"[37] rather than as a kind of property, but he modified it in favor of authors and at the expense of the bookdealers. The guild had tried to prevent such a blow long before it actually struck by getting an author to present its case. The result, Diderot's *Lettre sur le commerce de la librairie,* reiterated the old arguments about maintaining quality by restricting productivity in contradiction to Diderot's own liberal principles and Malesherbes's *Mémoires sur la librairie,* which had partly inspired the reform project. Apparently dismissing Diderot's *Lettre* as the work of a hired hack, Malesherbes's liberal successors, especially Sartine and Le Camus de Néville, pushed through the edicts of 1777 and so somewhat loosened the guild's stranglehold on the publishing industry.[38]

But the controversial item in the code of 1777 concerned the relations of guild members and authors: privilege was now clearly derived from authorship and belonged to the author and his heirs perpetually or expired after his death, if he had ceded it to a bookdealer and the dealer had had it for at least ten years. This provision brought many works into the public domain and provoked bitter complaints by the guild members, but it did not really undermine their monopoly.[39] The code reinforced their power to police the book trade and repeated in the strongest possible terms that no one outside the guild could engage in publishing. So the dynasties of printer-booksellers continued to dominate their industry until the Revolution. The greatest of them, Charles-Joseph Panckoucke, built up France's first press empire by lobbying in Versailles.[40]

There had never been any question of creating a free trade in books by abolishing the guild as Turgot had abolished the six great *jurandes*. The economic issue took another form; it arose from the ancient enmity between Parisian and provincial bookdealers. Provincial printing had not recovered since the trade war of the seventeenth century, but provincial booksellers survived in large numbers throughout the eighteenth century, and they drew much of their stock (often in the form of exchanges, measured in sheets rather than volumes) from outside France, where hundreds of enterprising printers turned out cheap pirated editions of French works. The state inadvertently produced a boom in this illicit trade in the 1770s by levying a tax on paper, a much more costly item in the budget of eighteenth-century printers than it is today.

Printer's *papier blanc* had been taxed from time to time, notably in 1680 and 1748, but not at a ruinous rate and not much, if at all, outside Paris—until March 1, 1771, when the abbé Terray, trying desperately to cut the deficit accumulated during the Seven Years' War, taxed it 20 sous per ream. In August 1771 he increased that rate by 10 sous as a result of the across-the-board tax of 2 sous per livre. Since exports of French paper went duty free, foreign printers and their provincial allies gained an enormous advantage. A ream of good white *papier d'Auvergne* cost 11 livres in Paris and 8 livres in Switzerland, according to one estimate.[41] To right the balance, Terray placed a duty of 60 livres per quintal on imports of French and Latin books on September 11, 1771. But this measure inadvertently undercut the exchange trade between provincial dealers and foreigners.

Seized by panic, publishers like the Société typographique de Neuchâtel suspended all shipments to France and cast about desperately for ways of cracking the tariff barrier while their customers in the provinces, men like Jean Marie Bruysset and Périsse Duluc of Lyons, agitated for the repeal of the duty.[42] The agitation paid: on November 24, 1771, the tax was reduced to 20 livres; on October 17, 1773, it went down to 6 livres 10 sous; and on April 23, 1775, Turgot withdrew it altogether. But this reversal of policy again tipped the economic balance in favor of the foreign publishers. An unsigned memorandum to the ministry reported: "It is from this time onward that the Swiss, realizing that they could undersell our books at half their price, have pillaged and ravaged our book trade. In fact, they market our books at three liards or one French sou per sheet; and since in addition to the cost of the paper tax and the high price of printing in France, we have to pay for the purchase of manuscripts, we often cannot make a profit when we sell that same sheet for two or three sous." As an example, the writer said that Panckoucke's new *Encyclopédie méthodique* would have to sell at 11 livres a volume for Panckoucke merely to cover production costs, while a pirated Swiss edition could sell in Paris at 6 livres a volume and produce a 40–50 percent profit.[43]

Until mid-1783 the business of foreign publishers and provincial dealers seems to have flourished at the expense of their Parisian rivals, but on June 12, 1783, Vergennes, the foreign minister, destroyed it with a stroke of the pen. He issued orders to the General Tax Farm requiring that all book imports—garnished with the usual seals, lead stamps, and customs slips called *acquits à caution*—be transmitted to the Chambre syndicale of the Parisian guild for inspection before being delivered to their final destination. Without tampering further with the taxation system or passing through formal, legal channels like the earlier edicts, this measure at once restored the guild's domination of the book trade. It meant that a crate of books sent from Geneva to Lyons now had to pass through the hands of the guild officials in Paris, which gave the Parisians an opportunity to weed out pirated editions and saddled the Lyonnais with a detour that would cost more than the books were worth. Even the extra trip from Rouen to Paris and back would ruin his business, a desperate Rouennais wrote.[44] Booksellers in Lille reported that they had no choice but to let imports pile up and rot in their damp customshouse.[45] The Lyonnais claimed that they had suspended all book imports—a matter of 2,000 quintals a year—and were in danger of suspending payments.[46] And while protests from provincial dealers flooded the *Direction de la librairie,* frantic letters flew around the circuit of publishers who fed the provincials from across France's borders. Boubers of Brussels, Gosse of The Hague, Dufour of Maestricht, Grasset of Lausanne, Bassompierre of Geneva, and dozens of others, all trembled for their commercial lives.

The Société typographique de Neuchâtel sent out an agent, J.-F. Bornand, to inspect the damage done to its supply lines. Bornand reported that Vergennes's "disastrous orders" had stopped all book traffic in Savoy and Franche-Comté. A side trip to Grenoble showed him that the southern route was "bristling with guards, so much so that in the outpost of Chaparillan they seized all the books in my trunk . . . while exhibiting the king's order instructing them not to let through any books at all."[47] The bookdealers in Lyons told Bornand such gloomy stories that he concluded, "It is necessary to give up on France."[48] They believed that Panckoucke was behind the crackdown, because he wanted to destroy his Swiss competitors, notably Heubach & Cie, of Lausanne, whose pirating had cut deeply into the sales of his edition of Buffon's *Histoire naturelle.* Bornand reported the same rumor from Besançon; and when he arrived in Paris, the booksellers turned their "scornful demeanor" on him with full force. One threatened to cause him "all possible harm; the Parisian booksellers have banded against the foreign booksellers and even against those in the provinces."[49] By mid-1785, the Neuchâtelois still found it impossible to get their books to the great clandestine trade center of Avignon,[50] and they abandoned attempts to reach Paris through smugglers stationed in Geneva, Besançon, Dijon, Châlons-sur-Saône, and Clairvaux. Their booming business in France had been cut to a trickle. It never recovered, because, as they explained to a Parisian confidant, "We don't know what means the other booksellers from here, Lausanne, and Bern are using. We know of none, except to ship through Paris with an *acquit à caution* ... All other channels are closed to us, because we do not want to take on risks, nor to expose ourselves to confiscations and fines."[51] Vergennes had cut the lifeline linking foreign producers and provincial distributors.

According to the provincial protests, Vergennes's orders would decimate the legal foreign trade in books. By making imports impossibly expensive, the new rules would produce an inevitable decline in exports, especially since much of the import-export business was conducted in exchanges of printed sheets rather than in money. The state saw the orders as a new policing technique, aimed at the destruction of pirated and prohibited books—the bread and butter of underground publishing. Both views may have been correct, but the clandestine trade probably suffered the most. The monopolistic practices of the Parisians had forced the provincials to seek shelter underground. There they formed alliances with foreign publishers, who sent them illegal works under cover of an *acquit à caution,* a customs permit that protected book shipments from all inspection between the border and their points of destination within France, where they were to be examined by the nearest official bookdealer. He would certify their legitimacy by endorsing the back of the *acquit* and returning it, by the driver who had delivered the books, to the border station where it had been issued. A dealer collaborating with an illegal publisher could either market the books himself (instead of impounding them), or he could relay them on toward Paris and collect a commission. Since domestic book shipments were rarely inspected en route, they could reach an entrepôt outside Paris, usually in Versailles, without risk and then could be smuggled in small quantities into the capitol.

The system worked quite well as long as provincial dealers could discharge the *acquits à caution.* But by placing that function in the hands of the Parisian guild, Vergennes undercut the whole operation. Of course there were other means of reaching the market, but it was no easy task to thread one's way through the internal customs barriers and to dodge the roaming inspectors of the General Farm, who received a reward and a portion of the goods after every confiscation. What the drivers and clandestine agents wanted was legal camouflage so they could send whole wagonloads rumbling down the middle of France's splendid highways to provincial guildhalls and to the very palace of the king. The clandestine trade was a matter of calculating risks and profit margins. Too chancy, too elaborate a system of smuggling would not pay. So when Vergennes changed the rules of the game, the foreign suppliers and provincial dealers faced disaster. If the papers of the Société typographique de Neuchâtel indicate the general reaction to the order of June 12, 1783, the whole underground industry fell into a depression that lasted for at least two years and perhaps until 1789.[52]

As far as foreign publishing was concerned, the French government had finally committed itself to a policy of laissez faire but not laissez passer.

Curiously, the graphs of legal French book production constructed by Robert Estivals and François Furet also show a spectacular drop in 1783, the low point of a slump extending roughly from 1774 to 1786.[53] Why this slump occurred is difficult to say. It does not seem to be related to Labrousse's prerevolutionary economic crisis or the Labrousse-like "cycles" that Estivals somehow sees in his statistics. Could it be connected with Vergennes's orders of June 12, 1783? The purpose of the orders stands out clearly in the text: to put an end to "the multitude of *libelles* printed in foreign countries and conveyed into the kingdom."[54] Even the petitions from the provincial bookdealers acknowledged that "the motive of the orders is to stop the flow of *libelles,* which arrive from foreign countries."[55] And a glance at Vergennes's correspondence with his ambassadors shows how much the *libelles* concerned him. In 1782 and 1783 he wrote as many letters to England about the need to suppress a smut factory run by émigré French *libellistes* as he did about the diplomatic preliminaries to the Treaty of Paris. He sent secret agent after secret agent (a bizarre collection of bogus barons and one police inspector disguised as an umbrella salesman) to buy off or kidnap the *libellistes.* No details of their fantastic, rococo intrigues were too trivial for Vergennes's attention, for he feared the effect of the *libelles* on public opinion in France. Well before the Diamond Necklace Affair, he exhorted the French chargé d'affaires to stamp out political pornography: "You know the malignity of our century and how easily the most absurd fables are received."[56] The orders of June 12, 1783, must have been part of this campaign, and they must have been fairly successful, judging from the consternation they produced in the world of underground publishing and the large collection of works like *Les amours de Charlot et Toinette* and *Essais historiques sur la vie de Marie-Antoinette* that the revolutionaries gleefully inventoried in the Bastille after 1789.[57]

There is no reason to connect the campaign against *libelles* with the drop in legal book production. Nonetheless, it seems possible that Vergennes was so determined to shut off the flow of *libelles* from outside France that he dammed up the channels of legitimate imports, too. His action could have created repercussions in the legal system of publishing, exactly as the provincial dealers argued. It would have forced even the most honest provincial booksellers to retrench, because it would have increased their expenses drastically and destroyed their exchange trade. It also would have eliminated their roles as middlemen (an important business in Lyons) in commerce between northern and southern Europe. As always, the Parisians might have profited from the provincials' losses. But provincial dealers drew some of the stock that they used for foreign exchanges from Paris. So Vergennes's offer also could have damaged part of the Parisians' market. It certainly reduced book imports on a national scale and, owing to the crucial importance of exchanges in the book trade, probably produced a corresponding drop in exports. Overall French book production therefore would have suffered, just as it suffered from the buffeting given it since 1771 by the succession of taxes and tariffs.

If these hypotheses are correct, they suggest that underground and legal publishing were not so separate and so inimical that they could not be injured by a common blow. A certain symbiosis probably developed between the two circuits. Each circuit relied heavily on injections of foreign books, and that foreign element must be measured if there is to be more exact knowledge about the circulation of ideas in the Old Regime. At this prestatistical stage, however, it seems legitimate to insist on one point: far from flourishing as a result of virtual freedom of the press, as is usually maintained, French publishing underwent a severe crisis on the eve of the Revolution, a crisis that has not been noticed by historians, because it did not manifest itself in formal documents, like the edicts on the book trade.[58]

The publishing crisis seems especially worthy of notice, because its economic and intellectual aspects were related in a way that reveals aspects of the prerevolutionary crisis. Economically, legal and clandestine publishing stood for antithetical ways of doing business. Faithful to the old "Colbertist" methods, the Parisian Communauté des libraires et imprimeurs produced a limited number of quality goods according to official specifications. It turned out traditional books for a traditional market, which it controlled by virtue of an official monopoly. With notable exceptions, like André François Le Breton, the publisher of the *Encyclopédie,* its members minimized risks, because they owed their profits to their privileges; and their privileges were family treasures, handed down from father to son and husband to widow. Furthermore, the guild fortified its monopoly by a share in the repressive power of the state. In publishing, as in so many other cases, the Old Regime was eaten away by privilege—not merely the juridical privileges dividing nobles from commoners, but the privilege of vested interests, which devoured the state like a cancer. In its last years, the government tried to rally and reform. But its efforts reactivated the century-old conflict between provincial and Parisian bookdealers, and the book duties of 1771–1775 followed by Vergennes's order of June 12, 1783, represented the final triumph of the Parisian publishing dynasties.

But this triumph was limited by the archaic character of the production system. Despite the flexibility introduced through the use of *permissions tacites* and the adventurous policies of a few guild members, privileged publishing failed to satisfy the demand created by an enlarged readership and by changing literary tastes. The reading patterns of the past weighed heavily in the traditional sector of publishing, as the statistics of Mornet and Furet demonstrate; and the reluctance of most traditional publishers to deviate from those patterns is perfectly understandable. Why should they abandon their privileges, risk their special status, and endanger their families' livelihood by producing new literature of uncertain legality? Innovation came through the underground. Down there, no legalities constrained productivity, and books were turned out by a kind of rampant capitalism. Not only did the state's misguided fiscal policies make it cheaper to produce new works outside France, but foreign publishers did a wild and woolly business in pirating old ones. As soon as their agents reported that a book was selling well in Paris, they began setting type for a counterfeit edition. Some of them also printed prohibited, hard-core *mauvais livres*. They were tough businessmen who produced anything that would sell. They took risks, broke traditions, and maximized profits by quantity instead of quality production. Rather than try to corner some segment of the market by a legal monopoly, they wanted to be left alone by the state and would even bribe it to do so. They were entrepreneurs who made a business of Enlightenment.

The enlightened themes of the books they produced—individualism, liberty, and equality before the law as opposed to corporatism, privilege, and mercantilist restrictions—suited their way of doing business. Perhaps the modes of production determined the product. If stretched that thin, the argument would turn into a kind of vulgar Marxist reductionism, but it suggests how far publishing history could be extended as a supplement to the conventional history of ideas.[59] Books are economic commodities as well as cultural artifacts; and as vehicles of ideas, they have to be peddled on a market. The literary marketplace of eighteenth-century France calls for closer analysis, for its books—whether privileged or philosophic, traditional or innovative—epitomized the character of the Old Regime.

SINCE THE OLD REGIME was a political as well as a social and economic system, a socioeconomic interpretation of its publishing ought to take account of political factors. What, in fact, were those books Vergennes wanted so desperately to keep out of France? They were listed in handwritten catalogues entitled "philosophical books," which circulated secretly and offered such delicious forbidden fruit as:

Vénus dans le cloître, ou la religieuse en chemise, figures
Système de la nature, 8°, 2 vol. 1775 très belle édition
Système social, 8°, 3 vol. 1775
Fausseté des miracles
La fille de joie, 8°, figures
Contrat social par Jean-Jacques Rousseau 12°
Journal historique des révolutions opérées en France par M. Maupeou, 3 vol. 8°
Mémoires authentiques de Mme. la comtesse Du Barry, 1775
Margot la ravaudeuse, 12°, figures
Lettres de l'abbé Terray à M. Turgot
Les droits des hommes et leurs usurpations[60]

The same underground publisher also circulated a formal printed catalogue, openly advertising its name, address, and items like the following:

> Bélisaire, par Marmontel, nouvelle édition augmentée, 8°, fig-ures, Lausanne, 1784: 1 livre.
> Bible (la Sainte), 8°, 2 vol., Neuchâtel, 1771: 6 livres.
> Bibliothèque anglaise, ou recueil des romans anglais, 14 vol., 12°, Genève, 1781: 15 livres.
> Bonnet (M. Charles), ses oeuvres complètes de physique et d'his-toire naturelle, 4°, 8 vol., figures, Neuchâtel, 1782: 81 livres.[61]

The books in the second catalogues may have been legal or pirated, but they did not offend religion, morality, or the French state. Those in the first cataloque offended all three and therefore earned the title "philosophical books"—a very revealing trade name, which recurs constantly in the com-mercial correspondence of underground publishers.

How offensive actually was this "philosophy"? *Les amours de Charlot et Toinette,* a work that was high on Vergennes's list of *libelles,* began with a description of the queen mastur-bating and then moved on to an account of her supposed orgies with the comte d'Artois, dismissing the king as fol-lows:

> On sait bien que le pauvre Sire,
> Trois ou quatre fois condamné
> Par la salubre faculté,
> Pour impuissance très complète,
> Ne peut satisfaire Antoinette.
> De ce malheur bien convaincu,
> Attendu que son allumette
> N'est pas plus grosse qu'un fétu;
> Que toujours molle et toujours croche,
> Il n'a de v . . . que dans la poche;
> Qu'au lieu de f . . . il est f . . .
> Comme le feu prélat d'Antioche.

It is well known that the poor Sire,
Three or four times condemned
By the salubrious faculty [of medicine],
For complete impotence,
Cannot satisfy Antoinette.
Quite convinced of this misfortune,
Considering that his match-stick
Is no bigger than a straw,
Always limp and always curved,
He had no p . . . except in his pocket;
Instead of f . . . , he is f . . .
Like the late prelate of Antioch.[62]

Crude stuff, but no less effective for its gross versification. A similar work, which pretended to defend the queen, and various courtiers and ministers as well, by refuting the calumnies against her in minute, scabrous detail, explained that the *libelles* circulated through several strata of society: "A vile courtisan puts these infamies in rhyming couplets and through the intermediary of flunkeys distributes them all the way to the market place. From the markets they reach artisans, who in turn transmit them back to the noblemen who first wrought them and who, without wasting a minute, go to the royal chambers in Versailles and whisper from ear to ear in a tone of consummate hypocrisy, 'Have you read them? Here they are. This is what is circulating among the common people in Paris.'"[63]

No doubt one could pick some smut from the gutter at any period in the history of Paris, but the gutters overflowed during the reign of Louis XVI; and the inundation worried Louis's chief of police, J.-C.-P. Lenoir, because, as Lenoir put it, "The Parisians had more of a propensity to believe the malicious rumors and *libelles* that circulated clandestinely than the facts printed and published by order or with the permission of the government."[64] Lenoir later reported that his attempt to suppress the circulation of *li-belles* "was undercut by courtiers who had scandalous works printed and who protected the printers. The Parisian police could only reach the bookdealers and peddlers who sold and distributed them. The peddlers were shut up in the Bastille, and that kind of punishment hardly mortified people of their stripe, poor devils who were in it for the money and who often did not know the names of the real authors and printers . . . During the years before the Revolution, the authorities were especially helpless in their efforts to curb *li-belles* against the government."[65]

The police took the *libelles* seriously, because they had a serious effect on public opinion, and public opinion was a powerful force in the declining years of the Old Regime. Although the monarchy still considered itself absolute, it hired hack pamphleteers like Brissot and Mirabeau to give it a good name.[66] It even attempted to manipulate rumors, for in the eighteenth century "public noises" (*bruits publics*) could lead to riots (*émotions populaires*). A riot broke out in 1750, for example, because of a rumor that the police were kidnapping working-class children to provide a literal blood bath for some royal prince of the blood.[67] It was the primitiveness of such "emotions" and the power of public opinion that made the regime vulnerable to *libelles*.

How badly the *libelles* damaged the public's faith in the legitimacy of the Old Regime is difficult to say, because there is no index to the public opinion of eighteenth-century France. Despite the testimony of expert observers like Vergennes and Lenoir,[68] it might be argued that the public found its dirty books amusing, nothing more. *Libellistes* had piled up trash for years without burying anyone. But there also could have been a cumulative effect that produced a deluge after Louis XV. Louis's private life provided plenty of material for the *Vie privée de Louis XV,* which in turn set the tone for a whole series of *Vies privées* about court figures. These scurrilous works hammered at the same points with such ferocity that they probably drove some home, at least in the case of a few leitmotivs: Du Barry's sexual success story (from brothel to throne); Maupeou's despotism (his search for a man to build a machine that would hang ten innocent victims at a time); and the decadence of the court (not merely a matter of luxury and adultery but also of impotence—in the *libelles* the high aristocracy could neither fight nor make love and perpetuated itself by extramarital infusions from more virile lower classes).[69] Louis XVI, notoriously unable to consummate his marriage for many years, made a perfect symbol of a monarchy in the last stages of decay. Dozens of pamphlets like *La naissance du Dauphin dévoilée* (another on Vergennes's list) provided dozens of revelations about the "real" lineage of the heir to the throne. And then the Diamond Necklace Affair produced an inexhaustible supply of muck to be raked. A king cuckolded by a cardinal: What better finale to a regime that was finished—better even than the rumor of the warming pan that brought public opinion to a boil in England on the eve of 1688.

It is easy to underestimate the importance of personal slander in eighteenth-century French politics, because it is difficult to appreciate that politics took place at court, where personalities counted more than policies. Defamation was a standard weapon of court cabales. And then as now, names made news, although news did not make the newspapers. Rigorously excluded from legal periodicals, it circulated in pamphlets, *nouvelles à la main,* and by *nouvellistes de bouche*—the real sources from which political journalism originated in France. In such crude media, politics was reported crudely—as a game for kings, their courtiers, ministers, and mistresses. Beyond the court and below the summit of salon society, the "general public" lived on rumors; and the "general reader" saw politics as a kind of nonparticipant sport, involving villains and heroes but no issues—except perhaps a crude struggle between good and evil or France and Austria. He probably read his *libelles* as his modern counterpart reads magazines or comic books, but he did not laugh them off, for the villains and heroes were real to him; they were fighting for control of France. Politics was living folklore. And so, after enjoying *La gazette noire's* titillating account of veneral disease, buggery, cuckoldry, illegitimacy, and impotence in the upper ranks of French society, he may have been convinced and outraged by its description of Mme. Du Barry, "passing directly from the brothel to the throne."[70]

This was more dangerous propaganda than the *Contrat social.* It severed the sense of decency that bound the public to its rulers. Its disingenuous moralizing opposed the ethics of little people to those of *les grands* on top, because, for all their obscenities, the *libelles* were strongly moralistic. Perhaps they even propagated a bourgeois morality that came to full fruition during the Revolution. "Bourgeois" may not be the proper term for it, but the *petits* who rose against the *gros* in the Year II responded to a kind of Gaulois Puritanism that had developed well before 1789. Gullible about the plots and purges of the Terror,[71] they had gullibly assimilated legends from their earlier *libelles.* Thus an aristocratic plot to kidnap bourgeois wives before the Revolution: "Do you have a pretty wife? Has she attracted the eye of some parvenu potentate, some fop who has gained power, some court aristocrat, for example? She is sequestered straight away. Do you want to discuss the matter? They send you to the galleys."[72]

Of course one can only speculate about what went on in the minds of such primitive readers, but it might have been *désacralisation,* occurring at levels well below the elite. Without this occurrence, it is hard to understand how the *Père Duchesne* could have had such an appeal or how people brought up to believe in the royal touch could have read about "the head of Female Veto [the queen] separated from her fucking neck"[73] without erupting in *émotion populaire.* The king had lost some of his mystical touch with the people long before Hébert's harangues about the "Austrian bitch" and her "fat cuckold." How great a loss it was, no one can say, but works like *Les rois de France régénérés* made the Bourbons look literally illegitimate. The administration feared those works, because it appreciated their power to make a mockery of the monarchy. The ridiculing of Louis XVI must have done a great deal of damage at a time when nobility was still identified with "seminal fluid"[74] and when the Salic Law still required that the royal "race" be transmitted through a magical unbroken chain of males. The magic had gone out of the Bourbons by the reign of Louis XVI. Lenoir reported that as the Revolution approached he could not get crowds to applaud the queen by paying them, although they had cheered spontaneously earlier.[75] And in 1789 Desmoulins described a four-year-old being carried around the Palais-Royal on the shoulders of a street-porter, crying out: " 'Polignac exiled a hundred leagues from Paris! Condé the same! Conti the same! The queen . . . !' I don't dare repeat it."[76] The *libelles* had done their work all too well.

The step from publishing to libeling was easily taken

outside the closed circles of the guild because nonguild publishers could only exist outside the law, and law in the Old
Regime meant privilege (*leges privatae,* private law).[77] The
nuances of legality and illegality covered a broad enough
spectrum, however, for many underprivileged bookdealers
to do a pretty legitimate business. The underground contained several levels. Its agents near the top may never have
touched *libelles,* while those at the bottom handled nothing
but filth. The Société typographique de Neuchâtel generally
pirated only good, clean books like the works of Mme. Riccoboni, but the neighboring house of Samuel Fauche and
his prodigal sons produced the very works that Vergennes
tried to suppress in London. Fauche also printed the political and pornographic writings of Mirabeau: *l'Espion dévalisé,
Ma conversion ou le libertin de qualité, Erotika Biblion,* and *Lettres de cachet.*[78] And yet when the last ten volumes of the
Encyclopédie appeared in 1765, they bore the false imprint "A
Neufchastel chez Samuel Faulche."

The underground genres easily got mixed up, and underground dealers often moved from one level to another.
Hard times forced them into lower reaches of illegality; for
as they sank deeper into debt, they took greater chances in
hope of greater profits. The crisis of the 1780s might have
produced precisely that result. Ironically, Vergennes might
have transformed some rather inoffensive pirates into pur-
veyors of *libelles* and actually increased the circulation of
"philosophical books" by decreasing the relatively above-
board traffic in pirated works. The Société typographique de Neuchâtel seems to have done more business in
libelles after 1783 than before Vergennes's crackdown.[79] As
the Revolution approached, provincial dealers who earlier
had merely discharged a few false *acquits à caution* may have
speculated more on shipments of works like *Les amours de*

Charlot et Toinette and passed around more catalogues of *livres philosophiques.* Or perhaps their customers' tastes changed in response to episodes like the Diamond Necklace Affair. It is impossible at this point to tell whether supply followed demand fairly neatly or whether demand was influenced by what could be supplied. Reading habits could have evolved as a result of the peculiar conditions determining literary output or could have been the determining factor themselves; or each element could have reinforced the other. Whatever combination of causes was at work, the Old Regime put *Charlot et Toinette, Vénus dans le cloître,* d'Holbach, and Rousseau in the same boxes and shipped them under the same code name. *Livres philosophiques* to the dealers, *mauvais livres* to the police, it made little difference. What mattered was their common clandestineness. There was equality in illegality; Charlot and Rousseau were brothers beyond the pale.

The very way in which these works were produced helped reduce them to the common denominator of irreligion, immorality, and uncivility. The foreigners who printed them felt no loyalty to France, the Bourbons, or, often, the Catholic Church. The dealers who distributed them operated in an underworld of "bandits without morals and shame." And the authors who wrote them had often sunk into a Grub Street life of quasi-criminality. The arch-*libelliste* Charles Théveneau de Morande was brought up in brothels and educated in prisons, and those milieux provided the material for his writing.[80] Perhaps the underground's impurities rubbed off on the books that passed through it: the message certainly suited the medium. But what a state of affairs! A regime that classified its most advanced philosophy with its most debased pornography was a regime that sapped itself, that dug its own underground, and that encouraged philosophy to degenerate into *libelle.* When philosophy went under, it lost its self-restraint and its commitment to the culture of those on top. When it turned against courtiers, churchmen, and kings, it committed itself to turning the world upside down. In their own language, the *livres philosophiques* called for undermining and overthrowing. The counterculture called for a cultural revolution—and was ready to answer the call of 1789.

Notes
Acknowledgments
Index

Notes

1. The High Enlightenment and the Low-Life of Literature

1. Chevrier to the Société typographique de Neuchâtel, Dec. 10, 1772, Papers of the Société typographique, Bibliothèque de la ville de Neuchâtel, Switzerland.

2. Among these histories, the following were found to be most useful: Maurice Pellison, *Les Hommes de lettres au XVIIIe siècle* (Paris, 1911); Jules Bertaut, *La Vie littéraire au XVIIIe siècle* (Paris, 1954); and John Lough, *An Introduction to Eighteenth-Century France* (London, 1960), chaps. 7 and 8.

3. Quoted in Marcel Reinhard, "Elite et noblesse dans la seconde moitié du XVIIIe siècle," *Revue d'histoire moderne et contemporaine*, 3 (Jan.–March 1956), 21. For Voltaire's view see the famous 23rd letter of his *Lettres philosophiques* (London, 1734).

4. The following is based on Mme. Suard's *Essais de mémoires sur M. Suard* (Paris, 1820), supplemented by the almost equally interesting reminiscences of D.-J. Garat, *Mémoires historiques sur la vie de M. Suard, sur ses écrits, et sur le XVIIIe siècle*, 2 vols. (Paris, 1820). Although Suard is a forgotten figure today, he was one of the most prominent writers of the High Enlightenment. He never produced a major work, but he made a reputation by journal articles, academic discourses, and translations, whose studied tastefulness may be appreciated from his *Mélanges de littérature*, 5 vols. (Paris, 1803–1805).

5. Garat described Raynal as follows (*Mémoires historiques*, I, 107): "In the capital of France and philosophy, he acted as a grand master of ceremonies, who introduced beginners with talent to talented celebrities and men of letters to manufacturers, merchants, farmers-general, and ministers."

6. Garat described Suard as the epitome of the savoir faire and respect for social rank that made a man of *le monde* (see especially

ibid., I, 133–136), and he defined *le monde* as a milieu of "men powerful by virtue of position, wealth, literary talent and birth ... those three or four conditions that are the real sources of power in society" (I, 263).

7. Of course well-born and wealthy philosophes like Montesquieu, d'Holbach, and Helvétius did not fit into this pattern. Humbler writers were expected to take mistresses or to marry when their fortune was made. Maupertuis, Marmontel, Piron, and Sedaine were famous and past fifty when they married.

8. Mme. Suard, *Essais de mémoires,* p. 59.

9. Ibid., p. 94.

10. Ibid., p. 137.

11. Archives Nationales, F17a 1212. Some unsigned, undated *Observations préliminaires* in the first dossier explained that the list was drawn up in order to implement an edict of Sept. 3, 1785, which announced the government's intention of aiding men of letters more systematically than had been done before. The author of the *Observations* (probably Gojard, *premier commis* to the controller general) evidently thought the proposed subsidies excessive: "Aside from the sums paid by the Royal Treasury to men of letters, and which amount to 256,300 livres, there are also pensions attached to journals and to the *Almanach royal;* and it is possible that they have been given to several authors who are applying today without having declared [that other income], as they should have done according to the terms of the first article of the edict." An incomplete (twenty-one names missing) version of the master list in the Archives Nationales was sold at an auction and later published by Maurice Tourneux in *Revue d'histoire littéraire de la France,* 8 (1901), 281–311. Lacking the supplementary information, which he vainly sought in series O of the Archives, Tourneux was unable to explain the circumstances of the pension scheme and wrongly linked it with the baron de Breteuil. Much of the material in F17a 1212 also covers the period 1786–1788.

12. Blin de Sainmore to the Contrôleur général, June 22, 1788, Archives Nationales F17a 1212, dossier 10.

13. Ibid., dossier 6.

14. Ibid., dossier 3.

15. Ducis to Loménie de Brienne, Nov. 27, 1787, ibid., dossier

6. See also the similar letter of A. M. Lemierre of March 8, 1788, dossier 10.

16. Caraccioli to the Directeur général des finances, Aug. 13, 1788, ibid., dossier 6. See also Caraccioli's letter April 8, 1785, dossier 10: "I am the only author of my advanced age who has never had either a pension or a grant."

17. Ibid., note in dossier 3.

18. Ibid., dossier 1.

19. Ibid., dossier 1.

20. The documents in the Archives Nationales would therefore tend to support the argument advanced by Marcel Reinhard in "Elite et noblesse."

21. Lenoir papers, Bibliothèque municipale d'Orléans, MS. 1422.

22. Pellisson, *Les Hommes de lettres,* p. 59.

23. See the appointments listed after the names of the academicians in the annual issues of the *Almanach royal.*

24. The most revealing of these is Lucien Brunel, *Les Philosophes et l'Académie française au dix-huitième siècle* (Paris, 1884).

25. Printed in Garat, *Mémoires historiques,* p. 342.

26. Charles Pinot-Duclos, *Considérations sur les moeurs de ce siècle,* ed. F. C. Green (Cambridge, Eng., 1939; 1st ed. 1750), p. 140, and, in general, chaps. 11 and 12.

27. On the strategical agreement and tactical differences between Voltaire and d'Alembert and their disagreements with the d'Holbach group (which apparently left Diderot somewhere in the middle) see John N. Pappas, *Voltaire and d'Alembert,* Indiana University Humanities Series, no. 50 (Bloomington, 1962).

28. D'Alembert, *Essai sur la société des gens de lettres et des grands, sur la réputation, sur les Mécènes, et sur les récompenses littéraires,* in *Mélanges de littérature, d'histoire et de philosophie* (Amsterdam, 1773: 1st ed. 1752), especially pp. 403, 367.

29. D'Alembert, *Histoire des membres de l'Académie française morts depuis 1700 jusqu'en 1771* (Paris, 1787), I, xxiv, xxxii.

30. See Henry Fairlie, "Evolution of a Term," *The New Yorker,* Oct. 19, 1968, pp. 173–206.

31. Although birth and death dates overlap too much to fall into clear categories, "generations" might be differentiated by the

experience of events. Whether we are thirty or fifteen, a chasm of experienced time separates those of us who did not live through World War II from those who participated in it or who read about it in the newspapers while it took place. Perhaps a similar line of experience divided the men who wrote and read the great works of the Enlightenment when they appeared in the mid-century from those who read them after they had already begun to congeal into "classics." Suard (1734–1817) recalled, "I entered *le monde* at the time of that explosion of the philosophical spirit which has marked the second half of the eighteenth century. I read *L'Esprit des lois* at the age of nineteen [that is, in 1753, five years after its publication]. I was in the provinces, and that reading delighted me. *L'Histoire naturelle* [of Buffon] and the works of Condillac appeared soon afterwards, the *Encyclopédie* in 1752, as did the *Découverte de l'irritabilité* by Haller" (quoted in Garat, *Mémoires historiques,* II, 445). For a survey of the literature on the problem of generations and periodization see Clifton Cherpack, "The Literary Periodization of Eighteenth-Century France," *Publications of the Modern Language Association of America,* 84 (March 1969), 321–328.

32. Mme. Suard, *Essais de mémoires,* p. 155.

33. Quoted in Louis de Loménie, *Beaumarchais et son temps* (Paris, 1856), II, 424. Suard did not object to *Le Mariage de Figaro* because he found it radical but because he considered its treatment of sex unsuitable for the stage (Mme. Suard, *Essais de mémoires,* p. 133). One could cite a dozen contemporary references indicating the same attitude. Even Lenoir, more involved in the business of sniffing out sedition than anyone in France, reported on Beaumarchais: "Almost all the plays of that author were prevented from opening on the grounds of being offensive to morality, but he succeeded by his intrigues in forcing his way through the censorship. More than once I received an order to let pass plays of his that had been held up for a long time without receiving the necessary approbation and permission" (Bibliothèque municipale d'Orléans, MS. 1423). The "revolutionary" message of *Le Mariage de Figaro,* if it exists, went unnoticed in prerevolutionary France. Is not the play's refrain a formula for political quietism: "Everything finishes with a song"? Beaumarchais was a wealthy, ennobled man-on-the-make like Voltaire, and he devoted much of his fortune to reediting Voltaire's works.

34. For information on literacy, education, and book production in eighteenth-century France see Michel Fleury and Pierre Valmary, "Les progrès de l'instruction élémentaire de Louis XIV à Napoléon III," *Population,* 12 (Jan.–March 1957), 71–92; Pierre Gontard, *L'Enseignement primaire en France de la Révolution à la loi Guizot (1789-1833)* (Lyons, 1959); Robert Estivals, *La Statistique bibliographique de la France sous la monarchie au XVIIIe siècle* (Paris and The Hague, 1965); and François Furet, "La 'librairie' du royaume de France au dix-huitième siècle," in *Livre et société dans la France du XVIIIème siècle,* 1 (Paris and The Hague, 1965), pp. 3-32. The *Almanach de la librairie* for 1781 lists 1,057 booksellers and printers, of whom about one-fifth did business in Paris. No editions of the *Almanach* go back before 1778, so comparisons cannot be made with the early eighteenth century. But the *Almanach royal* for 1750 lists 79 royal censors, and the *Almanach royal* for 1789 lists 181, an increase that represents a greater output of books, not greater severity in controlling them. It may never be possible to make estimates of the number of authors in the eighteenth century, not only because of a lack of statistics but also because of the problem of defining an author. Robert Escarpit made a brave but unsuccessful attempt in *La Sociologie de la littérature* (Paris, 1958).

35. *Mémoires et correspondance de Mallet du Pan pour servir à l'histoire de la Révolution française, recueillis et mis en ordre par A. Sayous* (Paris, 1851), I, 130. Lenoir estimated the number of applicants for pensions at 4,000 (probably a slip for 400). Bibliothèque municipale d'Orléans, MS. 1422.

36. L.-S. Mercier, *Tableau de Paris,* 12 vols (1789), X, 26–27.

37. Ibid., p. 29.

38. See his poem "Le Pauvre Diable" and the articles in the *Dictionnaire philosophique* from which the quotations are taken: "Auteurs," "Charlatan," "Gueux," "Philosophe," and "Quisquis."

39. *Le Petit Almanach de nos grands hommes* (1788), quotation p. 5. In the preface Rivarol explained that he would exclude all established writers from his survey: "I will gladly descend from these imposing colossi to the tiniest insects . . . to that innumerable mass of families, tribes, nations, republics, and empires hidden under a leaf of grass" (p. vi).

40. For a particularly striking example of this theme see the first chapters of J.-P. Brissot's *Mémoires,* ed. Claude Perroud (Paris, 1910).

Mercier often remarked on the influx of provincial writers and even wrote a sort of parable about it: *Tableau de Paris,* X, 129–130. He claimed that some of them roamed the capital in bands, so that the native Parisian writer "has to combat Norman writers, who form a corps, and especially the Gascons, who go around citing Montesquieu, to whom they consider themselves as successors" (XI, 103).

41. *Considérations sur les moeurs,* p. 141.

42. Voltaire, "Le Pauvre Diable," in *Oeuvres complètes de Voltaire* (n.p., 1785), XIV, quotation p. 162. Of course Voltaire used this theme to satirize his enemies, but it can be taken as social comment.

43. Ibid., p. 164.

44. *Tableau de Paris,* XI, 187. See especially the chapters entitled "Auteurs," "Des demi-auteurs, quarts d'auteurs, enfin métis, quarterons," "Misère des auteurs," "La Littérature du Faubourg Saint-Germain et celle du Faubourg Saint-Honoré," "Les Grands Comédiens contre les petits," and "Le Musée de Paris."

45. S.-N.-H. Linguet, *L'Aveu sincère, ou lettre à une mère sur les dangers que court la jeunesse en se livrant à un goût trop vif pour la littérature* (London, 1763), pp. v, vii. Linguet explained, p. iv, "I address myself to those ingenuous and inexperienced souls who could be deceived by the glory that they see surrounding the great writers."

46. *Correspondance littéraire, philosophique et critique par Grimm, Diderot, Raynal, Meister, etc.,* ed. Maurice Tourneux (Paris, 1880), XII, 402: "Since literature has become a job (*métier*), and, what's more, a job whose practice has been made easy and common, owing to the numerous models to emulate and the simplicity of its techniques."

47. J.-J. Garnier, *L'Homme de lettres* (Paris, 1764), pp. 134–135.

48. Mercier, *Tableau de Paris,* XI, 104–105: "The man of letters from the provinces finds in Paris an equality that does not exist at all among the men of his small town: here his origins are forgotten; if he is the son of a tavernkeeper, he can call himself a count; no one will dispute his claim." Mercier probably had Rivarol in mind when he wrote those lines.

49. On the financial relations between authors and publishers see Pellisson, *Les Hommes de lettres,* chap. 3; Lough, *An Introduction to Eighteenth-Century France,* chap. 7; and G. d'Avenel, *Les Revenues d'un*

intellectuel de 1200 à 1913 (Paris, 1922), although d'Avenel's study is flawed by an attempt to translate all financial transactions into francs of 1913. For vivid contemporary accounts of the dealings between authors and publishers see P. J. Blondel, *Mémoires sur les vexations qu'exercent les libraires et imprimeurs de Paris,* ed. Lucien Faucou (Paris, 1879), which hits the publishers very hard, and Diderot's *Lettre sur le commerce de la librairie* in his *Oeuvres complètes,* ed. J. Assézat and M. Tourneux (Paris, 1876), p. xviii, which also deals some damaging blows, although Diderot was evidently writing as their paid propagandist.

50. L.-S. Mercier, *De le littérature et des littérateurs* (Yverdon, 1778), pp. 38–39.

51. *Tableau de Paris,* VIII, 59.

52. For documentation of this trend in the subculture of scientists and pseudoscientists in prerevolutionary Paris see Robert Darnton, *Mesmerism and the End of the Enlightenment in France* (Cambridge, Mass., 1968), chap. 3.

53. A trade war in the late seventeenth century had left the publishing industry in the grip of the Communauté des libraires et des imprimeurs de Paris and the Parisian guild tightened its hold throughout the eighteenth century, despite the government's attempts to impose some reforms in 1777. The archaic, "Colbertist" conditions of the book trade may be appreciated from the texts of the edicts regulating it: see *Recueil général des anciennes lois françaises,* ed. F. A. Isambert, Decrusy, and A. H. Taillandier (Paris, 1822–1833), XVI, 217–251, XXV, 108–128. The transition from seventeenth- to eighteenth-century conditions is explored in the thesis by Henri-Jean Martin, *Livre, pouvoirs et société à Paris au XVIIe siècle (1598–1701),* 2 vols. (Geneva, 1969). On the even more monopolistic conditions in the theater see Jules Bonnassies, *Les Auteurs dramatiques et la Comédie française aux XVIIe et XVIIIe siècles* (Paris, 1874).

54. See Chapter 2.

55. Because Grub Street remains unexplored territory (I hope at least to map it in a later work), there are no secondary works on it. For an example of how it wrapped its tentacles around one future revolutionary see Chapter 2. See also the fascinating biography by Paul Robiquet, *Théveneau de Morande: étude sur le XVIIIe siècle* (Paris, 1882). Morande acted as the dean of the *libellistes* and lived with a

collection of underworld characters that makes some of the extravagant comments in *Le Neveu de Rameau* seem mild indeed.

56. Charles Théveneau de Morande, *La Gazette noire par un homme qui n'est pas blanc* (1784, "imprimé à cent lieues de la Bastille"), p. 212. The literature on salons and cafés is brought together in the works of Pellisson and Bertaut, cited above. See also the revealing remarks by Karl Mannheim in *Essays on the Sociology of Culture,* ed. Ernest Manheim (London, 1956), pp. 91–170.

57. The only copy of *Les Nouvelles de la République des lettres et des arts,* 7 vols. (Paris, 1777–1787) that I have been able to locate is incomplete: Bibliothèque Nationale, Réserve Z 1149–1154. See also La Blancherie's *Correspondance générale sur les sciences et les arts* (Paris, 1779), Rz. 3037 and 3392. There is a great deal of information on the *musées* and *lycées* of the 1780s scattered throught the *nouvelles à la main* published as *Mémoires secrets pour servir à l'histoire de la République des lettres en France* and commonly known as the *Mémoires secrets* of Bachaumont.

58. See especially Linguet's widely read *Annales politiques, civiles et littéraires du dix-huitième siècle,* which attacked the cultural elite with declamations like the following (VI, 386): "There was nothing in France that was not subordinate to it. The ministry, the judiciary, science, literary bodies, everything had been invaded by it: [the "faction" of the established philosophes] controlled everything, even reputations. It alone opened the gateway to glory and wealth. It filled every position with philosophizing parvenus. The academies as well as the courts were in its grip; the press, the censors, the journals were at its command."

59. See Jean Bouchary, *Les Manieurs d'argent à Paris à la fin du XVIIIe siècle* (Paris, 1939–1943), I, and Jean Bénétruy, *L'Atelier de Mirabeau: quatre proscrits genevois dans la tourmente révolutionnaire* (Geneva, 1962).

60. *Dictionnaire philosophique,* article entitled "Quisquis."

61. "Extraits de divers rapports secrets faits à la police de Paris dans les années 1781 et suivantes, jusques et compris 1785, concernant des personnes de tout état et condition [ayant] donné dans la Révolution," Lenoir papers, Bibliothèque municipale d'Orléans, MS. 1423. As their gossipy tone indicates, these reports should not be taken as factually accurate, but they do suggest the general character of life at the bottom of the literary world. In a note

at the end of the reports, Lenoir explained that he cut out sections that would incriminate respectable persons but that the remaining excerpts were untouched and could be verified by comparison with other police records (which have been destroyed since he wrote). In general, Lenoir's papers seem reliable. In the case of Manuel, for example, they contain several remarks about Manuel's life in the literary underworld which are corroborated by his dossier in the Archives Nationales, W 295, and by an anonymous *Vie secrète de Pierre Manuel* (n.p., 1793).

62. Bibliothèque municipale d'Orléans, MS. 1423.

63. J. F. de La Harpe, *Lycée ou cours de littérature ancienne et moderne* (Paris, Year VII to Year XIII), XI, pt. 2, p. 488. Fabre's play, *Les Gens de lettres,* was published posthumously in *Mélanges littéraires par une société de gens de lettres* (Paris, 1827).

64. See Marat's letters to Roume de Saint Laurent in *Correspondance de Marat, recueillie et annotée par Charles Vellay* (Paris, 1908).

65. This interpretation, which maintains that the *libelles* increased in number and importance during the regime's last years, is based only on impressions from extensive reading in the pamphlet collections of the Bibliothèque Nationale and the British Museum, but it is supported by the similar impressions of Louis XVI's lieutenant general of police: see Lenoir's essay, "De l'administration de l'ancienne police concernant les libelles, les mauvaises satires et chansons, leurs auteurs coupables, délinquants, complices on adhérents," Bibliothèque municipale d'Orlèans, MS. 1422.

66. For a more detailed discussion of *libelle* literature see Chapter 6.

67. Charles Théveneau de Morande (anonymously), *Le Gazetier cuirassé: ou Anecdotes scandaleuses de la cour de France* (1771, "imprimé à cent lieues de la Bastille, à l'enseigne de la liberté"), p. 128.

68. Ibid., pp. 167–168.

69. Ibid., pp. 169–170.

70. As examples of Morande's characteristic emphasis on impotence and sodomy see ibid., pp. 51–52, 61.

71. Ibid., pp. 79–80.

72. Ibid., pp. 182–183.

73. Ibid., pp. 131–132.

74. Ibid., pp. 80–81.

75. Ibid., p. 53.

76. Ibid., pp. 36–37.

77. Ibid., p. 80. This remark introduced the following reference (p. 80) to Maupeou's fellow minister, the Duke d'Aiguillon: "The peerage used to be in France a rank where the slightest stain was inadmissable; but today a peer [that is, d'Aiguillon] can empoison, ruin a province and intimidate witnesses, provided he possesses the art of the courtier and can lie well."

78. Ibid., p. 31.

79. Ibid., p. 109: "A new book has just appeared, which challenges the kings of France to prove their divine institution by producing the treaty that the eternal father signed with them; the author of that book defies them to do so."

80. Ibid., pp. 157–158.

81. See Carra's notes to his translation of John Gillies's *Histoire de l'ancienne Grèce* (Paris, 1787), I, 4, 11, II, 387–389, V, 387, VI, 98. Carra produced an influential *Mémoire* attacking Calonne just before the opening of the Assembly of Notables in 1787 (it was reprinted in Carra's *Un Petit mot de réponse à M. de Calonne sur sa Requête au Roi,* Amsterdam, 1787) and continued to pummel him in *libelles* like *M. de Calonne tout entier* (Brussels, 1788). He also turned on Lenoir (*L'an 1787: Précis de l'administration de la Bibliothèque du Roi sous M. Lenoir,* 2nd ed., Liège, 1788), because Lenoir had not only advised Calonne against giving Carra a pension but had also tried, with the help of some academicians, to get him dismissed from a subordinate post in the Bibliothèque du Roi, which was Carra's only feeble source of income: see the Lenoir papers, Bibliothèque municipale d'Orléans, MSS. 1421 and 1423. Not surprisingly, Carra's prerevolutionary pamphlets fairly sizzle with hatred of the literary patricians who *did* get the pensions, sinecures, and seats in the academy and of the *grands* who dealt them out.

82. See his implicit contrast of bourgeois and aristocratic morality and of England and France in *Le Gazetier cuirassé,* pp. 83–86, 171, 173.

83. Ibid., p. 131.

84. His victims included Voltaire, d'Alembert, and their companions in the salon of Mme. Geoffrin: see ibid., pp. 178, 181.

85. Charles Théveneau de Morande (anonymously), *La Gazette noire par un homme qui n'est pas blanc; ou oeuvres posthumes du Gazetier*

cuirassé (1784, "imprimé à cent lieues de la Bastille"), pp. 194–195. See also the strikingly similar passage in *Vie privée de Louis XV, ou principaux événements, particularités et anecdotes de son règne* (London, 1781), IV, 139–140.

86. "Rousseaus of the gutter," a term applied to Restif de la Bretonne in the eighteenth century and that fits many of Restif's Grub Street comrades.

87. As an example of this widespread identification with Rousseau in opposition to Voltaire see *Le Tableau de Paris,* XI, 186.

88. For a striking account of a fortune laboriously built up by pensions and sinecures and then demolished by the Revolution see the *Mémoires de l'abbé Morellet sur le dix-huitième siècle et sur la Révolution,* 2 vols. (Paris, 1921). Chaps. 5–7, vol. II, gives a fascinating picture of an old veteran of the Enlightenment trying to communicate with young *sans-culottes,* who had no interest in the mid-century treatises he produced to prove the soundness of his principles but who wanted answers to questions like, "Why were you happy before the 10th of August and have you been sad since then?" (II, 124). Morellet could not make sense of the *sans-culottes* any more than they could understand him: a cultural revolution separated them.

89. After the abolition of the monopoly of the Comédie française, 45 new theaters sprang up in Paris; 1,500 new plays were produced between 1789 and 1799, 750 in the years 1792–1794, in contrast to the mere handful produced annually before the Revolution. These new plays may have derived more from the popular *foire* theater and *drames poissardes* than from the Comédie française, which catered to aristocratic audiences and even had direct access to the king, thanks to its governing board, made up of gentlemen of the king's bedchamber. Perhaps the genres of Grub Street (the *libelle* type of pamphlet and the *Père Duchesne* type of newspaper) gained ground as the Parisian populace gained power: the *lumpen* intelligentsia certainly knew how to speak the language of the common people. Most striking of all was the revolution that the Revolution wrought in journalism. Only a few dozen periodicals, none containing much news, circulated in Paris during the 1780s. At least 250 genuine newspapers were founded in the last six months of 1789, and at least 350 circulated in 1790. On the theater see John Lough, *Paris Theatre Audiences in the Seventeenth and*

Eighteenth Centuries (London, 1957); Jules Bonnassies, *Les Auteurs dramatiques;* and Beatrice Hyslop, "The Theatre During a Crisis: The Parisian Theatre During the Reign of Terror," *Journal of Modern History,* 17 (1945), 332–355. On the press see Eugène Hatin, *Bibliographie historique et critique de la presse périodique française* (Paris 1866); Eugène Hatin, *Histoire politique et littéraire de la presse en France* (Paris, 1859), especially chaps. 2–8; and Gérard Walter, *Hébert et le Père Duchesne* (Paris, 1946).

90. A. Rivarol and L. de Champcenetz, *Petit Dictionnaire des grands hommes de la Révolution* (1790). For a typical comment see p. vii: "It is by a perfect agreement between the rejects of the court and the rejects of fortune that we have arrived at this general impoverishment which alone testifies to our equality."

91. *Réimpression de l'ancien Moniteur* (Paris, 1861), V. 439.

92. Henri Grégoire, *Rapport et projet de décret, présenté au nom du Comité de l'instruction publique, à la séance du 8 août* (Paris, 1793). See also the *Discours du citoyen David, député de Paris, sur la nécessité de supprimer les académies* (Paris, 1793), made during the same session of the Convention; the polemics between Morellet and Chamfort (S. R. N. Chamfort, *Des académies,* Paris, 1791, and abbé André Morellet, *De l'Académie français,* Paris, 1791); and the debates on the cultural implications of the Revolution in the *Moniteur,* for example, VII, 115–120, 218–219, XVII, 176, XXII, 181–184, 191–193, XXIII, 127–128, 130–131. The classic statement of the revolutionaries' hatred for the Old Regime's cultural elitism remains Marat's *Les Charlatans modernes, ou lettres sur le charlatanisme académique* (Paris, 1791).

93. Albert Soboul touches on this theme in *Les Sans-culottes parisiens en l'an II* (Paris, 1958), pp. 670–673, and in "Classes populaires et rousseauisme," *Paysans, sans-culottes et Jacobins* (Paris, 1966), pp. 203–223.

94. Walter, *Hébert,* chaps. 1–2. See also R.-N.-D. Desgenettes (who knew Hébert as a starving hack writer before 1789), *Souvenirs de la fin du XVIIIe siècle et du commencement du XIXe siècle* (Paris, 1836), II, 237–254; and the description of the prerevolutionary Hébert printed in a Robespierrist *libelle* attacking him, *Vie privée et politique de J.-R. Hébert* (Paris, Year II), p. 13: "Without a shirt, without shoes, he only left the tiny room he rented on the seventh

floor in order to borrow some pennies from his friends or to pilfer them."

95. Gustave Lanson, *Voltaire,* trans. R. A. Wagoner (New York, 1966), p. 48.

2. A Spy in Grub Street

1. Daniel Mornet, *Les origines intellectuelles de la Révolution française* (1715–1787), 5th ed. (Paris, 1954), p. 410.

2. For a detailed account of Brissot's early life see Eloise Ellery, *Brissot de Warville: A Study in the History of the French Revolution* (Boston and New York, 1915).

3. J.-P. Brissot, *Réplique de J. P. Brissot à Charles Théveneau Morande* (Paris, 1791), p. 20. Brissot set his total loss from the Lycée at 18,000 livres (p. 21).

4. This is the Society's evaluation of Brissot's debt, according to its copy of a letter it sent to him on Oct. 12, 1784. Papers of the Société typographique, Bibliothèque de la ville de Neuchâtel, referred to henceforth as STN.

5. An accompanying list of books and prices has been omitted.

6. A Parisian bookseller who specialized in the underground trade and handled most of Brissot's works.

7. Brissot to STN, Oct. 22, 1784.

8. For a detailed account of Clavière's subsidies and the services he received in return see Robert Darnton, "Trends in Radical Propaganda on the Eve of the French Revolution (1782–1788)," Ph.D. diss., Oxford, University, 1964, pp. 179–195.

9. Bibliothèque de la ville de Neuchâtel, MS. 1137.

10. J. P. Marat, "Traits destinés au portrait du jésuite Brissot," an article in *L'Ami du peuple,* June 4, 1792, reprinted in *Annales révolutionnaires,* 5 (1912), 689.

11. Ibid., p. 685.

12. Marat to Brissot, in J.-P. Brissot, *Correspondance et papiers,* ed. Claude Perroud (Paris, 1912), p. 78. See also Brissot to Marat, June 6, 1782, pp. 33–35.

13. Jean François-Primo, *La jeunesse de Brissot* (Paris, 1939).

14. Ellery, *Brissot de Warville,* p. 268.

15. Claude Perroud's account of Brissot's life, probably the most influential one in French, in his edition of Brissot's *Correspondance et papiers,* p. xxxv.

16. Hippolyte Taine, *Les origines de la France contemporaine: La Révolution,* 15th ed. (Paris, 1894), II, 133.

17. Albert Mathiez, *La Révolution française* (Paris, 1922), I, 186. Mathiez's hostile portrait of Brissot resembles that by his master, Jean Jaurès, who did not, however, mention the spying charge. Jean Jaurès, *Histoire socialiste de la Révolution française,* ed. Albert Mathiez (Paris, 1928), III, 69.

18. Pierre Gaxotte, *La Révolution française* (Paris, 1928), p. 233.

19. Jules Michelet, *Histoire de la Révolution française,* Bibliothèque de la Pléiade, ed. Gérard Walter (Paris, 1952), I, 850–851, 862, II, 47; M. F. A. de Lescure, ed., *Mémoires de Brissot* (Paris, 1877), pp. xl, lvi; Louis Blanc, *Histoire de la Révolution française* (Paris, 1847–1862), VI, 289–292, VIII, 500. Although the other historians of the Revolution have not pronounced on Brissot's alleged spying, they have unavoidably assessed his role as a leader of the Girondins. The more recent assessments by Georges Lefebvre, J. M. Thompson, and Crane Brinton credit his honesty and idealism, if not his political genius. They show more indulgence for him, oddly, than did Lamartine, who voiced skepticism about the integrity of the "homme mixte, moitié d'intrigue, moitié de vertu," at least in the beginning of his *apologia* for the Girondins; by the end, Brissot walked to the guillotine with his colleagues as the apotheosis of moderate revolutionary idealism. See Georges Lefebvre, *La Révolution française,* Peuples et civilisations, XIII (Paris, 1951), 226; J. M. Thompson, *Leaders of the French Revolution* (New York, 1962), pp. 67–91; Crane Brinton, *A Decade of Revolution, 1789–1799,* The Rise of Modern Europe, XI (New York and London, 1934), 106; and Alphonse de Lamartine, *Histoire des Girondins* (Paris, 1847), I, 235–241 (quotation p. 241), VII, 36.

20. F. A. Aulard, *Danton* (Paris, 1903), p. 8.

21. Taine, *Les origines,* II, 133, in Widener Library, Harvard University, Cambridge, Mass., Fr. 1327.144.5.

22. F. A. Aulard, *Les orateurs de la Révolution: La Législative et la Convention* (Paris, 1906), I, 218–263, quotation p. 221.

23. André Amar, "Acte d'accusation contre plusieurs membres de la Convention Nationale, présenté au nom du Comité du Sûreté

Générale, par André Amar, membre de ce Comité," *Réimpression de l'ancien Moniteur* (Paris, 1841), Oct. 25, 1793, XVIII, 200. The charge, together with other references to Brissot's prerevolutionary career, was lost in the verbose, confusing, and inconclusive testimony about the intrigues and policies of the Girondins, as reported in the *Moniteur* and the *Bulletin du Tribunal criminel révolutionnaire* (Paris, 1793), nos. 34–64, pp. 133–256. The biased editors of these publications may have cut a reply by Brissot to the accusation of spying, for they interrupted his testimony at one point with the same remark: "L'accusé fait ici une longue et verbeuse apologie de sa conduite" (ibid., p. 181). Saint-Just had little to say about Brissot's prerevolutionary career: his report is in the *Moniteur,* July 18 and 19, 1793, XVIII, 146–150, 153–158.

24. Brissot, *Mémoires,* II, 277.

25. *François Chabot à Jean-Pierre* [sic] *Brissot* (1792).

26. Cloots clearly aimed his attack at Brissot but did not mention him by name. The speech is in F. A. Aulard, *La Société des Jacobins: Recueil de documents pour l'histoire du club des Jacobins de Paris* (Paris, 1889–1897), IV, 520.

27. *Vie privée et politique de Brissot* (Paris, Year II), p. 12.

28. *Oeuvres de Maximilien Robespierre,* ed. Marc Bouloiseau, Georges Lefebvre, Jean Dautry, and Albert Soboul (Paris, 1958), IX, 592.

29. Joachim Vilate, *Les mystères de la mère de dieu dévoilés* (Paris, Year III), p. 51.

30. *Jean-Pierre* [sic] *Brissot démasqué* (originally published in Feb. 1792), in *Oeuvres de Camille Desmoulins,* ed. Jules Claretie (Paris, 1874), I, 267. Desmoulins did not repeat the charge in his *Histoire des Brissotins* published in May 1793.

31. Rivarol's letter, reprinted in *Ecrits et pamphlets de Rivarol, recueillis pour la première fois et annotés par A.-P. Malassis* (Paris, 1877), contains the remark, exactly as Desmoulins reported it, on p. 115. Following an article by Maurice Tourneux in *L'intermédiaire des chercheurs et des curieux,* 24 (Jan. 25, 1891), 62, Ellery (*Brissot de Warville,* pp. 243–244) traces the Rivarol letter to *Les Actes des Apôtres,* no. 261. This number, however, contains only some irrelevant "Fragments de la correspondance secrète du Baron de Grimm avec la première fonctionnaire publique de toutes les

Russies." Tourneux attributed the Rivarol letter to another issue of *Les Actes des Apôtres* in his edition of the *Correspondance littéraire, philosophique et critique par Grimm, Diderot, Raynal, Meister, etc.* (Paris, 1880), XVI, 265, but I have not been able to find the original. Rivarol and Champcenetz expressed their views of the Revolution's leaders in *Petit dictionnaire des grands hommes de la Révolution* (1790), which contains a satirical attack on Brissot.

32. Brissot, *Mémoires,* II, 277.

33. J.-P. Brissot, *Réplique de J. P. Brissot à la Premiére et dernière lettre de Louis-Marthe Gouy, défenseur de la traite des noirs et de l'esclavage* (Paris, 1791), p. 42.

34. *Journal de Paris,* March 13, 1792. See also Pange's articles in the *Journal de Paris* of March 18 and 25, 1792, and the anonymous attacks on Brissot in the issues of March 6 and 16, 1792. Brissot's pamphlet, *Les moyens d'adoucir la rigueur des lois pénales en France* (Châlons-sur-Marne, 1781), praised Lenoir on p. 43.

35. *Journal de Paris,* March 13, 1792. Chénier's letter criticized the *lâcheté* of such praise, but it shied away from a direct challenge to Brissot on the spying issue, contrary to the inaccurate account of it in Vernon Loggins, *André Chénier: His Life, Death and Glory* (Athens, Ohio, 1965), p. 161.

36. *Le Patriote français,* March 7, 1791 (italics in the original). For background on this quarrel see ibid., March 13, 1791.

37. Ibid., Oct. 7, 1790.

38. *Bulletin du Tribunal Criminel Révolutionnaire,* no. 45, p. 177. An even more fanciful version of Brissot's career, attributed to Joel Barlow, made him an "agent of the police" well after the fall of the Bastille: "A Sketch of the Life of J. P. Brissot by the Editor" in a translation of Brissot's *Nouveau voyage dans les Etats-Unis,* entitled *New Travels in the United States of America Performed in M.DCC. LXXXVIII by J. P. Brissot de Warville* (London, 1794), II, xxx.

39. The most effective in the barrage of pamphlets that Morande delivered against Brissot was *Réplique de Charles Théveneau Morande à Jacques-Pierre Brissot sur les erreurs, les oublis, les infidélités et les calomnies de sa Réponse* (Paris, 1791). The accusation of spying also failed to appear in the somewhat milder volleys of pamphlets exchanged between Brissot and Stanislas de Clermont-Tonnerre in the autumn of 1790.

40. Etienne Dumont, who kept a sense of objectivity in his friendship with Brissot, considered him a virtuous but dangerously partisan zealot: *Souvenirs sur Mirabeau et sur les deux premières assemblées législatives,* ed. Joseph Bénétruy (Paris, 1951), pp. 178, 192, 203. Other friends of Brissot, notably Pétion and Mme. Roland, produced stronger but more biased declarations of faith in his honesty.

41. Bibliothèque municipale d'Orléans, MS. 1422. After looking through these papers, Georges Lefebvre found no reason to doubt their authenticity: "Les papiers de Lenoir," *Annales historiques de la Révolution française,* 4 (1927), 300. On Lenoir and the police of Paris see Maxime de Sars, *Le Noir, lieutenant de police 1732–1807* (Paris, 1948).

42. *Le Patriote français,* Aug. 10, 1790. It may be relevant to note that in 1781 Brissot expressed horror at police spying: *Théorie des lois criminelles* ("Berlin," 1781), II, 177. For the character of the anti-Lenoir pamphleteering see Jean-Louis Carra's opening attack, *L'An 1787. Précis de l'administration de la bibliothèque du roi sous M. Le Noir* (Liège, 1788).

43. Brissot, *Mémoires,* II, 23.

44. J.-P. Brissot, *J. P. Brissot, membre du comité de recherches de la municipalité à Stanislas Clermont* (Paris, 1790), pp. 34–35. The most important gap in the papers at the Bibliothèque de L'Arsénal comes in MS. 12454, which contains nothing about Brissot but a great deal about his fellow prisoners of 1784, notably his old friend the Marquis de Pelleport, who was arrested in connection with Brissot on the charge of producing *libelles* against members of the French court. Other police records concerning Brissot may have been destroyed with the Hôtel de Ville in 1871.

45. Bibliothèque de l'Arsénal, MS. 12517, fol. 77 *bis.*

46. P. L. Manuel and others, *La Bastille dévoilée, ou recueil de pièces authentiques pour servir à son histoire* (Paris, 1789), *troisième livraison,* p. 78. How much of this work can be attributed to Manuel is doubtful. He seems to have been one of several writers who used the papers of the Bastille as a source for some sensational, lucrative, and safely expurgated pamphleteering.

47. Archive Nationales, W295; Manuel, *La Bastille dévoilée,* pp. 105–106.

48. Bibliothèque municipale d'Orléans, MS. 1422.

49. Bibliothèque municipale d'Orléans, MS. 1423, entitled "Rapport des inspecteurs ayant les départements de la librairie et des étrangers." Robert Pigott was a radical English Quaker, who was still in touch with Brissot during the early years of the Revolution, when he contributed articles to *Le Patriote français*.

50. Jacques Peuchet, *Mémoires tirés des archives de la police de Paris* (Paris, 1838), III, 17. Peuchet added that he himself did not credit this report (p. 18), but it would not contradict the picture of Mirabeau's checkered career that emerges from Charles de Loménie's *Les Mirabeau, nouvelles études sur la société française au 18ᵉ siècle* (Paris, 1889), III and IV, and Jean Bouchary's *Les manieurs d'argent à Paris à la fin du XVIIIᵉ siècle* (Paris, 1939), I. The latter has been incorporated in Joseph Bénétruy's *L'Atelier de Mirabeau: Quatre proscrits genevois dans la tourmente révolutionnaire* (Geneva and Paris, 1962). In an almost illegible note among his papers, Lenoir scribbled, "The famous Comte de Mirabeau had been employed by the lieutenant of police, the famous Brissot de Warville also. The police employed them in producing and [circulating?] pamphlets." Bibliothèque municipale d'Orléans, MS. 1422.

51. Brissot, *Mémoires*, II, 7–8. See also Paul Robiquet, *Théveneau de Morande, étude sur le XVIIIᵉ siècle* (Paris, 1882).

52. Brissot, *Réplique . . . à Morande,* p. 25. Brissot added, "I have always especially held in horror the genre of personal libel." Brissot did not challenge the authenticity of the letter from his agent, Vingtaine, dated April 3, 1784, which Morande printed in his *Réplique . . . à Brissot,* p. 106. The extensive correspondence about the *libellistes* in the archives of the Ministère des affaires étrangères, Correspondance politique, Angleterre, MSS. 541–549, treats Brissot as a companion but not an accomplice of them.

53. Marat, "Traits destinés," p. 686. On Sept. 16, 1781, the Society wrote to Brissot, refusing to print an obscene work that he had sent on behalf of Desauges; yet it printed a pirated edition of *Les liaisons dangereuses,* which Brissot reviewed with horror in his *Journal du Licée* [sic] *de Londres* (London, 1784), I 389–391, and his *Correspondance universelle sur ce qui intéresse le bonheur de l'homme et de la société* (London, 1783), where he maintained, "A novel with an equivocal moral message is a very dangerous poison" (p. 124). The Society sold, but did not print, much pornography, including some

written by Mirabeau and published in Neuchâtel by a former partner, Samuel Fauche.

54. Brissot, *Mémoires*, I, 104–106.

55. Brissot to STN, July 26, 1781.

56. Brissot to STN, Jan. 12, 1782.

57. Brissot to STN, April 23, 1781. Brissot also indicated an official source for his report of the government's measure against the continuation of Linguet's *Annales politiques, civiles et littéraires du dix-huitième siècle* by Mallet du Pan; "You can be sure that none of Mallet's journals have got through here. They have all been confiscated. I know that from the very man who had them confiscated." Brissot to STN, Aug. 18, 1782.

58. Quandet to STN, June 20, 1781. Quandet was referring to a seizure of a shipment of the nineteen-volume *Description des arts et métiers,* which was published by the Society and banned from France, owing to the machinations of one of the Society's French competitors.

59. Brissot to STN, March 30, 1782.

60. *Le Patriote français,* July 31, 1790.

61. Brissot to [Martin], Oct. 21, 1784, in Brissot, *Correspondance et papiers,* pp. *83–85*. The context of this letter indicates that its unnamed addressee was Martin.

62. Brissot to STN, Sept. 22, 1782.

63. J. F. Bornand to STN, Feb. 19, 1785.

64. *Journal du Licée de Londres,* I, 223. On p. 225 Brissot described the state of his *âme électrisée* after reading the *Confessions* for the third time.

65. Brissot, *Mémoires*, I, 14, 18. Brissot acknowledged the model for his "portrait of Phédor"—"The reading of Rousseau's Confessions, which I am now taking up for the sixth time, reminds me of some traits that belong to him [Phedor]" (I, 18)—and for his memoirs—"I shall imitate Rousseau" (I, 24).

3. A Pamphleteer on the Run

1. This and the following extracts of Voltaire's poem come from "Le Pauvre Diable," in *Oeuvres complètes de Voltaire* (Paris, 1877), pp. 99–113.

2. Le Senne does not appear in any standard biographical dictionary, bibliography, or catalogue of printed books, not even in the gossipy *Mémoires secrets pour servir à l'histoire de la république des lettres en France* or in Voltaire's correspondence, where the names of a great many obscure writers turn up. This study is therefore based almost entirely on a unique source: the Papers of the Société typographique de Neuchâtel (hereafter cited as STN) in the Bibliothèque de la ville de Neuchâtel, Switzerland.

3. Lans de Boissy to STN, March 9, 1780: "It is very nice to believe in God, especially in Switzerland, but that doesn't provide much amusement; and your journal can only succeed by having a philosophic tincture." For further details see Lans's letters of Jan. 21 and Feb. 19, 1780, and the undated "Prospectus" in his dossier, which stresses the journal's potential role in the philosophes' fight against *fanatisme.*

4. Bosset to STN, May 17, 1780. In describing his negotiations with d'Alembert to the home office, Bosset added, 'Il m'a paru tenir beaucoup à la partie lucrative de ses oeuvres."

5. Le Senne included the prospectus in his letter to the STN of Feb. 3, 1780.

6. Le Senne to STN, Feb. 3, 1780.

7. Ibid.

8. Le Senne to STN, March 18, 1780.

9. These remarks occurred in a memorandum entitled "Réponse aux conditions proposées," undated but evidently from May 1780, in Le Senne's dossier.

10. Le Senne to STN, March 26, 1780.

11. Bosset to STN, May 15 and 17, 1780.

12. Panckoucke's success in obstructing the entry of the *Journal helvétique* was confirmed a year later by an agent of the STN, who reported, "Panckoucke is moving heaven and earth, nothing is advancing in the offices of the Keeper of the Seals." Thiriot to STN, May 5, 1781. On the construction of Panckoucke's press empire see Suzanne Tucoo-Chala, *Charles-Joseph Panckoucke & la librairie française 1736–1798* (Pau and Paris, 1977).

13. Le Senne to STN, May 20, 1780.

14. Le Senne to STN, May 14, 1780.

15. Quandet de Lachenal to STN, Oct. 26, 1781.

16. Le Senne to STN, Feb. 3, 1780.

17. Le Senne to STN, March 18, 1780.

18. Undated memorandum from Le Senne's dossier, written sometime in the spring of 1780.

19. Le Senne to STN, April 2, 1780.

20. Le Senne to STN, April 8, 1780.

21. Le Senne to STN, April 19, 1780.

22. Le Senne to STN, May 24, 1780.

23. Le Senne to STN, May 27, 1780.

24. Le Senne to STN, April 19, 1780.

25. Le Senne to STN, June 11, 1780.

26. Bosset to STN, June 12, 1780.

27. Bosset described Cugnet's proposal in his letter of June 12, 1780.

28. Le Senne to STN, May 27, 1780. Le Senne described the Cugnet project in more detail in a letter dated May 29, 1780.

29. Le Senne to STN, June 11, 1780.

30. Bosset to STN, June 19, 1780.

31. Le Senne to STN, July 25, 1780.

32. Le Senne to STN, Oct. 5, 1780.

33. Cugnet to STN, Oct. 12, 1780.

34. Cugnet to STN, April 2, 1781.

35. Le Senne to STN, Sept. 20, 1780.

36. Le Senne to STN, Oct. 5, 1780.

37. Le Senne to STN, Oct. 12, 1780.

38. Ibid.

39. STN to Le Senne, Nov. 19, 1780. The last letter from Cugnet was dated Oct. 12, the same day, or thereabout, as Le Senne's flight from Paris. See also the STN's letter to Cugnet of Nov. 21, in which it complained that it had sent three persons to deal with him and none of them had been able to find his shop.

40. Le Senne to STN, Dec. 2, 1780.

41. STN to Le Senne, Dec. 10, 1780.

42. D'Alembert to STN, Dec. 30, 1780. This is a copy in the STN papers. There is no reason to doubt its authenticity, although I have not been able to find the original. Ostervald and Bosset knew d'Alembert reasonably well, having negotiated with him at length over the publication of his works. On June 14, 1780, Bosset wrote

home about the following session with him: "He showed me some manuscripts, which would make an octavo volume of opuscules that he intended to give us to print. I proposed various arrangements to him for this item. It seemed to me that the one he would like most, which he proposed to me himself, would be for us to advance the cost of the printing and paper and then for him to split the profits with us ... After that he will have about three volumes of eulogies, but they are not ready yet ... He is talking about coming to Switzerland." Le Senne had participated in these negotiations. He seems to have occupied a place near the center of d'Alembert's entourage, and he was one source for the remark attributed to Frederick II at the time when Frederick agreed to have a service said for the soul of Voltaire: "Although I don't much believe in eternity, I consent to it." Bosset to STN, June 23, 1780. See also Bosset's letter of June 16, 1780.

43. D'Alembert to Frederick II, July 24, 1780, in *Oeuvres de d'Alembert* (Paris, 1822), V, 431: "M. de Catt will give to Your Majesty a new memorandum and some authentic certificates in favor of the poor curé of Neuchâtel, who is being persecuted by his fanatical bishop. Your Majesty is requested to take this detail into consideration and to obtain justice for this poor devil of a priest, who has expected it and asked for it for a long time." The "of Neuchâtel" must have been a slip of the pen.

44. Le Senne to STN, Dec. 18, 1780. Le Senne's "Observations patriotiques" could have been the Neckerite treatise on "L'Administration physique et morale de la France," which he had proposed to the STN earlier. But he made so many proposals, handled so many manuscripts, and changed titles so often that it is impossible to identify the works he mentioned in his letters.

45. STN to Le Senne, Dec. 24, 1780.

46. Le Senne to STN, Dec. 28, 1780.

47. STN to Le Senne, Jan. 4. 1781.

48. Le Senne to STN, Jan. 9, 1781.

49. *Mémoires secrets pour servir à l'histoire de la république des lettres en France* (London, 1777–1789), 36 vols., entries for June 4, June 30, and July 11, 1780.

50. Le Senne to STN, Jan. 9, 1781.

51. Le Senne to STN, Feb. 9, 1781.
52. STN to Le Senne, Feb. 25, 1781.
53. Quandet de Lachenal to STN, March 7, 1781.
54. STN to Quandet, March 11, 1781.
55. The analysis of Le Senne's embezzlement is based primarily on the STN's correspondence with Quandet, especially the STN's letter of March 11, 1781, and Quandet's letters of March 23 and April 2, 1781.
56. Le Senne to STN, April 23, 1781.
57. Cugnet to STN, April 2, 1781. Cugnet added that Le Senne was "in very bad odor" in Paris and explained that he had bought the books from Le Senne because the abbé had not been able to pay for their transport and because the abbé Bretin, who had originally paid the transport bill upon their arrival in Brunoy, would not release them until he had been reimbursed. Thus, despite what he wrote to the STN, Le Senne had never had the books in his possession and probably was destitute at the time of his flight from Paris.
58. STN to Cugnet, April 8, 1781.
59. On the breviary project see Le Senne to STN, May 8, May 25, and July 11, 1781; STN to Le Senne, May 17, June 2, and July 17, 1781; and STN to the Abbot of Cîteaux, June 2, 1781. The abbot never answered the STN's letter.
60. Le Senne to STN, May 25, 1781.
61. Le Senne to STN, July 11, 1781.
62. Le Senne to STN, Aug. 27, 1781.
63. Le Senne to STN, Nov. 26, 1781.
64. STN to Le Senne, Dec. 9, 1781.
65. Le Senne to STN, Dec. 22, 1781.
66. Le Senne to STN, March 17, 1782.
67. Le Senne to STN, June 4, 1782. See also Le Senne's letters of April 3, April 25, June 23, and Aug. 2, 1782.
68. Le Senne to STN, June 23 and Aug. 8, 1782.
69. Quandet to STN, Oct. 2, 1782.
70. Le Senne to STN, Aug. 15, 1782.
71. Le Senne to STN, April 26, 1784.
72. Le Senne to STN, Sept. 18, 1784.
73. "Le Pauvre Diable," p. 99.

74. Denis Diderot, *Le Neveu de Rameau,* ed. Georges Monval (Paris, 1891), p. 91.

75. Pat Rogers, *Grub Street: Studies in a Subculture* (London, 1972).

76. Le Senne to STN, May 27, 1780.

77. On this theme see John McManners, *French Ecclesiastical Society Under the Old Regime: A Study of Angers in the Eighteenth Century* (Manchester, 1960), chaps. 9–11.

78. Aside from the correspondence itself, where this theme stands out clearly, see John N. Pappas, *Voltaire and d'Alembert* (Bloomington, Ind., 1962).

79. *Le Neveu de Rameau,* p. 164.

80. Ibid., pp. 165–166.

81. Ibid., p. 47.

82. Ibid., pp. 109, 113.

4. *A Clandestine Bookseller in the Provinces*

1. Mauvelain to STN, April 14, 1781, Papers of the Société typographique de Neuchâtel, Bibliothèque de la ville, Neuchâtel, Switzerland. All references are to these papers, unless indicated otherwise.

2. Mauvelain to STN, May 8, 1781.

3. Mauvelain to STN, June 5, 1781.

4. Mauvelain to STN, May 19, 1782.

5. Mauvelain to STN, Jan. 10, 1783.

6. Mauvelain to STN, Jan. 29, 1783.

7. Mauvelain to STN, April 9, 1783.

8. Mauvelain to STN, May 3 and June 7, 1783.

9. Mauvelain to STN, May 17, 1784.

10. Mauvelain to STN, Nov. 2, 1783.

11. Mauvelain to STN, May 31, 1784.

12. Mauvelain to STN, June 16, 1784.

13. Mauvelain to STN, May 10 and June 16, 1784.

14. Mauvelain to STN, Sept. 24, 1784.

15. STN to Mauvelain, Sept. 26, 1784.

16. Faivre to STN, Aug. 14, 1784.

17. Faivre to STN, Sept. 23, 1784.

18. Mauvelain to STN, Dec. 31, 1784.

19. Mauvelain to STN, March 12, 1785.

20. Mauvelain to STN, May 27, 1785.

21. STN to J.-P. Brissot, Feb. 13, 1787.

22. Charles Théveneau de Morande, *Le Portefeuille de Madame Gourdan, dite la comtesse* (Spa, 1783), reprinted as *Correspondance de Madame Gourdan, dite la comtesse* (Paris, 1954), p. 41.

23. *La Chronique scandaleuse* (Paris, 1783), p. 38.

24. *Les Fastes de Louis XV* (Villefranche, 1782), II, 27.

25. Ibid., p. 296.

5. *A Printing Shop across the Border*

1. Thomas to STN, July 19, 1778. On this episode in the recruiting campaign see Pyre to STN, June 16, 1777, and STN to Pyre, July 1, 1777.

2. Christ to STN, Jan. 8, 1773.

3. STN to Pyre, Oct. 14, 1777.

4. STN to Vernange, May 24, 1777.

5. Claudet to STN, June 18, 1777.

6. STN to Claudet, May 8, 1777.

7. STN to Duplain, July 2, 1777.

8. STN to Vernange, June 26, 1777.

9. "Banque des ouvriers" of the STN, entry for Jan. 16, 1779.

10. Pfaehler to STN, March 3, 1772.

11. Mme. Bertrand to Ostervald of the STN, Feb. 12, 1780.

12. Offray to Ducret of the STN, Dec. 1770, cited in Jacques Rychner, "A l'ombre des Lumières: coup d'oeil sur la main-d'oeuvre de quelques imprimeries du XVIIIème siècle," *Studies on Voltaire and the Eighteenth Century,* 155 (1976), 1948-1949. When Jacques Rychner completes his dissertation on the STN, it will be possible to follow the peregrinations of the journeyman printers in splendid detail.

13. Ibid.

14. See, for example, Nicolas Contat *dit* Le Brun, *Anecdotes typographiques où l'on voit la description des coutumes, moeurs et usages singuliers des compagnons imprimeurs,* ed. Giles Barber (Oxford, 1980), pt. II, chap. 2.

15. Some of these data appear in chapter 5 of my book, *The Business of Enlightenment: A Publishing History of the "Encyclopédie," 1775–1800* (Cambridge, Mass., 1979), but most of them remain unpublished.

16. Leon Voet, *The Golden Compasses* (Amsterdam, 1972), II, 351.

17. Contat, *Anecdotes typographiques,* pt. I, chap. 3.

18. Ibid., pt. II, chap. 1.

19. Ibid., chap. 2.

20. Ibid., pt. I, chap. 6.

6. Reading, Writing, and Publishing

1. Walter Benjamin, "Unpacking My Library: A Talk about Book Collecting," in *Illuminations,* ed. Hannah Arendt (New York, 1968).

2. Daniel Mornet, "Les enseignements des bibliothèques privées (1750–1780)," *Revue d'histoire littéraire de la France,* 17 (1910), 449–492.

3. Although he carefully qualified the conclusions in his article, Mornet made more sweeping statements in his later work. He wrongly implied that his research on the *Social Contract* was valid for the period after 1780: "This redoubtable book was hardly talked about before 1789." Daniel Mornet, "L'influence de J.-J. Rousseau au XVIIIe siècle," *Annales Jean-Jacques Rousseau,* 8 (1912), 44. See also Daniel Mornet, *Rousseau, l'homme et l'oeuvre* (Paris, 1950), pp. 102–106, and Daniel Mornet, *Les Origines intellectuelles de la Révolution Française,* 5th ed. (Paris, 1954), p. 229. Robert Derathé accepted Mornet's interpretation: "Les réfutations du *Contrat Social* au XVIIIe siècle," *Annales de la Société Jean-Jacques Rousseau,* 32 (1950–1952), 7–12. And Alfred Cobban extended it: "Rousseau's *Contrat social* had no ascertainable influence before the Revolution and only a very debatable one during its course"; see his "The Enlightenment and the French Revolution," reprinted in *Aspects of the French Revolution* (New York, 1968), p. 22. The fullest version is Joan McDonald, *Rousseau and the French Revolution, 1762–1791* (London, 1965).

4. See R. A. Leigh, "Jean-Jacques Rousseau," *The Historical Journal,* 12 (1969), 549–565.

5. Although Rousseau's treatise was too abstruse to provoke the sort of controversy that followed *Emile* and his discourses (except in Switzerland), its influence, like all ideological influence, is difficult to measure. If repression is any indication of importance, it should be noted that the French state never formally condemned the *Contrat social* but did not permit it to circulate freely. The revolutionaries found it locked up with other seditious literature in the *pilon* of the Bastille. Bibliothèque de l'Arsenal, MS. 10305, "le pilon de la Bastille."

6. Escarpit's book was published in the widely read "Que Sais-Je" series and has already gone through four editions. As an example of its influence see Louis Trenard, "La sociologie du livre en France (1750-1789)," *Actes du cinquième Congrès national de la Société française de littérature comparée* (Paris, 1965), p. 145.

7. Robert Escarpit, *Sociologie de la littérature,* 4th ed. (Paris, 1968), p. 46. It should be noted also that the development of writing as a *métier* in the eighteenth century did not correspond to the sociological phenomenon of professionalization. See the article "Professions" by Talcott Parsons in the *International Encyclopedia of the Social Sciences,* XII, 536-547.

8. David Pottinger, *The French Book Trade in the Ancien Régime, 1500-1791* (Cambridge, Mass., 1958).

9. The studies, to be cited henceforth by name of author, are: François Furet, "La 'librairie' du royaume de France au 18e siècle," in *Livre et société dans la France du XVIIIème siècle,* 1 (Paris and The Hague, 1965); Jean Ehrard and Jacques Roger, "Deux périodiques français du 18e siècle: 'le Journal des savants' et 'les Mémoires de Trévoux.' Essai d'une étude quantitative," in the same volume; Daniel Roche, "Un savant et sa bibliothèque au XVIIIe siècle: les livres de Jean-Jacques Dortous de Mairan, secrétaire perpétuel de l'Académie des sciences, membre de l'Académie de Béziers," *Dix-huitième siècle,* 1 (1969), 47-88; François Bluche, *Les magistrats du Parlement de Paris au XVIIIe siècle, 1715-1771* (Paris, 1960), pp. 291-296, which incorporates the findings of an unpublished study by Régine Petit, *Les bibliothèques des hommes du parlement de Paris au XVIIIe siècle* (1954); and Jean Meyer, *La noblesse bretonne au XVIIIe siècle* (Paris, 1966), pp. 1156-1177.

10. Furet, p. 19.

11. Ehrard and Roger, p. 56.

12. Mornet, "Les enseignements des bibliothèques privées," p. 473.

13. Quotation cited in Raymond Birn, "Le Journal des savants sous l'Ancien Régime," *Journal des savants* (Jan.–March 1965), p. 28, and in Eugène Hatin, *Histoire politique et littéraire de la presse en France* (Paris, 1859–1861), II, 192.

14. Jean-Louis and Marie Flandrin, "La circulation du livre dans la société du 18e siècle: un sondage à travers quelques sources," *Livre et société*, 2 (Paris and The Hague, 1970), 52–91. The Flandrins studied three private or at least uncensored literary journals, which discussed philosophic works that could not be mentioned in the pages of quasi-official, heavily censored periodicals like the *Journal des savants*. But the Flandrins' three journals show the opposite bias from those studied by Ehrard and Roger. They discussed mainly sensational books—books that made news—and thus do not represent the general literary tastes of their readers any more than do the *Journal des savants* and the Jesuit *Mémoires de Trévoux*.

15. Trenard, "La sociologie du livre en France."

16. The main problem in constructing these graphs was to find comparable units and statistics for them in the eight studies under analysis. In order to make comparisons possible, it was necessary to redo some of the mathematics and to reconvert some of the data that appeared in graph form in the two articles published in *Livre et société*. The graphs all refer to the mid-century, although they represent slightly different time spans. The subjects that do not appear on them mostly concern the various "arts" catalogued under the heading *sciences et arts*. Because that heading seemed too broad to mean much to the modern reader, it was replaced by the subcategory "sciences." Composed of four subsubcategories—*physique, médecine, histoire naturelle,* and *mathématiques*—the "sciences" could be computed in every case except those of Mornet and Bluche-Petit. Mornet gave no statistics on mathematical books, but the omission probably concerned much less than 1 percent of all his titles and so did not affect the general pattern. Bluche did not differentiate "sciences" from *sciences et arts* at all. Although the subcategory "sciences" varied widely in other cases (from 10 percent to 70 percent of the general category), it seemed reasonable to estimate it

at half of Bluche's *sciences et arts* or 7 percent of the total—a rough approximation indicated by broken lines that the reader may prefer to discount. Mornet's figures covered only *romans* and *grammaires* in the category "belles-lettres," which probably left out a little over half that category, judging from the distribution in Furet's *permissions publiques* and *permissions tacites*. The category probably would have occupied between 10 percent and 20 percent of Mornet's total and is indicated at 15 percent by broken lines. Unlike the others, Mornet did not classify travel literature with history, as was the practice in the eighteenth century. Had he done so, his "history" division would have expanded by another 1.5 percent. Meyer's "belles-lettres" also is approximate and therefore appears in broken lines.

A graph combining Furet's studies of *permissions publiques* and *permissions tacites* was constructed from computations based on his original data, because it was hoped that an overall picture of literary output would emerge by combining statistics from those two very different sources. Suggestive as it is, this composite bar graph contradicts all the others. For example, it somewhat resembles the graph based on Mornet's statistics, but Mornet would have the French reading far fewer religious works (6 percent) in relation to science (3 percent) and especially history (30 percent) than would Furet, whose combined graph shows 20 percent religion, 9 percent science, and 11 percent history.

Because all eight studies kept close to the eighteenth-century classification scheme, they do not give much help to the modern reader in search of the Enlightenment. Does he associate Enlightenment with *philosophie,* one of the eight subcategories under *sciences et arts?* If so, he must contend with four sibling subsubcategories: *philosophie ancienne, logique, morale,* and *métaphysique.* The last two seem promising, but (except in Roche's statistics, which include two additional subsubcategories) the data do not distinguish them from their two predecessors. The four studies that provide statistics on *philosophie* as a whole suggest it comprised a small, stable portion of eighteenth-century reading: the *permissions publiques* fix it at 3 percent (1723–1727), 3.7 percent (1750–1754), and 4.5 percent (1784–1788); the *permissions tacites* at 6 percent (1750–1759), 5 percent (1770–1774), and 6 percent (1784–1788); the reviews in the *Journal des savants* at 3 percent

(1715–1719), 4 percent (1750–1754), and 5 percent (1785–1789); and it made up 7 percent of Dortous de Mairan's library. Not much evidence for the spread of *Lumières*. But then the Enlightenment cannot be identified with any of the eighteenth-century categories or their subdivisions.

It would also be possible to express Pottinger's study of 200 eighteenth-century authors in a bar graph, because he produced a statistical table of their publications, taking Mornet's work as a model. But, as explained above, Pottinger's selection of writers is so arbitrary and his statistics are so incomplete and unrepresentative that the graph would not mean very much. Nonetheless, for purposes of comparison, his findings ought to be mentioned (Pottinger, *The French Book Trade,* pp. 30–31): religious works 11 percent of the total produced by his authors, science 20 percent, history 20 percent, law 2 percent, belles-lettres 10 percent.

17. The figure is based on the Maggiolo study of literacy as presented by Michel Fleury and Pierre Valmary in "Les progrès de l'instruction élémentaire de Louis XIV à Napoléon III d'après l'enquête de Louis Maggiolo (1877–1879)," *Population* (1957), pp. 71–92, estimating the population at 26 million.

18. After 1969, when this essay was written, quantitative studies of book diffusion began to proliferate. The most important were the articles by Julien Brancolini, Marie-Thérèse Bouyssy, Jean-Louis Flandrin, and Maria Flandrin in *Livre et société,* 2 (Paris and The Hague, 1970); Jean Quéniart, *L'Imprimerie et la librairie à Rouen au XVIIIe siècle* (Paris, 1969); René Moulinas, *L'Imprimerie, la librairie et la presse à Avignon au XVIIIe siècle* (Grenoble, 1974); Michel Marion, *Recherches sur les bibliothèques privées à Paris au milieu du XVIIIe siècle* (1750–1759) (Paris, 1978), and the articles appearing regularly in *Revue française d'histoire du livre.* As a result, we now have a much richer picture of eighteenth-century reading habits. The picture remains confused, however, because the monographs cover different kinds of data and often contradict one another. The run of bar graphs could be extended indefinitely, but where will it all lead?

19. The following account is based primarily on the papers of the STN. Other important sources were the papers of Jean-Charles-Pierre Lenoir, *lieutenant-général de police* of Paris from 1774 to 1775 and 1776 to 1785, in the Bibliothèque municipale d'Orléans, MSS. 1421–1423; the Archives de la Chambre syndicale de

la Communauté des libraires et imprimeurs de Paris and the Collection Anisson-Duperron of the Bibliothèque Nationale (especially fonds français, MSS. 21862, 21833, 22046, 22063, 22070, 22075, 22081, 22109, 22116, 22102); the papers of the Bastille and related papers on the book trade in the Bibliothèque de l'Arsenal (especially MSS. 10305, 12446, 12454, 12480, 12481, 12517); and the Ministère des affaires étrangères, Correspondance politique, Angleterre, MSS 541–549. For information on the underground book route through Kehl and Strasbourg as opposed to Neuchâtel and Pontarlier, the relevant papers in the Archives de la ville de Strasbourg (mainly MSS. AA 2355–2362) were consulted but turned out to be less useful than the others. Research on publishing under the Old Regime by now has made J.-P. Belin, *Le commerce des livres prohibés à Paris de 1750 à 1789* (Paris, 1913) somewhat dated. For information about the most important secondary works see the bibliographies in Nicole Herrmann-Mascard, *La censure des livres à Paris à la fin de l'Ancien Régime, 1750–1789* (Paris, 1968), and Madeleine Ventre, *L'imprimerie et la librairie en Languedoc au dernier siècle de l'Ancien Régime, 1700–1789* (Paris and The Hague, 1958). The present essay was written before the thesis of H.-J. Martin became available, but it relies heavily on his article, "L'édition parisienne au XVIIe siècle: quelques aspects économiques," *Annales: économies, sociétés, civilisations,* 7 (July–Sept. 1952), 303–318. Another suggestive article is Léon Cahen, "La librairie parisienne et la diffusion du livre français à la fin du XVIIIe siècle," *Revue de synthèse,* 17 (1939), 159–179.

20. A typical example is the memoire of Aug. 2, 1783, by Périsse Duluc, syndic of the Chambre syndicale of Lyons in the Bibliothèque Nationale, MSS. français 21833, fol. 96.

21. Revol to STN, July 4, 1784.

22. For example, the Société typographique de Neuchâtel received a letter dated Oct. 30, 1783, from François Michaut, its agent on the Swiss side of the French border, which explained, "You are in a ticklish situation, because the porters are worried that if they are caught they will be condemned for smuggling in books that attack religion or that denigrate certain persons in authority ... If you only want to ship books whose content is irreproachable, the porters will ask you to guarantee that fact and you will find some in

our area who will charge 12 livres per quintal for delivery to Pontarlier or even a league farther if necessary. Aside from that it is necessary to give each porter a drink before departure. I should point out to you, Messieurs, that at that price the porters do the best they can without assuming responsibility for the merchandise." Michaut observed with some pride that "in effect my position is rather advantageous for clandestine border crossings" but warned, "in the villages and all along the route there are agents roaming about, and even if a shipment is in order they stop the wagoners and search through their loads." He therefore stressed the need of having a man to dupe or bribe the agents of the General Farm on the French side of the border: "I don't know anyone better qualified to do that than le sieur Faivre." Faivre did not hesitate to recommend himself. On Oct. 14, 1784, he informed the STN, "Your crates will cross the border next Saturday. I have prepared everything and have persuaded the porters to return by promising them that they will be satisfied and will get a drink . . . I am about to make a deal with one of the agents of the Farm, who will let us get through without any trouble at night and will show me the paths where we can cross the border in safety."

23. STN to J.-P. Brissot, April 29, 1781.

24. Mme. La Noue to STN, Sept. 8, 1782. Mme. La Noue was sensitive to complaints that she overcharged and underprotected her customers. On Dec. 9, 1780, she wrote to the STN in her usual semiliterate French, "Don't worry at all about the safety of your goods. Once they are in my hands I do everything possible to keep them sheltered from mishaps. You may have complete confidence in my way of doing business." But on Jan. 13, 1783, she confessed that six of its crates had been confiscated at her doorstep: "The wagoner was followed so closely that when he began to unload three persons from the police seized the six crates. The wagoner did not dare resist because of the threats they made. For two weeks now they have been harassing me with questions and trying to get me to say who the crates belong to and where they came from. But I have refused."

25. Paul de Pourtalès to STN, June 23, 1784.

26. See the Desauges dossier in the Bibliothèque de l'Arsenal, MS. 12446. On April 4, 1775, Desauges père wrote dyspeptically from the Bastille to his son, who had just been released: "You have to roll with the blows. But I'll admit to you that I am damned tired

of this place." The Desauges dossier in Neuchâtel, MS. 1141, shows the sharp practices of underground bookdealers at their most cutthroat.

27. Mme. J. E. Bertrand to STN, Oct. 7, 1785.

28. J.-F. Bornand to STN, Aug. 10, 1785. Poinçot occasionally smuggled books from Versailles to Paris for Desauges at 12 livres the quintal, which apparently was cheap compared with the charges of Mme. La Noue: 3 livres per "large article," which her nephew delivered to appointed hiding places on the outskirts of Paris (see Desauges to STN, Nov. 24, 1783, and Mme. La Noue to STN, June 22, 1781).

29. Among his tasks, Bornand had to try to cope with the "palaver" of Mme. La Noue (Bornand to STN, Feb. 19, 1785), the ruses of Poinçot and Desauges, and the impecuniousness of authors: "When it comes to money, authors are a sad resource" (Bornand to STN, March 9, 1785).

30. Giles Barber, "French Royal Decrees Concerning the Book Trade, 1700–1789," *Australian Journal of French Studies,* 3 (1966), 312.

31. A. J. L. Jourdan, O. O. Decrusy, and F. A. Isambert, eds., *Recueil général des anciennes lois françaises* (Paris, 1822–1833), XXI, 230.

32. Ibid., p. 218.

33. Ibid., p. 217.

34. George V. Taylor, "Noncapitalist Wealth and the Origins of the French Revolution," *American Historical Review,* 72 (1967), 469–496.

35. P. J. Blondel, *Mémoire sur les vexations qu'exercent les libraires et imprimeurs de Paris,* ed. Lucien Faucou (Paris, 1879), especially pp. 18–25, 45.

36. Quotations from *Recueil général des anciennes lois françaises,* XXV, 109, 119, 110.

37. Ibid., p. 109.

38. Because of the complicated problems of dating Diderot's *Lettre,* relating it to earlier documents that influenced Diderot's argument, and establishing a correct version of the text, it is important to read the *Lettre* in the critical edition by Jacques Proust (Paris, 1962). But even the old edition in Diderot's *Oeuvres complètes,* ed. J. Assézat and Maurice Tourneux (Paris, 1876), XVIII, 6, included a

note by someone in the Direction de la Librairie (d'Hémery?) which observed that Diderot wrote the *Lettre* "according to the advice of the booksellers and material that M. Le Breton provided, whose principles are diametrically opposed to the proper administration of *privilèges.*" Although the *Lettre* contains some heartfelt statements about liberty and the tribulations of authors, its logic is twisted to favor publishers and it reproduces the old arguments advanced by the guild. It is therefore difficult to accept Brunel's claim that Diderot did not write the *Lettre* either as an ally or as a paid propagandist of Le Breton and the other privileged publishers. Lucien Brunel, "Observations critiques et littéraires sur un opuscule de Diderot," *Revue d'histoire littéraire de la France,* 10 (1903), 1–24.

39. The code of 1777 weakened some of the Parisian guild's power by giving authors the right to sell their own works and by providing for two public book sales in Paris every year. It favored provincial publishers by permitting them to print the increasing number of books that it caused to fall into the public domain—an acknowledgment of the fact that they had engaged in illegal activities for lack of "a legitimate way to employ their presses." *Recueil général des anciennes lois françaises,* XXV, 109. The edicts of 1777 thus attempted to "put an end to the rivalry that divides the booksellers of Paris against those of the provinces, to promote the general welfare of this important branch of commerce, and to unite all the booksellers in a single family, which will have but a single interest." Ibid., pp. 119–120. But this rivalry went too deep to be settled by such small concessions to the provincial dealers, who continued to protest against exploitation by the Parisians throughout the 1780s. The 1777 code also extended and strengthened the guild system in the provinces, because "His Majesty has recognized that it would be dangerous to permit isolated printing shops to remain in a state of independence, which favors abuses." Ibid., p. 112. So the reorganization of the guilds did not substantially weaken them or impair their policing function.

40. D.-J. Garat, *Mémoires historiques sur la vie de M. Suard, sur ses écrits et sur le XVIIIe siècle* (Paris, 1820), I, 274.

41. Bibliothèque Nationale, MSS. français 21833, foll. 87–88. This account of French tax and tariff legislation is derived from several documents in MS. 21833, particularly foll. 89–91, 129–140.

42. The tariff legislation was a constant theme in the commercial correspondence of the Société typographique de Neuchâtel for the first half of the 1770s. The Society even sent one of its partners on a business trip through eastern France to sell books, to find new ways of making fraudulent shipments, and to learn as much as possible about tariff policy. According to the instructions in his travel-log, he was to seek out "J. M. Bruysset, a cold and cunning man: (1) Engage him in conversation about the French book trade in general; find out from him whether the tariff will actually be collected or lowered." STN, MS. 1058, "Carnet de voyage, 1773, J. E. Bertrand." The Bruysset house was one of the most effective lobbyists against the tariff, judging from the memoranda in the Bibliothèque Nationale, MSS. français 21833, especially foll. 87–88, 129–140. The tariff damaged the illegal trade, because pirated works were usually shipped through legal channels, at least at the border, under false *acquits à caution* and therefore paid duty.

43. Bibliothèque Nationale, MSS. français, 21833, foll. 87–88. This memoire reads as though it were the work of Panckoucke. One sou per sheet was the normal printing charge of the Société typographique de Neuchâtel, whose flourishing business in the mid-1770s seems to have resulted from the combination of France's favorable tariff policy and the cheap conditions of printing in Switzerland.

44. Ibid., foll. 111–115. The dealer showed, by a very detailed argument, that a six-hundred-pound crate would cost him 61 livres, 15 sous, in extra charges, would cause enormous delays and damage through mishandling, and would make it impossible for him to collect insurance for damaged shipments.

45. Ibid., fol. 70.

46. Ibid., fol. 107: "The booksellers at some distance from Paris, and those from Lyon in particular, immediately countermanded the orders for shipments that were to be made to them, sent back crates that were already en route, canceled purchases, and renounced their plans to print works for which they now see an insufficient market. In short, there already is no more active intercourse between French and foreign booksellers."

47. J. F. Bornand to STN, April 12, 1784.

48. J. F. Bornand to STN, April 9, 1784.

49. J. F. Bornand to STN, Feb. 19, 1785.

50. STN to Garrigan, a bookseller in Avignon, Aug, 23, 1785: "Of course we sincerely share the regret about the interruption of our commerce, which you express by your letter of the tenth of this month, but you are well aware that the fatal cause of it all is to be attributed entirely to the undiminished severity of the ordinances about the importation of foreign books in the kingdom. Things are still in such a bad state that we cannot get a single crate of books through our nearest border station, except by taking out an *acquit à caution* for Paris; so that your crates would have to make an enormous detour and would have to undergo inspection by the Parisian guild, which is completely unfeasible."

51. STN to Mme. J. E. Bertrand, early Oct. 1785.

52. The archives in Strasbourg, an important center of the clandestine trade, complement those in Neuchâtel in that they show a determined effort by the government to stop traffic in prohibited works. Strasbourg's *préteur royal* received frequent reports from local officials about seizures of illegal shipments from the publishers across the Rhine; and he also received strict orders from his own superior, the keeper of the seals (letter of April 26, 1786, in Archives de la ville de Strasbourg, MS. AA2356): "The book trade prohibited by our laws surrounds you on all sides; and it will penetrate by any means that you allow, if you do not disallow them all . . . I therefore exhort you, you and the municipal officers of your city, to take the appropriate measures." Despite this rigor, printers in Kehl seem to have got a great many books—political pamphlets and *libelles* as well as Beaumarchais's Voltaire—through the traps laid for them in Strasbourg. The town's semiautonomy, guaranteed by the capitulations of 1681, may have made it relatively easy to penetrate.

53. See Furet, p. 8, and Robert Estivals, *La statistique bibliographique de la France sous la monarchie au XVIIIe siècle* (Paris and The Hague, 1965), p. 296.

54. Bibliothèque Nationale, MS. français 21833, fol. 107.

55. Ibid., fol. 108; see also foll. 99-104.

56. Vergennes to d'Adhémar, May 12, 1783, Ministère des affaires étrangères, Correspondance politique, Angleterre, MS. 542. The details of "this infernal combination of intrigue, cupidity, and deceit," as Vergennes called it (Vergennes to Lenoir, May 24, 1783,

ibid.)—and which I plan to recount in a latter work—can be found in the series 541–549.

57. Bibliothèque de l'Arsenal, MS. 10305. The inventory also included *Le gazetier cuirassé, L'espion dévalisé, Vie privée de Louis XV, Le diable dans un bénitier,* and other classics of the London school of *libellistes.* It specified that they had been shipped to some of the customers of the STN, notably Poinçot, Blaizot, and Mme. La Noue. Poinçot himself drew up the inventory.

58. For the conventional view that the government's policy was severe in theory and permissive in practice see J.-P. Belin, *Le commerce des livres prohibés à Paris de 1750 à 1789* (Paris, 1913), and the restatement of Belin's interpretation in Nicole Herrmann-Mascard, *La censure des livres à Paris à la fin de l'ancien régime, 1750–1789* (Paris, 1968). Both books dismiss the June 12, 1783, orders in two sentences—the same sentences, curiously, almost word-for-word (Belin, p. 45; Herrmann-Mascard, p. 102).

59. It also might serve as a corrective to the Marxist tendency to treat the Enlightenment as bourgeois ideology. One version of this tendency argues that ideas such as social contract, individualism, liberty, and equality before the law derived from capitalist methods of exchange, which involve contractual obligations between legally free and equal individuals: Lucien Goldman, "La pensée des 'Lumières,'" *Annales: économies, sociétés, civilisations,* 22 (1967), 752–770. Considering the multitude of writers who expressed such ideas before the development of capitalism, this argument seems less convincing than its opposite, which relates the Enlightenment to a tradition of aristocratic liberalism: Denis Richet, "Autour des origines idéologiques lointaines de la Révolution française: élites et despotisme," ibid., 24 (1969), 1–23.

60. STN, MS. 1108.

61. Ibid. In contrast, the manuscript catalogue offered the following under the letter "B": *"La belle allemande, ou les galanteries de Thérèse, 1774; Bijoux indiscrets* par Diderot, 8° figures; *Le bonheur,* poème par Helvétius; *Le bon sens, ou idées naturelles, opposées aux idées surnaturelles."*

62. Reprinted in A. Van Bever, *Contes et conteurs gaillards au XVIIIe siècle* (Paris, 1906), pp. 280–281. In notes that he assembled

for his memoirs, the former lieutenant general of police J.-C.-P. Lenoir associated this work with a widespread outbreak of libeling in the 1780s (Bibliothèque municipale d'Orléans, MS. 1423): "The morals of the successor of Louis XV being beyond reproach, the new king was invulnerable to calumny from that side during the first years of his reign. But in 1778 the attacks began to be directed at his weakness, and the first calumnies against his person took place only a short time before the maligning of the queen. M. de Maurepas— who until then had been oblivious to the epigrams and songs made against him [Maurepas] and who used to amuse himself at all the libels, at all the private and scandalous anecdotes that were concocted and printed with impunity—M. de Maurepas was informed that some writers had put together a sort of speculation among themselves, that they had organized a correspondence system through which some of them sent the latest scandals with background material to the others, who wrote it up and had it printed in The Hague and London. From there they had it smuggled into France in small quantities by foreign travelers. A secretary in the English embassy notified him [Maurepas] that an abominable *libelle* entitled *Les amours de Charlot et d'Antoinette* was about to be smuggled into France."

63. *Le portefeuille d'un talon rouge contenant des anecdotes galantes et secrètes de la cour de France*, reprinted under the title *Le coffret du bibliophile* (Paris, n.d.), p. 22. Lenoir's manuscripts confirm this account (Bibliothèque municipale d'Orléans, MS. 1422): "It is no longer doubtful that it was MM. de Montesquiou, de Créqui, de Champcenets, and other courtiers, who in league with Beaumarchais, Chamfort, and other writers still alive today composed *libelles* against the court, against the ministers, and even against the ministers who employed them. It is more than probable that Beaumarchais wrote a libel with engraved illustrations entitled *Les amours de Charlot et d'Antoinette* and that he brought it to London, where it was printed."

64. Ibid.

65. Ibid. Lenoir's remarks might seen to contradict the above interpretation about a crackdown on underground publishing, but they refer primarily to the circulation of *libelles* inside Paris, not to the traffic from outside France to the capital. There seems to have

been a considerable domestic production of *libelles,* which survived the police's attempts to impound them because of influential "protection" and the immunities of *lieux privilégiés* like the Palais-Royal, where the police could not penetrate. See ibid., MS. 1421.

66. See Chapter 2.

67. Lenoir later tried to investigate the rumor and the riot but without success. Bibliothèque municipale d'Orleans, MS. 1422.

68. Lenoir developed his observations most fully in an essay entitled "De l'administration de l'ancienne police concernant les libelles, les mauvaises satires et chansons, leurs auteurs coupables, délinquants, complices ou adhérents," ibid.

69. [Charles Théveneau de Morande], *Le gazetier cuirassé: ou anecdotes scandaleuses de la cour de France* ("imprimé à cent lieues de la Bastille à l'enseigne de la liberté," 1771), p. 92: "The French nation is so enfeebled today that robust persons are wildly expensive. It is said that a beginning lackey in Paris is as well paid by the women who use him as a stud racehorse is in England. If this system spreads, one or two generations will suffice to restore the general physique." In *Le libertin de qualité,* reprinted in *L'Oeuvre du Comte de Mirabeau,* ed. Guillaume Apollinaire (Paris, 1910). Mirabeau described aristocratic immorality in great detail. After recounting a depraved duchess's abandonment of her lover, he remarked (p. 232), "She replaced him with a prince, and on the moral side of things they really suited each other very well. On the physical side she had her lackeys: they are the daily bread of a duchess."

70. [Charles Théveneau de Morande], *La gazette noire par un homme qui n'est pas blanc: ou oeuvres posthumes du gazetier cuirassé* ("imprimé à cent lieues de la Bastille, à trois cent lieues des Présides, à cinq cent lieues des Cordons, à mille lieues de la Sibérie," 1784), p. 194.

71. See Richard Cobb, "Quelques aspects de la mentalité révolutionnaire," *Revue d'histoire moderne et contemporaine,* 6 (1959), 81–120, and "The Revolutionary Mentality in France," *History,* 42 (1957), 181–196.

72. *La gazette noire,* p. 7. For a similar example of such rumors about the promiscuous use of police by *gens en place* see M. de Lescure, ed., *Correspondance secrète inédite sur Louis XVI, Marie-Antoinette, la Cour et la ville de 1777 à 1792* (Paris, 1866), II, 157–158.

73. The subheadline of the account of the queen's guillotining in *Le Père Duchesne,* undated (Oct. 1793).

74. Pierre Goubert, *L'Ancien Régime* (Paris, 1969), I, 152.

75. Bibliothèque municipale d'Orléans, MS. 1423.

76. Quoted in Frantz Funck-Brentano and Paul d'Estrée, *Les nouvellistes* (Paris, 1905), p. 304.

77. Goubert, *L'Ancien Régime,* p. 152. The connection between privilege and monopoly is brought out clearly in the first definition of *privilège* given in the *Dictionnaire de l'Académie française* (Paris, 1778): "The capacity, granted to an individual or a community, to do something or to enjoy some advantage to the exclusion of others."

78. See Charly Guyot, *De Rousseau à Mirabeau: pèlerins de Môtiers et prophètes de 89* (Neuchâtel and Paris, 1936), chap. 4.

79. Although the increased severity in the policing of the book trade cut down on its business in France, the Société typographique de Neuchâtel still did its best to supply works like the following, which it entered in its *Livres de commission* (STN MS. 1021, foll. 173-175) after receiving an order from Bruzard de Mauvelain in Troyes, dated June 16, 1784: "6 *Les petits soupers de l'Hôtel de Bouillon;* 6 *Le diable dans un bénitier;* 6 *L'espion dévalisé;* 1 *Correspondance de Maupeou;* 1 *Recueil de remontrances au Roi Louis XV;* 2 *Mémoires de Madame de Pompadour;* 2 *Vie privée de Louis XV;* 12 *Fastes de Louis XV;* 6 *Histoire philosophique* 8°, 10 vol.; 6 *Erotika biblion* 8°; 1 *La Mettrie;* 1 *Boulanger complet, antiquité, Christianisme, et despotisme;* 1 *Helvétius complet;* 6 *Lettres de Julie à Calasie, ou tableau du libertinage à Paris;* 1 *La dernière livraison de Jean-Jacques* 12°; 6 *Chronique scandaleuse;* 6 *Les petits soupers du comte de Vergennes;* 6 *Le passe-temps, d'Antoinette.*"

80. See Paul Robiquet, *Théveneau de Morande: étude sur le XVIIIe siècle* (Paris, 1882).

Acknowledgments

Chapter 1 originally appeared as "The High Enlightenment and the Low-Life of Literature in Prerevolutionary France," *Past and Present: A Journal of Historical Studies,* no. 51 (May 1971), 81–115. World Copyright: The Past and Present Society, Corpus Christi College, Oxford, England.

Chapter 2 originally appeared as "The Grub Street Style of Revolution: J.-P. Brissot, Police Spy," *The Journal of Modern History,* 40 (1968), 301–327. Reprinted by permission of The University of Chicago Press. Copyright © 1968 by the University of Chicago.

Chapter 3 is an abridged version of a more detailed study, "The Life of a 'Poor Devil' in the Republic of Letters," in Jean Macary, ed., *Essays on the Age of Enlightenment in Honor of Ira O. Wade* (Geneva and Paris: Librairie Droz, 1977), pp. 39–92. Reprinted by permission of Librairie Droz.

Chapter 4 is a condensed version of a full-length study that appeared in Paul J. Korshin, ed., *The Widening Circle: Essays on the Circulation of Literature in Eighteenth-Century Europe.* (Philadelphia: University of Pennsylvania Press, 1976), pp. 11–83. Reprinted by permission of the University of Pennsylvania Press.

Chapter 5 was originally given as part of the Engelhard Lectures on the History of the Book, a program of the Center for the Book in the Library of Congress.

Chapter 6 originally appeared as "Reading, Writing, and Publishing in Eighteenth-Century France: A Case Study in the Sociology of Literature," *Daedalus* (Winter 1971), pp. 214–256. Copyright © 1971 by Robert Darnton.

The Index was prepared by Susan Darnton.

Index

Académie des Inscriptions, 9
Académie des Sciences, 21
Académie Française, 3, 6, 7, 8–9, 11, 13, 21, 24
Académie Royale de Musique, 21
Académie Royale de Peinture et de Sculpture, 21
Académies, and privileges, 21, 39
Acquits à caution, 191–195
Aiguillon, Emmanuel Arnaud de Vignerod du Plessis de Richelieu, duc d', 5, 32, 33
Alembert, Jean Le Rond d', 3, 4, 6, 11, 13–14, 15; as patron of Le Senne, 73–97, 101–112; his declining reputation, 106; his death, 107–108; and philosophic propaganda, 111–112
Almanach des Muses, 25
Almanach Royal, 6
Amar, André, 51
America, United States of, 61
Amsterdam, vii
Annales politiques, civiles et littéraires du dix-huitième siècle, 73
Année littéraire, l', 73
Archives Nationales, 7
Aretino, Pietro, 29
Arnaud, abbé François d', 3, 5, 12
Artois, Charles-Philippe de Bourbon, comte d', 200
Aubert, Jean-Louis, abbé, 8
Audouin, Pierre-Jean, 26
Aulard, Alphonse, 50, 58

Authors: established, 2–15; hacks, *see* Grub Street; population of, 169–173; generations of, 170; "provincialization" of, 171; professionalization of, 171–172; privileges of, 189
Auxerre, 105, 107–108, 115
Avignon, 192

Bailly, Jean-Sylvain, 38, 49, 57
Balzac, J.-L. Guez de, 12
Barnave, Antoine-Pierre, 56
Bastille, 41–69 passim; archives of, vi, 59
Bauprais, la veuve (bookseller), 75, 99–101, 115
Bayreuth, margrave of, 6
Beaumarchais, Pierre-Augustin Caron de, 15
Beauvau, Charles-Just, prince de, 4, 7
Bellelay, 88, 94, 115
Benjamin, Walter, 167
Bern, 102, 115, 152
Bernardin de Saint-Pierre, Henri, 8
Bernardins, Collège des, 84, 85, 86, 92, 111
Besançon, 46, 130, 131, 152
Bicêtre, 26
Blanc, Louis, 50
Blancs Manteaux, 88, 89, 91, 95, 98
Blondel, Pierre-Jacques, 188
Bluche, François, 173, 178, 179, 181

Boisgelin, Raymond de, archbishop of Aix, 12
Booksellers' guild, vi, 86, 113–114, 185–192, 194, 197–199
Book trade: clandestine, 122–125, 127–132, 135–147, 183–187, 193–199, 206–208; anticlerical, 127, 141–142; prices, 129, 131, 136; legal, 185–193, 195–199; edicts regulating, 185–192, 195–196; provincial and foreign, 190–197
Bornand, Jacob-François, 184, 192
Bosset de Luze, Abraham, 73–78, 83–86, 91
Bouillon, 82
Boulogne-sur-Mer, 44
Braun, Rudolf, 153
Bretin, abbé, 84, 85
Brienne, E. C. Loménie de, 12
Brissot de Warville, Jacques-Pierre, 20, 21, 35, 38, 41–70, 123, 202; his London Lycée, 42–43, 62; and the Société typographique de Neuchâtel, 44–48, 64–67; as police spy, 49–68
Brittany, Parlement of, 178
Brussels, 192
Budapest, vii
Buffon, Georges-Louis Leclerc, comte de, 4, 14, 192

Cabinets littéraires, 107
Cafés, 23
Cailhava de L'Estendoux, Jean-François, 3, 8
Calonne, Charles Alexandre de, 7, 34
Caraccioli, Luigi, 9
Carra, Jean-Louis, 10, 17, 20, 28, 34, 38, 59
Chabot, François, 52
Châlons-sur-Saône, 193
Chamfort, Nicolas de, 3, 8, 12, 38
Champcenetz, Louis Edmond de, 17

Chartres, 42, 69, 94, 96, 110
Chastellux, François Jean, marquis de, 5, 12
Châtelet, comte de, 85
Chénier, André, 27, 55
Choiseul, Etienne-François, duc de, 5
Cistercians, 102–103
Clairvaux, 193
Clavière, Etienne, 46–47, 62, 67, 68
Clergy, General Assembly of the, 187
Cloots, Anacharsis, 52
Coigny, J.-A.-F. de Flanquetot, duc de, 6
Colbert, Jean-Baptiste, 21, 185, 186
Collot d'Herbois, Jean-Marie, 17, 38
Comédie Française, 21, 27
Committee of General Security, 51
Committee of Public Safety, 51
Condillac, Etienne Bonnot de, 15, 117
Condorcet, Antoine-Nicolas, marquis de, 38, 40
Contat, Nicolas, 159–160
Contrat social, 167, 168, 204
Court de Gébelin, Antoine, 24
Crébillon, Claude-Prosper Jolyot (Fils), 17
Cubières-Palmézeaux, Michel de, 3, 8
Cugnet (bookseller), 83–87, 89–91, 98–102, 110, 113–114, 116; his wife, 93

Danton, Georges Jacques, 50
Delacroix, Jean-François, 26
Delille, Jacques, abbé, 3, 12
Delisle de Sales, J.-B.-C. Izouard, 10
Desauges, 184
Des Essarts, Nicolas-Toussaint Le Moyne, 8
Desforges d'Hurecourt, 42–43, 62
Desmoulins, Camille, 17, 38, 52–53, 57, 67, 205

Diamond Necklace, Affair of the, 35, 60, 195, 203, 207
Diderot, Denis, 4, 14, 15, 20, 71, 109, 116, 118–120, 141, 189
Dijon, 93
Dorat, Claude-Joseph, 3
Du Barry, Jeanne Bécu, comtesse, 33, 35, 146, 203, 204
Ducis, Jean-François, 8
Duclos, Charles Pinot, 4, 12–13, 14, 18
Dumont de Sainte-Croix, J.-C.-N., 9
Dumouriez, Charles-François, 61
Duport, Adrien, 56
Duport du Tertre, F.-J., 26
Duras, Henri de Durfort, duc de, 12

Edict of Nantes, 169
Ehrard, Jean, 173, 176, 177, 179
Encyclopédie, 148–150, 153
England, 169, 195
Enlightenment: and Revolution, viii, 37–40; authors, their popularity, 1–2, 141, 167–168, 182
Escarpit, Robert, 168–173
Estivals, Robert, 195

Fabre d'Eglantine, Philippe, 10, 17, 28, 38
Fauche, Samuel, 206
Félice, Barthélemy de, 150, 153–154
Feuillants, 54, 56
Flandrin, Jean-Louis and Maria, 177
Fontenelle, Bernard Le Bovier de, 4
Frankfurt, vii
Franklin, Benjamin, 159
Frederick II, 76, 92, 104
Fréron, Elie, 27, 73, 116
Fribourg, 102, 108, 115
Fronde, 29, 169
Furet, François, 173–176, 177, 179, 195, 198

Garat, Dominique-Joseph, 3, 8
Garden, Maurice, 153

Garnier, J.-J., 19
Gaxotte, Pierre, 50
Gazette de France, 4, 5, 10, 76
Geneva, 62, 150, 151, 192, 193
Genlis, S.-F. Ducrest de Saint-Aubin, comtesse de, 44, 56
Geoffrin, Marie-Thérèse, 4
Girondins, 50–56, 69, 123
Gluck, Christoph Wilibard von, 40
Gorsas, Antoine-Joseph, 10, 17, 26, 38
Goupil de Palières, 63–64
Gouy d'Arsy, marquis de, 53–54
Graffigny, Françoise Paule d'Issembourg de, 167
Grammont, Béatrix de Choiseul-Stainville, duchesse de, 5
Grégoire, Henri, 39
Grenoble, 192
Grimm, Friedrich Melchior, baron de, 53
Grosley, P.-J., 137
Grub Street, ix, 16–40, 134, 207–208

Hague, The, 192
Hébert, Jacques, 38, 39, 57, 205
Helvétius, Claude-Adrien, 84, 141
Historiographers, 8, 11
Holbach, Paul Thiry, baron d', 4, 14, 114, 141, 144, 207
Houdetot, Elisabeth, comtesse d', 4

Jacobins, 52, 55, 93, 94, 97
Joseph II, 102, 104
Journal de littérature, des sciences et des arts, 77
Journal de Paris, 6, 24, 54, 55
Journal des savants, 10, 176
Journal encyclopédique, 74, 83
Journal helvétique, 72–78, 92, 97, 112
Journalism, 112–113, 142–144, 146–147, 176–177, 203–204

Keralio, Louis-Félix Guinement de, 8

La Blancherie, P.-C. de, 24
Labrousse, C.-E., 195
Lafayette, Marie Joseph, marquis de, 53, 55, 56, 61
La Harpe, Jean-François de, 3, 6, 7, 12, 15, 22, 28, 38
Lamartine, Alphonse de, 170
Lameth, Théodore, 53, 55–56
La Mettrie, Julien Offroy de, 141
Lanjuinais, Jean-Denis, 39
La Noue, madame (bookseller), 184
Launay, marquis de, 60
Lausanne, 154, 192
Laus de Boissy, Louis de, 72
Le Breton, André François, 197
Lenoir, Jean-Charles-Pierre, 7, 10, 201–202, 205; on Brissot as a police spy, 49–68 passim; his opposition to booksellers' guild, 86–87, 98
Le Sage, Alain René, 20
Lescure, F.-A. Mathurin de, 50
Le Senne, abbé: relations with the Société typographique de Neuchâtel, 72–108; as bookseller, 84–87, 98–101, 107; anticlerical works, 94–96, 106, 108, 110–111
Lespinasse, Julie-Jeanne-Eléonore de, 4
Libel, *libelles* (see Pamphlets)
Libraries, composition of, 177–182
Linguet, Simon-Henri, 18, 24, 73, 112, 144
Lisbon, vii
Literacy, 16
Livres philosophiques, 1–2, 122, 174, 199–208
London, 42, 62–63, 79, 82
Lons-le-Saunier, 55
Louis XIV, 169, 170
Louis XV, 169, 170, 202–203
Louis XVI, 170, 203, 205
Loustalot, Elisée, 38
Louvet de Couvray, Jean-Baptiste, 38

Louvre, 83, 87, 98
Luzarches, 90
Lycées, 24; Brissot's London Lycée, 42, 62
Lyons, 178, 183, 191, 196

Mably, Gabriel Bonnot de, 14, 15
Maestricht, 192
Mairan, Dortous de, 178, 179
Mairobert, Mathieu François Pidansat de, 143
Malesherbes, C.-G. de Lamoignon de, 93, 103–104, 110, 174, 187, 189
Mallet du Pan, Jacques, 16
Manuel, Pierre Louis, 17, 26, 35, 38, 59, 60–61, 65–66, 141
Marat, Jean Paul, 20, 28, 38, 49, 52, 57, 63, 67
Marchais, madame de, 5
Maret, Hugues-Bernard, 38
Marie-Antoinette, 56, 200–201
Marmontel, Jean-François, 3, 7, 11, 12, 15, 22, 38
Marot, Clément, 168
Marseilles, vii
Martin (secretary of police), 64–67
Mathiez, Albert, 50
Maupeou, René Nicolas de, 32, 33, 203
Maury, Jean-Sifrein, abbé, 3, 22
Mauvelin, Bruzard de, 123–128, 131–134
Mémoires de Trévoux, 176
Mémoires secrets, 96, 143
Mercier, Louis Sébastien, 10, 17–18, 19, 20, 26, 38, 64, 126, 141
Mercure, 4, 7, 10, 11, 24, 76–77, 176
Meyer, Jean, 173, 178, 181
Michelet, Jules, 50
Mirabeau, Honoré Gabriel Riqueti, comte de, 25, 60, 62, 129, 136, 141, 144, 202, 206
Molière, J.-B. Poquelin, 28
Monde, Le, 4–16, 21–22
Montagnards, 51–52, 53, 56

Montesquieu, Charles de Secondat, baron de, 4, 14, 141
Morande, Charles Théveneau de, 25, 30–35, 58, 62, 141, 207
Morellet, André, abbé, 3, 7, 22, 117
Mornet, Daniel, 41, 167–168, 176–182 passim, 198
Mouchy, Antoine, 61
Musées, 24

Naples, vii
Napoleon, 169
Necker, Jacques, 4, 6, 79, 116
Neuchâtel, vi, 26, 71, 74–75, 92, 105, 149
Néville, Le Camus de, 189
Newton, Sir Isaac, 28, 173
Nivernais, duc de, 6, 7

Orléans, duc d' (Philippe Egalité), 49, 56, 61
Ormesson de Noiseau, Louis François-de-Paul Lefèvre d', 27
Ostend, 63
Ostervald, Frédéric-Samuel, 73–78, 87–103 passim

Palais Royal, 24, 87, 143
Palissot, Charles, 116
Pamphlets (*libelles*), 29–36, 38, 144–146, 195–196, 199–208
Panckoucke, Charles-Joseph, 4, 76, 189, 191, 192
Pange, François de, 54–55, 57
Panis, Etienne-Jean, 27
Paper, 190
Parlement of Paris, 178, 187
Patriote français, Le, 54, 55, 56, 66, 69
Pensions, 7–11
Permissions (for books), 16, 174, 177, 179
Petit, Régine, 173, 178
Peuchet, Jacques, 62
Physiocrats, 110

Piccini, Niccolo, 40
Piis, Pierre-Antoine Augustin de, 8
Poitiers, 1
Pontarlier, 128
Pope, Alexander, 109
Pornography, 142, 199–208
Porrentruy, 102
Pottinger, David, 171–172
Prévost, Antoine François, abbé, 19
Printing, printers: recruitment by Société typographique de Neuchâtel, 148–155; wages, 149, 151–153; work patterns, 155–159; ceremonies, 159–161; slang, 162–163, 165–166; horseplay, 163–165
Privileges, 76, 86, 123, 135; of institutions, 21–22; of books, 174–175, 186–187; of booksellers, 187–189, 191–192, 197–199
Procope, Le (café), 23
Propaganda, 9, 146–147, 195–196, 199–208; anticlerical, 94–96, 103, 106, 108, 110–111
"Protection," 6–7
Provins, 97, 101, 110
Prudhomme, Louis-Marie, 26, 38

Quandet de Lachenal, Nicolas-Guillaume, 65–67, 78, 98–101, 106, 116
Quiquincourt, 86, 106

Rameau's nephew, 71, 109, 117–121
Raynal, Guillaume-Thomas-François, abbé, 4, 64, 85, 117, 126, 141, 142
Reading, 135–136, 146–147; changing tastes in, 173–182
Régence, La (café), 23
Reims, 101
Restif de la Bretonne, Nicolas, 17, 159, 171
Revol, Jacques, 183
Riccoboni, Marie-Jeanne Laboras de Mézières, 167

Richelieu, A.-J. du Plessis, duc de, 169

Rivarol, Antoine, 9, 17, 22, 38, 53, 57, 67

Robespierre, Maximilien, 52, 168

Roche, Daniel, 173, 178, 179

Roger, Jacques, 173, 176, 177, 179

Rohan, Edouard, prince de, 35, 56

Roucher, J.-A., 3

Rouen, 99

Rousseau, Jean-Jacques, 4, 15, 35–36, 64, 68–69, 84, 87, 141, 168, 207

Rousseau, Pierre, 74

Roux, Jacques, 118

Rulhière, Claude-Carloman de, 3, 12

Sainmore, Blin de, 8

Saint-Hyacinthe, Thémiseul de, 167

Saint-Just, Louis de, 51, 58

Saint-Lambert, Jean-François, marquis de, 8

Salic Law, 205

Salons, 4–5, 23

Sartine, A.-R.-J.-G. Gabriel de, 189

Saurin, Bernard-Joseph, 5, 8; his widow, 4, 8

Slave trade, 54

Smuggling (of books), 84–86, 104, 113–114, 116, 128–132, 183–185, 193–195; insurance costs, 131

Société des Amis des Noirs, 54

Société Royale de Médecine, 21, 26

Société typographique de Neuchâtel, vi–vii, 44–48, 63–67, 206; correspondence with Le Senne, 72–108; sales in France, 84–87, 98–101, 104, 107, 113–114, 124, 127–128; correspondence with

Mauvelain, 123–128, 131, 132–134; analysis of sales, 135–147

Sociology of literature, 167, 168–173

Soleure, 102, 115

Soulavie, Jean-Louis Giraud, abbé, 9

Spying, 61–62

Suard, Jean-Baptiste-Antoine, 3–6, 11, 15, 40

Swift, Jonathan, 109

Taine, Hippolyte, 50–51

Target, Guy-Jean-Baptiste, 3

Terray, Joseph-Marie, abbé, 33, 190

Tessé, madame de, 5

Thomas, Antoine-Léonard, 3, 12, 15, 22

Thompson, E. P., 153

Tocqueville, Alexis de, 22

Trenard, Louis, 178

Troyes, 101, 102, 104–105, 123, 125, 127–128, 130, 134, 135–136

Turgot, Anne-Robert-Jacques, 188, 190, 191

Vergennes, Charles Gravier, comte de, 43, 194–206 passim

Versailles, 184, 194

Vicq d'Azir, Félix, 26

Vidaud de Latour, Jean-Jacques, 7

Voiture, Vincent, 12

Volney, C.-F. de, 53

Voltaire, François-Marie Arouet, 2–3, 4, 11, 17–18, 25, 35, 71–72, 87, 108–118 passim, 141, 168, 177

Warsaw, vii

Yverdon, 150, 153, 154